CASS LIBRARY OF AFRICAN STUDIES

GENERAL STUDIES

No. 73

Editorial Adviser: JOHN RALPH WILLIS

Centre of West African Studies, University of Birmingham

A BORGU CANOE-MAN.
(Photo by Mr. E. Firmin.)

Frontispiece.

NIGERIA

ITS PEOPLES AND ITS PROBLEMS

BY

E. D. MOREL

THIRD EDITION

With a New Introduction

by

KENNETH DIKE NWORAH

FRANK CASS & CO. LTD.
1968

Published by
FRANK CASS AND COMPANY LIMITED
67 Great Russell Street, London WC1
by arrangement with John Murray (Publishers) Limited

First edition	1911
Second edition	1912
Third edition	1968

Printed in Great Britain by
Thomas Nelson (Printers) Ltd., London and Edinburgh

TO THE MEMORY

OF

MARY KINGSLEY

WHO POINTED THE WAY

INTRODUCTION
TO
THE THIRD EDITION

EDMUND DENE MOREL, the only child of Georges
Edmund Morel-de-Ville of the Avenue D'Eylea and
Emmeline de Horne of Peckham, combined the virtues
and vices of his French and English parentage. He is
said to have inherited the French exactitude, acuteness
and logicality when he made a point, and demonstrated the English stubborness, impatience, audacity and
scorn for other people's views when he knew they were
in the wrong. This combination naturally made him
formidable when he attacked or defended a view.
Either as author, critic, journalist or humanitarian,
Morel was primarily sustained by an unfailing faith in
the efficacy of his opinions.[1]

As a background to his interest in African affairs,
we may trace another combination of two personal
circumstances. His mother was descended from the de
Hornes, a remarkable Quaker family of religious
fanatics. This probably imbued in young Morel that
reformist and humanitarian impulse traditionally associated with Quakerism. Moreover, as a young man,
he was in the employ of Alfred Jones, the senior partner
of the Liverpool shipping firm of Elder Dempster and
Company Limited, where he must have come into contact with most baleful aspects of West Africa. There
and then he plunged into the literature of West Africa,

[1] See F. Seymour Cocks, *E. D. Morel: The Man and His Works* (London,
1920).

vii

and learnt almost everything that he wished to know, so that when, in 1899, Mary Kingsley introduced him to John Holt, the Liverpool merchant and humanitarian, Morel was already one of the most informed people in Britain on West African subjects.[1]

At the same time as he was studying African affairs in Liverpool, Morel was also broadening his contacts. His most intimate associate was John Holt. In assessing the latter's career, the mercantile activity is always emphasised. But it must be noted that his *raison d'être* was humanity, not commerce.[2] He had, of course, " as a Trader worked hard and tried to keep pace with others in enterprise and pushfulness in the establishment of the fabric of British commerce in West Africa, and in the development of the resources of Southern Nigeria."[3] Apparently harsh and brusque, Holt was nevertheless morally stern and an uncompromising fighter against injustice and the exploitation of human misery. His intense individuality was reinforced by a natural open-mindedness which in his case was another stimulus to his negrophilism. This quality therefore produced in him that belief in fair, honest and just treatment of men, his condemnation of bad laws, and was the genesis of his free-trade zeal. He sought to right the wrongs believed to have been done to West Africans, and his actions were duly appreciated by ' Coast ' natives.[4]

The first meeting between Holt and Morel seemed like the meeting of men from strange worlds. Apparently, there was little in common between two men who were soon to become bed-fellows. Holt felt that Morel had been sent to procure commercial intelligence for

[1] See Introduction to Second Ed., of E. D. Morel's, *Affairs of West Africa*. Cass, 1968.
[2] K. Dike Nworah, *Humanitarian Press-Groups and British Attitudes to West Africa* (Unpublished Ph.D. London thesis, April 1966) p. 28.
[3] Holt to Morel, 22 October, 1903, F8/1, E. D. Morel Papers.
[4] See Mrs. A. Stopford Green, 'A Founder of the Society' in *Journal of the African Society*, October, 1915.

his rival in business, Alfred Jones. Morel's assessment was that Holt was " an abrupt and ill-bred " old man.[1] Gradually, however, common elements were discernible. Both had lived tough lives. Morel had lost his father in infancy, and had worked hard in Liverpool, giving part-time French lectures to make ends meet. He had also seen what West Africa was like from his contacts in Liverpool and omnivorous application to its literature. At the same time, he had learned to trust himself. In the same way, Holt was self-reliant, tough and courageous. He had gone to Fernando Po in 1862 at the age of twenty-one; had indulged in the cut-throat competition methods of those days, and had triumphed without the favour of charter, grant or concession. Moreover, he had no contempt for the Africans he met there. Therefore, despite their disparity of age and cultural bearings, " an extensive, almost daily, confidential, warm and often fatherly correspondence grew between Holt and Morel ". Holt provided a wealth of first hand, intimate information, increased his human contacts, gave him business advice and help, and at times flattered him. Morel, for his part, put on the mantle of enlightened commerce, and stood with Holt on almost every issue that came up about West Africa at the time.[2]

This relationship was, as with Mary Kingsley and Holt, one of mutual inspiration and perpetual education. From the beginning Holt helped to bring Morel to the limelight. It was Holt who introduced him to Mrs. Alice Stopford Green, the daughter of the Reverend Stopford of Meath and the wife of John Richard Green, the historian. During the ten years following her husband's death in 1883, Mrs. Green's house in Kensington Square became the centre of a brilliant group

[1] Holt to Morel, 31 July, 1901, F8/1.
[2] See Robert Wuliger, *The Idea of Economic Imperialism with Special Reference to the Life and Work of E. D. Morel* (Unpublished London Ph.D. thesis, 1959) p. 15.

of friends, among whom were Florence Nightingale, Mary Kingsley, Bishop and Mrs. Creighton, the Humphrey Wards, Bishop Stubbs, John Morley, R. B. Haldane, H. A. L. Fisher and Winston Churchill. Morel's association with Mrs. Green proved most valuable. As Vice-President of the African Society, she knew almost every Colonial Governor and Colonial Office official. She introduced Morel to such important men as Sir Harry Johnston, de Cerdi, Arthur Brisbane and others. She helped very much to bring Morel into contact with responsible journalism, which probably influenced his later critical methods.

It was also both Holt and Mrs. Green who suggested that Morel should address the Women's Liberal Association at its annual meeting in June, 1901.[1] He had advised Morel, who addressed the women on "England's Relations to Her Native Races in West Africa," to use the occasion to meet influential people who could help him later.[2] Holt's generous judgements of Morel's efforts encouraged him, as he put it because " to feel that you whom poor Miss Kingsley used to call her political leader think so well of my efforts " was a precious asset and a great moral tonic.[3] Holt also protected Morel from his enemies. For example, late in 1899 when A. L. Jones (his employer) threatened to deal with Morel for an alleged disrespect to the Liverpool Chamber of Commerce, it was to Holt that Mary Kingsley appealed not to side with Jones on the matter. She told Holt that Morel " was a struggling young man with a family ", and that she would be " sorry for them " if Jones co-operated with George Goldie in the latter's " nagging " to " get rid of him. "[4] At other times, when Morel suffered from the underhand

---

[1] The meeting was held at the Memorial Hall, Farringdon Street, London.
[2] Holt to Morel, 26 May, 1901, F8/1, E. D. Morel Papers.
[3] Morel to Holt, 28 October, 1902, 18/1, John Holt Papers in the archives of John Holt and Company Ltd., India Buildings, Water Street, Liverpool.
[4] Kingsley to Holt, 25 July, 1899, 16/4 John Holt Papers.

attacks of other foes, he was sustained by the friendship, kindness and support of Holt, who often cheered
his spirits when he was gloomy and provided him
" with that stimulus which a nature like Morel's wanted
so badly at times."[1]

Once he was assured of Holt's support, Morel
virtually seized the initiative in the politics of dissent
in the interest of Africans and British commercial
power. His chief claim to universal fame was his
championship of native rights which in his day were
being undermined by a reckless and swift application
of European capitalism in tropical Africa. Morel
contrasted two methods of administering tropical Africa
and therefore, two divergent policies. One method was
to dispossess the African of his rights in land, to
declare that African territories and products were the
property of some European State or corporation, and
then to exploit them in the interest of European
capitalism, using the African merely as a slave or a
hired labourer. This method, according to Morel only
led to the degradation of the African, and eventually
to the ruin of his country. The reasons, he believed,
were both psychological and economic. If the African
was deprived of his land right, he would put no effort
into his work. He became unhappy, and if force were
substituted to induce him to work, the regime would
become atrocious, as in the case of the Congo. In any
case, possessing no property of his own, the African
would have nothing with which to purchase the
manufactured goods of Europe. Consequently, imports would fall; trade would dwindle; the cost of products might increase; and then the British Government
might be called upon to advance imperial loans to the
colonies.[2]

The alternative method, which Morel supported, was

---

[1] Morel to Holt, 25 December, 1902, 18/1, John Holt Papers.
[2] See E. D. Morel: *Great Britain and the Congo* p. 86.

a policy of preservation of the right of the African in land. He wanted the African to be recognized as a free man, a human being who needed some help in the development of his country, not as a mere tool of industry. He saw this question of Land Tenure as the key to the whole question of African administration: " Native ownership in land," he says, " must need be the foundation-stone of all normal European rule in the African tropics, because the economical aspects of normal European rule is the development of commercial relations, and any relationship between the European and the native is impossible, unless the native has articles to sell with which to purchase manufactured goods—in other words, as long as the native has free access to the soil, he will develop his land, he will put forth every effort to increase its productive value; he will exchange its products with manufactured goods sent from Europe; a normal commercial relationship will be set up; imports and exports will expand, the prosperity of the whole country will increase, and incidentally, the workers of Britain, of France, or Belgium will benefit, first by the employment created by the manufacture of the goods exported to West Africa, secondly by the increased supply of valuable foodstuffs and raw materials." He, therefore, regarded the policy of expropriation as both injurious to British trade and demoralising to the African.[1]

Having armed himself with a formidable theory of colonial government, Morel immediately proceeded to stir up the colonial conscience in Britain. Like Mary Kingsley, who had blazed the trail, Morel found himself still confronted with a public which knew little or nothing about African problems and was largely indifferent to their implications. Reducing his own theory to a three-point programme, he reminded the

[1] Ibid. pp. 86–87.

British public in his writings that a system of African rights to the land really had existed in West Africa from time immemorial, and that this system was just and adapted to the needs of that country. Secondly, he consistently maintained that the West African, when treated as a free man, was hard-working and capable, with little administrative supervision, of developing his country. Viewed from this standpoint, his anger with Grogan and his impatience with Leo Weinthal are understandable. Thirdly, he never equivocated on the issue of free-trade which he saw as the natural process of trade most beneficial to true British and African interests.[1]

Many of these ideas were derived from the British social experience. Earlier in the Nineteenth Century, Henry George, an American land reformer, had published his *Progress and Poverty*, advocating the " single-tax " formula which he thought would sweep away all private ownership of land, and convert all occupiers into tenants of the State, by appropriating rent. When he came to Britain on an organised lecture-tour in 1884, he attracted great audiences and soon gained adherents. Most prominent among these were Morel and Josiah Wedgewood, the radical member of Parliament for Newcastle.

However, since Britain did not clearly respond to their doctrines on land, they felt that the Colonial Empire might provide a better ground to test the theories of this " Georgian " radicalism. Hence in alliance with others, Morel and Wedgewood advocated land reforms in West Africa. This was timely since it synchronized with the intentions of the Colonial Officials in Nigeria, particularly Sir Percy Girouard, to

[1] See Cocks, op. cit., pp. 43–52.
Grogan insisted on the lazy African myth. See *Affairs of West Africa* pp. 178–182.
Weinthal, the racist editor of the *African World*, believed that nothing could save the African from damnation.

put the land administration and policy in Northern Nigeria on a permanent basis. The Northern Nigerian Land Committee, on which Wedgewood served as a member, produced a report which, although it escaped being brought under the principles of economic rent advocated by Henry George, stated the two cardinal principles of public ownership and native security. Almost immediately after, another movement, led by Morel and supported by Wedgewood and other Liberal and Labour parliamentarians, sought to introduce the principles, though not the form, of the Northern Nigerian Land Law to other West African Colonies. This led to a welter of educated African and Chiefly opposition, but this could not prevent the movement from pushing its arguments far enough to impel the Colonial Office to appoint a Commissioner to report on the situation in the Gold Coast in 1911, and later a West African Lands Committee in 1912 with Morel and Wedgewood among its members.[1]

Before the appointment of the latter Committee, however, Morel had wanted to visit West Africa, particularly Northern Nigeria. In March 1909, he had told Holt about his plans provided he could arrange with some newspapers to pay his expenses and purchase the matter he would contribute for publication.[2] Once he could find someone to manage the *African Mail*, in his absence, Morel felt certain that apart from increasing his income, he would enhance his power in West African affairs if he visited the country. By May, 1910, after financial arrangements with *The Times* and the *Morning Post* which had agreed to pay for the tour and buy the forthcoming articles, Morel had made up his mind to go to Northern Nigeria in October of that year. The generosity of his friend William Cadbury, the Quaker and chocolate manufac-

[1] See K. Dike Nworah, op. cit., pp. 303–316.
[2] Morel to Holt, 23 March, 1909, 29 May, 1910.

turer of Birmingham, really made the tour possible. Holt
had arranged every possible facility and help from his
Company in West Africa for Morel so that at 3.10 p.m. on
22 October, 1910, when the *Jonathan Holt* "steamed
gaily away ", E. D. Morel left Liverpool for West Africa.[1]

After a pleasant passage nearly marred by bad
weather, he arrived at Warri on 17 November, 1910.
He travelled inland to Northern Nigeria, visiting
important centres there. On his homeward journey to
Lagos, he visited the Bale of Ibadan and the Alake of
Abeokuta, and discussed the liquor traffic with them.
In Lagos, he was received by the native community
and lodged with Sir Walter Egerton at Government
House. At Freetown, a deputation of about forty
Muslim chiefs received him, and paid deep respect to
the man whom they later remembered as " the whiteman with the straight eye." An enthusiastic reception
proposed to be staged in his honour was cancelled
because his ship travelled earlier than scheduled. But
most of the whitemen there refused to meet a man who
fraternized with blackmen![2]

In March 1911, Morel returned to Britain. The
importance of this journey was immense, as he regained
his energy which the Congo Reform Association had
severely strained. He had seen the African in his
natural *habitat*, and was now in a better position to
advise or criticise the officials with the integrity of
first-hand knowledge. The trip, by way of his newspaper articles, also proved financially profitable and
thus strengthened his independence. But one of the
greatest results of his visit is the present book: *Nigeria:
Its Peoples and its Problems*. It is a revised compilation of the articles he had published in *The Times* and
Morning Post, but its appearance in book form
obviously excited new interest.

---

[1] Mrs. Morel to Holt, 22 October, 1910.
[2] Cocks, op. cit., p. 37.

INTRODUCTION TO THE THIRD EDITION

The importance of the book at the time can be assessed from the wide review it received from some of the most important sources. Dedicated to the memory of Mary Kingsley, Morel showed himself an upholder of her tradition and a faithful apostle of her aims. Holt's eulogy was thus poetic: " If the spirits of the departed can visit our sphere, you have constantly led her spirits with you during all the years you have written and fought for the lives and liberties of the Negro in his own country."[1]   H. S. W. Edwardes, a Colonial Official at Bida, was of the opinion that the book " stands alone as a weighty and reasoned statement of the problems we have to grapple with."[2]

The unanimous verdict of the newspapers contrasted with the discord that greeted his first book, *Affairs of West Africa*. *The Economist* saw the present one as not only a vivid picture of a possession second only to India among British tropical dependencies, but also an eloquent plea for the only policy which could make the partition of Africa a blessing to the African and not a curse. Sir Harry Johnston in the *Daily Chronicle* recommended it to " all officials of civilized governments dealing, or intending to deal, largely with the opening up of tropical Africa . . ." *The Times*, which had found fault with an earlier volume, now saw this one as altogether " one of distinctive value to the student and administrator ". Summing it up as " a study in applied anthropology," the *Morning Post* advised that it should be read " by every thinking Englishman." *The Spectator* saw it as a travel account by an unbiased traveller, in which the dry bones of history become living flesh! *The Nation* was particularly struck by the book's accurate picture, its " sound sense and sympathy ". *The Academy* rejoiced in the opinion that though it was humanitarian in principle,

[1] Holt to Morel, 9 November, 1911.
[2] H. S. W. Edwardes to Morel, 25 November, 1911.

the book was free from that detestable narrowness of outlook which rendered many humanitarian proposals incompatible with colonial progress. *Truth* praised the adequate, temperate and conclusive treatment of the central question: that the civilization of the negro races on their own lines of natural development as against the two schools of thought—the " damned nigger " school, which would make him a hewer of wood and a drawer of water for all time, and those who would make him in a moment a twentieth-century European and Christian. It would be unfair to doubt the merit of these views; for Morel, in the book and elsewhere, could be said to have proffered constructive advice to the officials, though much of the advice, although praising the work of these officials, often took the form, in which it appeared that only Morel could carry out the necessary colonial reforms.[1]

This view was even entertained, though differently expressed, by some of his admirers. Thus the *Athenaeum* found Morel's projected reforms so thoughtful that it wished he were in the House of Commons to advocate his views. The *Review of Reviews* wondered whether the then British Government could not create a post for Morel which would give him official authority to act as peripatetic tribune of the natives throughout the whole of the British dominions in tropical Africa. Holt also believed that Morel possessed " the constructive statesmanship " which " few of our government (men) have," and hoped that it would be better if they put Morel in a position to utilise it.[2]

It was this aspiration to be in a position of power and authority which induced Morel to enter practical politics. Supported by Holt, Cadbury, Mrs. Green and other influential members of the Liberal Party, Morel was sponsored as Liberal Candidate for Birkenhead.

[1] F3, E. D. Morel Papers.
[2] Holt to Morel, 15 November, 1911.

INTRODUCTION TO THE THIRD EDITION

When on 8 November, 1912 he was officially nominated, and adopted as candidate, Morel gave a summary of his position in British politics. He stood for equitable distribution of wealth socially produced, for maximum wage standards, Irish Home Rule, Welsh Disestablishment, the Insurance Act, and the principle of the Licensing Bill of 1908. He advocated women's suffrage, diminution of the powers of the House of Lords, land reform and spoke and wrote against Tariff Reform. On foreign policy, he favoured the Concert of Europe idea, advocated friendship with Germany, and a defensive navy for Britain. He was opposed to the idea of national conscription, and isolationist policy. His advocacy of public control of the Secret Treaties and foreign policy became crystallized in the Union of Democratic Control which tried to socialize foreign policy administration during and after the first World War. It was for his tireless and ubiquitous organisation of the U.D.C. that A. S. P. Taylor eulogized Morel as the " Foreign Secretary of Dissent ".[1]

Although Morel tried to widen his interest by harping on domestic and foreign policy issues, he never totally allowed the urge for political expediency at home to undermine his urge for colonial conscience. As the possibility of an election became more elusive (not held until 14 December, 1918 after he had resigned as liberal candidate), Morel saw no electoral disadvantage in bringing home to Englishmen those moral ideas which he saw as the basis of true imperialism. At the Church Congress at Southampton on 2 October, 1913, he once again supported his thesis for African land rights, and warned the public against the policy which led to " social misery and a land-less proletariat "; against forcing loans upon African natural rulers in the interest of cosmopolitan finance and for the greater profit of armament firms ". He spoke against im-

[1] See E. D. Morel Papers F2/1 for Morel's speeches and activities.

posing European culture and legal names and institutions upon African Societies not suited for them, and chastised the Church for the " staggering abruptness " with which it transmitted exotic ideas and habits to Africa.[1]   In 1908, Holt had expressed the wish that John Morley (because of his speech on India Reform which had relevance to West Africa) would join their enlightened party.[2]

Morel however, criticised Morley's views expressed in the Lord's, that it was " impossible to prevent the condition of labourers in the tropics from being unpleasantly akin to slavery ", it might be : " disastrous to the maintenance of a high standard of rule by the whiteman in the tropical belt."[3] Not only, therefore, was Morel practically against the physical coercion of Africans, and in support of legitimate and equitable commercial transactions, he also set a theoretical high standard of colonial ethics.

After the death of Holt, and with the Lands Committee Report, in 1915, Morel became more interested in international issues related to the war, during which he was imprisoned at Pentonville for an indiscreet dissemination of literature against the war.   On his release, however, he remained radically devoted to his Union of Democratic Control on which platform he was elected to Parliament for Dundee in 1922.   But, before he could prove his parliamentary mettle, he became ill, and died suddenly in 1924.

The life of E. D. Morel must be fascinating to all those interested in African questions, and particularly, in the politics of the left.   He possessed the vital qualities for public agitation; a capacity for prolonged effort which made it possible for him to reconcile his West African work with the demands of the Congo Reform Association, and later with the Union of Democratic Control;

[1] Morel's *Notes* F2/1 E. D. Morel Papers.
[2] Holt to Morel, 19 December, 1908, F8/3.
[3] Morel's *Notes* F2/1.

and a single mind which sustained him against all doubts when his fortunes were low. His personal relations with the officials, with Members of Parliament, with editors of newspapers, made him an inestimable asset to any movement he led. But it was his own editorial power, his vast and incisive knowledge of African affairs, not to mention his sincerity and honesty, that added significance to the movements that became associated with his name. At times, however, he took extreme views of issues. Moreover, lack of financial independence necessarily undermined the sanctity of his ideals, while a few instances of political expediency threatened them. But apart from his destined commitment to the cause of enlightened commerce, he was both a sincere advocate and a critic of experience.

KENNETH DIKE NWORAH

KINGS COLLEGE, LONDON
August 1966

PREFACE TO THE SECOND EDITION

THE First Edition of this work has been very generously received. I have to express my warm appreciation for the many kindly criticisms which have appeared in the Press, and for the friendly words of correspondents who have written to me. My chief pleasure is the thought that I may have contributed in making the work of British officials in Nigeria better known, and, in particular, that the principles of Native Policy applied in Northern Nigeria, and described in the book, should have received so emphatic and universal an endorsement from those who have perused my attempt to explain them to the Public. This is specially comforting to a student who is firmly convinced that through those principles alone can tropical Africa be successfully administered by the white races, and who, in the humble capacity of an independent free-lance, has for some fifteen years preached the doctrine they embody. It is also a source of satisfaction that the amalgamation of the two Nigerias, urged in the book, should now be well on its way to accomplishment, and under the direction of so distinguished and experienced a public servant as Sir Frederick Lugard, with whose personality the foundation of Northern Nigeria will ever be associated. That the feasibility of consolidating the various Yoruba States, urged in Chapter VII., should now likewise be giving rise to official studies on the spot is welcome news. As an outsider, I may, perhaps, venture to express the hope that the unrivalled knowledge of Yoruba customs and history possessed by Mr. R. E. Dennett, and the confidence in which Mr. W. A. Ross, the Resident at Oyo is held by the Alafin—the titular head of Yorubaland—will be utilized in any scheme of reconstruction which may be evolved. I apologize to the two officials mentioned for venturing to make free with their names.

Among the features of administrative work in Northern Nigeria, described in this volume, none, perhaps (unless it be the Land Legislation) has received more commendation at the hands of reviewers than the National Schools at Nassarawa. And in this connection I cannot forbear making a strong appeal to the Public to support a scheme, than which there can be no branch of imperial responsibility more important or far-reaching in its effects for good—a scheme of Native Education *in harmony with the national life of the people.* The funds at the disposal of the Northern Nigeria Government are altogether inadequate to extend the work as it should be developed, and there is immediate need for external assistance which the Colonial Office, I understand, is prepared to welcome. Let me briefly recapitulate what has already been done, and what is required.

Early in 1909 proposals for a National System of Education were submitted to the Colonial Office by Mr. Hanns Vischer, peculiarly fitted to the task assigned to him of director of education by his African travels, his knowledge of Hausa and Arabic and of native life in the Soudan, and his study of the various educational systems in Khartoum, Lagos, and elsewhere. The principle governing the proposals was the preservation of native language, customs, and character ; their aim was the establishment of schools managed by the natives themselves under British guidance—schools which should form part and parcel of the native life. A school had already been started, with a good deal of difficulty, by

PREFACE TO THE SECOND EDITION

Major Burdon, the Resident at Sokoto in 1906 ; and one by Mr. Temple, then Resident at Kano. Following upon the acceptance of Mr. Vischer's proposals, a central school was opened at Kano in September, 1909, reinforced by native Mallamai (teachers) from Sokoto and pupils from Katsina.

The sneers and suspicions with which these efforts were first received rapidly subsided, and with the assistance of the Emirs of Kano, Katsina, and Zaria, the confidence of the people was gradually won over.

The Central Schools at Nassarawa (Kano) now comprise (A) a School for the sons of Chiefs ; (B) a School for teachers (Mallamai) ; (C) a technical School with an agricultural branch ; (D) an elementary School.

The object of School (A) is to train men who later on will be able to administer the country, understanding the needs of their people and the methods of the British Administration, bound to us not by fear or by commercial interests only, but by ties of co-operation and sentiment. The object of School (B) is to train teachers for Branch Schools throughout the country. The object of School (C) is to train the native artisan—carpenters, blacksmiths, leather-workers and tanners, embroiderers, etc., and to adapt his methods to modern requirements while avoiding any but the most simple of European tools, so that when the pupil returns to his home he can fashion the same tools for himself or procure them from European merchants at a price not beyond his means. Such handicrafts as those mentioned are, of course, old and established ones in which the natives are already proficient in a local sense. The export of goat-skins to Europe is considerable, but the value is lessened by generally defective tanning. I brought back with me a number of specially well-tanned (native tanned) skins, and binders and shoemakers who have handled them declare that they are amongst the finest specimens of

xxiii

leather they have come across. Expert opinion is that, properly tanned, the Nigerian skins will rival the best imports from India. The agricultural branch of School (C) is concerned with the teaching of seed selection, afforestation, and the improvement of agriculture and stock raising. The pupils of Schools (A) and (B) attend these classes as part of their curriculum. The object of School (A) need not be further particularized.

A word remains to be said as to the curriculum. That of (A) and (B) includes arithmetic, reading, history, geography, elementary surveying and hygiene. That of (D) includes the three " R "'s and elementary surveying and hygiene.

All instruction is given in the vernacular, and all instruction is based upon already existing knowledge. Thus, in the initial stage of geography, the pupils are first taught to make a plan of their hut, compound, and immediate surroundings ; they are then taught their own local geography ; the history classes begin with local native records.

All pupils receive instruction in the religion their parents desire. At present only Mohammedans are dealt with.

All pupils pay school fees and buy their school material.

The success of the movement has been wonderful. In two short years not only has confidence in our intentions become rooted, but positive enthusiasm has been enlisted among one of the most intelligent races in the whole of Africa. The Schools are already being looked upon by the natives generally not as something alien thrust upon the country by the white man, *but as institutions of their own*. At the present moment there are over three hundred pupils from all the provinces at Nassarawa, and all the most powerful Chiefs in the country support the enterprise.

So much for what has been done.

PREFACE TO THE SECOND EDITION

Now for what remains to be accomplished. The work is now solidly rooted. Its expansion is a vital necessity. From nearly every province come urgent requests for the opening of local schools. It is desired to start an elementary school in all the more important towns of the Protectorate.

The general work is full of the utmost promise. Education in tropical Western Africa has at length been started on right lines. The results—if the devoted labours of Mr. Hanns Vischer and his European and Nigerian assistants are not hampered for lack of funds—will prove of incalculable benefit. The opportunity is unique, and the task taken in hand is one of the truest and soundest Imperialism.

A sum of £50,000 is required to place these schools on a permanent footing and to allow of their expansion to meet the needs of the moment.

I would like to place on record my profound conviction that a rich man could perform no more enduring benefit upon Africa and upon British rule in Africa, than by subscribing liberally to this great work.

I pass from this to two questions raised in my book which were bound to give rise to adverse comment in certain quarters. I refer to the criticisms contained in the volume as regards certain aspects of Christian missionary effort in Nigeria and to my remarks on the liquor traffic in Southern Nigeria. In truth I have been surprised rather at the amount of support than at the censure with which the views I thought it but honest to express have been received. Apart from personal abuse in one or two religious and temperance papers, and a few equally abusive letters, my unorthodoxy on these points has been most fairly treated. Nevertheless it has given pain—specially on the religious side—to some old friends and co-workers in another cause which I would fain have avoided giving had I felt it possible to suppress opinions that [however open to objection] it seemed to me there was utility in recording. Whether my views on particular weaknesses in the spirit, practice, and effects of missionary propaganda contain elements of soundness or not, I must repudiate the charge of attacking missionaries as missionaries, or of a desire to depreciate the generally self-sacrificing character of missionary effort *per se*. Nothing in my book warrants it, and I am glad to see that one of the most prominent Church organs, the *Church Times*, remarks in the course of its review : " Let it be clearly understood that he (the Author) is not that cheapest of things, an Englishman sneering at missionaries." With that certainly unprejudiced verdict I am well content.

As regards the liquor traffic in Southern Nigeria, the only thing I will say is this. My contribution to the discussion falls into two parts, viz. a general survey of the problem combined with a criticism of the action of the Native Races Committee and of some of its Clerical friends and supporters. That is one part. The other is an attempt to put forward constructive recommendations for the future. Of the two, the former is the less important. The criticisms that have been made upon it are (*a*) that I have been too severe upon the Committee and its friends. If so, I am sorry, but would point out that the Committee and its friends have been particularly ruthless towards those who did not share their views, most of whom, being Officials, have not been able to defend themselves against attacks always sweeping, sometimes personal, and, often, I think, very unjust. As, however, there seemed no need in a Second Edition to revive a controversy which has now virtually burnt itself out, I have re-modelled the chapter on the liquor traffic, omitting therefrom discussion of the past action of the Native Races Committee. (*b*) That I have posed as a " half-hearted apologist " for the liquor traffic, which is a bad traffic. I am not conscious of having posed as an apologist. I have dealt with specific statements advanced and publicly discussed, and have said precisely what I thought about them. I recognize in the liquor traffic a real potential danger if unrestricted. I do not like the traffic. I wish it did not exist. But the dreadful things said about it are not, in my opinion, true. (c) That illicit distilling is not a danger that need be feared. I cannot agree. (d) That I contradict myself when I say at one and the same time that it is impossible to prevent the Southern Nigerian from drinking alcohol in some form or another because the race has never been a teetotal one, and that the spread of the Mohammedan religion is an automatic antidote to drinking. The contradiction is only apparent. The vast majority of the Southern Nigerians are Pagans. So long as they remain Pagans they will drink, because they always have drunk. If they do not drink " gin," they will drink something else—more of their own fermented beverages, upon the physiological effects of which, compared with imported spirit, medical and other opinion is divided. They are not immoderate but moderate drinkers. Those who have become Christians, or nominal Christians, who have become Europeanized, have not, speaking generally, become abstainers. On the contrary. The Christianized Southern Nigerians drink dearer and more potent spirits, the spirits drunk by the European, not the " trade " spirits drunk by the Pagans, which, as now imported, are weaker than the usual class of spirits. It is here that, to my mind, the greatest danger for the future lies. If the Southern Nigerians become a non-spirit drinking race, it will not be through legislation, but by their conversion to a religion which prohibits indulgence in alcoholic liquors. The question will then resolve itself into a struggle between the spiritual force of Islam and natural tendencies.

PREFACE TO THE SECOND EDITION

The constructive part of my remarks have not been seriously criticized. Until they are shown to be faulty I may be forgiven for believing—and my belief is strengthened by the failure of this year's Liquor Conference at Brussels—that it is along the lines I have indicated that the problem of the liquor traffic must be tackled. The *gradual* introduction of direct taxation is the road to follow, for it leads to the goal of making the administration progressively independent of revenue from customs-taxes on imported spirits. This policy can be combined with the other various measures I have ventured to indicate. But if direct taxation is brusquely imposed and enforced, as it was in Sierra Leone, the Southern Nigerian will resist it by force, for of the majority of the inhabitants of Southern Nigeria it may be said that we have been in touch with them for periods varying from fifty to ten years, and that we have never yet exacted tribute from them. And the idea of making sober people more sober by killing them, burning their villages and destroying their farms (the inevitable accompaniments of warfare) is to me inexpressibly revolting, un-Christian—and stupid.

It has been pointed out to me that the *jangali* (cattle) tax in Northern Nigeria (*vide* p. 170) is now paid in silver ; that the Administrative Staff in the province of Bauchi (*vide* p. 182) is no longer so undermanned as it was when I passed through the country, and that the trading licences to Europeans (*vide* p. 174) are now being abolished.

E. D. MOREL.

February, 1912.

PREFACE TO THE FIRST EDITION

I HAVE to express, in the first place, my indebtedness to the Editor and Management of the *Times* and of the *Manchester Guardian* for permission to reproduce the articles and maps which appeared in the columns of those newspapers, and to all those who have so generously helped me to overcome an accident to my camera by placing their own admirable photographic work at my disposal.

In the second place, I desire to record my sincere appreciation for the courtesy I received from the Colonial Office in connection with a recent visit to Nigeria ; and to Sir Walter and Lady Egerton, Sir Henry Hesketh Bell, Mr. Charles Temple (Acting-Governor of Northern Nigeria) and their Staffs for the kindness and hospitality extended to me while there.

Also to the Management and Staff of the Southern and Northern Nigeria railways ; in particular to the Director of the Public Works Department of the Northern Protectorate, Mr. John Eaglesome and to Mrs. Eaglesome, and to Mr. Firmin, the Resident Engineer of the Southern Nigeria line at Jebba.

My travels in the country were facilitated in every way possible, and the kindness everywhere shown me in both Protectorates far transcended any claim which ordinary courtesy to a stranger might have suggested.

To the British merchants established in Nigeria I am under similar obligations, more particularly to Messrs. John Holt & Co., Ltd., who were good enough to place their steamers at my disposal. To Messrs. Elder Dempster & Co. I am similarly indebted.

My special thanks are due to my friends Mr. and Mrs. William A. Cadbury and Mr. John Holt and his sons, for much personal kindness in connection with my journey. I am indebted to Mr. Trigge, of the Niger Company, Mr. W. H. Himbury, of the British Cotton Growing Association, and many others who have responded with unwearied patience to my importunate questionings.

I have also to express my sense of obligation to the Native Community of Lagos—Christian, Mohammedan and Pagan—for the cordial public reception they accorded to me in that place ; and for the address with which they were good enough to present me. Also to the leading Native gentlemen of Freetown for the kind hospitality they extended to me during my short stay at the capital of Sierra Leone, and to the Mohammedan Chiefs representing many different tribes of the hinterland, who there foregathered, under Dr. Blyden's [1] roof, to bid me welcome, and for the addresses they presented to me.

West Africa is a land of controversy. There is not, I think, any question of public interest concerned with it that does not give rise to acute differences of opinion into which some influence—the climate, perhaps—and the fact that the country is going through a difficult transition stage, seems not infrequently to infuse a measure of bitterness. I fear it is unavoidable that some of the opinions expressed in this volume, if they give pleasure in certain quarters, will give displeasure in others. I can only ask those who may be affected in the latter sense to believe that the writer has really had no other object in view than that of setting forth the facts as he saw them, and to draw from those facts the inferences which commended themselves to a judgment no doubt full of imperfections, but able, at any rate, to claim sincerity as its guiding motive.

E. D. MOREL.

August, 1911.

I regret to hear of Dr. Blyden's death since the first edition of this volume appeared.

INTRODUCTION

My chief object in presenting to the public in book form a collection of articles recently published in the *Times* * as revised, together with additional matter, has been that of increasing—if haply this should be the effect—public interest in the greatest and most interesting of our tropical African Protectorates. It has been my endeavour throughout not to overload the story with detail, but to paint, or try to paint, a picture of Nigeria as it is to-day ; to portray the life of its people, the difficulties and tasks of its British governors, and the Imperial responsibilities the nation has contracted in assuming control over this vast region.

Parts II., III., and IV. consist of an attempt at a serious study of these things.

Part I. consists of a mere series of pen and ink sketches, so to speak ; impressions jotted down in varying moods. The value, if, indeed, they have any value at all, of these disjointed ramblings lies in the glimpse they may afford of native character and the nature of the country, thus helping, perhaps, to bring Nigeria a little nearer to us.

I ought, perhaps, to apologize for not having incorporated a history of the British occupation of Nigeria. But, apart from the circumstance that Captain Orr, now Colonial Secretary for Cyprus, and for many years Resident in Northern Nigeria, is, I understand, about to publish a volume on that subject written with the inside knowledge

* With the exception of the articles on Cotton, which appeared in the *Manchester Guardian.*

which he so peculiarly possesses : the thing has already been done by others.

It seemed to me that if any public utility at all were to be attached to my own modest effort, it could more fittingly be sought in the direction of handling, from an independent outsider's point of view, problems of actuality in their setting of existing circumstances and conditions ; and in emphasizing a fact sometimes apt to be forgotten. I mean that in these Dependencies the Native is the important person to be considered, quite as much from the Imperial as from any other standpoint, interpreting Imperialism as personally I interpret it, to signify a good deal more than painting the map red and indulging in tall talk about " possessions " and about " inferior races." In Nigeria, the Nigerian is not, as some persons appear to regard him, merely an incidental factor but the paramount factor. Nigeria is not a Colony; it is a Dependency.

The West African native has two classes of enemies, one positive, the other unconscious. The ranks of both are not only recruited from members of the white race : they are to be found among members of the West African's own household. The first class corresponds to the school of European thought concerning tropical Africa, whose adherents object to the West African being a land-owner, and whose doctrine it is that in the economic development of the country the profits should be the exclusive appanage of the white race, the native's *rôle* being that of labourer and wage-earner for all time.

In the fulfilment of the *rôle* thus assigned to him, some of the adherents of this school, those with the longest sight, would be quite prepared to treat the individual native well ; others would cheerfully impose their will by brutal violence. That is a temperamental affair which does not touch the essence of the deeper issue.

To this class of enemies belong some of the educated or half-educated Europeanized natives whom our educational

and religious system divorces from their race, and
who, having no outlet and bereft of national or racial
pride, betray the interests of their country into the hands
of its foes.

The second class is to be met with among the ranks of
those who, by striking at slavery and abuse, have rendered
enormous benefit to the West African, but who were also
unwittingly responsible for fastening upon his neck a heavy
yoke, and who, not only with no motive of self-interest,
but, on the contrary, with the most generous desire to
minister to his welfare, are to-day in danger of ministering
to his undoing.   It is not easy to affix any particular label
to those influences which, in the political field, contributed
so powerfully in handing over the Congo to Leopold II.
(afterwards strenuously co-operating in freeing its peoples
from his grasp) and in placing two million West Africans
in Liberia under the pettily tyrannous incompetence of a
handful of American Blacks.   They are partly educational,
partly philanthropic, partly religious.   The basis of sentiment animating them appears to be that a kindness is
being done to the West African by the bestowal upon him
of European culture, law, religion and dress, and that,
having thus unmade him as an African, those responsible
are in duty bound to support the product of their own
creation in its automatic and inevitable revolt against
authority, whether represented by the Native Ruler or by
the European Administrator.   In the form it at present
takes, and in the circumstances too often accompanying
it, this is not a kindness but a cruel wrong.

Let me try to make my meaning perfectly clear in
regard to this latter case.   I make no attack upon any
organization or body.   I criticize the trend of certain
influences, and I willingly admit, as all must do, even those
who most dread their effects, that these influences have
their origin in centres imbued with genuine altruism.
Also that of one side of them nothing but good can be

said—the destructive side, the side which is ever prepared to respond to the call of human suffering. Neither do I suggest that education can, or should, be arrested. I simply lay down this double proposition. First, that educational and allied influences, whose combined effect is to cause the West African to lose his racial identity, *must* produce unhappiness and unrest of a kind which is not susceptible of evolving a compensating constructive side. Secondly, that in no period of time which can be forecast, will the condition of West African society permit of the *supreme* governing power being shared by both races, although short of the casting vote, so to speak, policy should everywhere be directed towards consolidating and strengthening Native authority.

Still less do I make any reflection upon the educated West African as such. Among these Westernized Natives are men to be regarded with the utmost respect, for they have achieved the well-nigh insuperable. They have succeeded, despite all, in remaining African in heart and sentiment ; and in retaining their dignity in the midst of difficulties which only the most sympathetic alien mind can appreciate, and, even so, not wholly. To Mary Kingsley alone, perhaps, was it given to probe right down to the painful complexities of their position as only a woman, and a gifted woman, specially endowed, could do. Of such men the great Fanti lawyer, John Mensah Sarbah, whose recent and premature death is a calamity for West Africa, was one of the best types. The venerable Dr. E. Wilmot Blyden, whose race will regard him some day as its misunderstood prophet, is another. One could name others. Perchance their numbers are greater than is usually supposed, and are not confined to men of social distinction and learning. And these men wring their hands. They see, and they feel, the pernicious results of a well-meaning but mistaken policy. They appreciate the depth of the abyss. But they lack the power of combination, and their position is delicate to a degree which Europeans, who do not realize the innumerable undercurrents and intrigues of denationalized West African society are unable to grasp.

Between these two schools of thought, the " damned nigger " school and the denationalizing school (that, without appreciating it, plays into the hands of the first), which threaten the West African in his freedom, his property and his manhood, there is room for a third. One which, taking note to-day that the West African *is* a landowner, desires that he shall continue to be one under British rule, not with decreasing but with increasing security of tenure ; taking note that to-day the West African *is* an agriculturist, a farmer, a herdsman, and, above all, to the marrow of his bones, a trader, declines to admit that he should be degraded, whether by direct or indirect means, to the position of a hireling ; taking note that customary law it is which holds native society together, calls for its increased study and demands that time shall be allowed for its gradual improvement from within, deprecating its supersession by European *formulæ* of law in the name of " reform," for which the country is not ripe and whose application can only dislocate, not raise, West African social life. A school of thought which, while prepared to fight with every available weapon against attempts to impose conditions of helotism upon the West African, earnestly pleads that those controlling the various influences moulding his destinies from without, shall be inspired to direct their energies towards making him a better African, not a hybrid. A school of thought which sees in the preservation of the West African's land for him and his descendants ; in a system of education which shall not anglicize ; in technical instruction ; in assisting and encouraging agriculture, local industries and scientific forestry ; in introducing labour-saving appliances, and in strengthening all that is best, materially and spiritually,

INTRODUCTION

in aboriginal institutions, the highest duties of our Imperial rule. A school of thought whose aim it is to see Nigeria, at least, become in time the home of highly-trained African peoples, protected in their property and in their rights by the paramount Power, proud of their institutions, proud of their race, proud of their own fertile and beautiful land.

E. D. MOREL.

August, 1911.

CONTENTS

PART I
THOUGHTS ON TREK

PART II
SOUTHERN NIGERIA

PART III
NORTHERN NIGERIA

xxxvii

CONTENTS

PART IV

ISLAM, COTTON GROWING, AND THE LIQUOR TRAFFIC

LIST OF ILLUSTRATIONS

LIST OF ILLUSTRATIONS

xl

PART I

THOUGHTS ON TREK

CHAPTER I

ON WHAT HAS BEEN AND MAY BE

AFTER trekking on horseback five hundred miles or so, you acquire the philosophy of this kind of locomotion. For it has a philosophy of its own, and with each day that passes you become an apter pupil. You learn many things, or you hope you do, things internally evolved. But when you come to the point of giving external shape to them by those inefficient means the human species is as yet virtually confined to—speech and writing—you become painfully conscious of inadequate powers. Every day brings its own panorama of nature unfolding before your advance ; its own special series of human incidents— serious, humorous, irritating, soothing—its own thought waves. And it is not my experience that these long silent hours—for conversation with one's African companions is necessarily limited and sporadic—induce, by what one would imagine natural re-action, descriptive expansiveness when, pen in hand, one seeks to give substance to one's impressions. Rather the reverse, alack ! Silent communing doth seem to cut off communication between brain and pen. You are driven in upon yourself, and the channel of outward expression dries up. For a scribbler, against whom much has been imputed, well-nigh all the crimes, indeed, save paucity of output, the phenomenon is not without its alarming side, at least to one's self. In one's friends it may well inspire a sense of blessed relief.

One day holds much—so much of time, so much of

space, so much of change. The paling stars or the waning moon greet your first swing into the saddle, and the air strikes crisp and chill. You are still there as the orange globe mounts the skies, silhouetting, perchance, a group of palms, flooding the crumbling walls of some African village, to whose inhabitants peace has ceased to make walls necessary—a sacrifice of the picturesque which, artistically, saddens—or lighting some fantastic peak of granite boulders piled up as though by Titan's hand. You are still there when the rays pour downwards from on high, strike upwards from dusty track and burning rock, and all the countryside quivers and simmers in the glow. Sometimes you may still be there—it has happened to me —when the shadows fall swiftly, and the cry of the crown-birds, seeking shelter for the night on some marshy spot to their liking, heralds the dying of the day. From cold, cold great enough to numb hands and feet, to gentle warmth, as on a June morning at home ; from fierce and stunning heat, wherein, rocked by the " triple " of your mount, you drowse and nod, to cooling evening breeze. You pass, in the twenty-four hours, through all the gamut of climatic moods, which, at this time of the year, makes this country at once invigorating and, to my thinking, singularly treacherous, especially on the Bauchi plateau, over which a cold wind often seems to sweep, even in the intensity of the noontide sun, and where often a heavy overcoat seems insufficient to foster warmth when darkness falls upon the land.

So much of time and change—each day seems composed of many days. Ushered in on level plain, furrowed by the agriculturist's hoe, dotted with colossal trees, smiling with farm and hamlet ; it carries you onward through many miles of thick young forest, where saplings of but a few years' growth dispute their life with rank and yellow grasses, and thence in gradual ascent through rock-strewn paths until your eye sees naught but a network of

4

hills ; to leave you at its close skirting a valley thickly overgrown with bamboo and semi-tropical vegetation, where the flies do congregate, and seek, unwelcomed, a resting-place inside your helmet.   Dawning amid a sleeping town, heralded by the sonorous call of the Muslim priest, which lets loose the vocal chords of human, quadruped and fowl, swelling into a murmur of countless sounds and increasing bustle ; it will take you for many hours through desolate stretches, whence human life, if life there ever was, has been extirpated by long years of such' lawlessness and ignorance as once laid the blight of grisly ruin over many a fair stretch of English homestead.   Yes, you may, in this land of many memories, and mysteries still unravelled, pass, within the same twenty-four hours, the flourishing settlement with every sign of plenty and of promise, and the blackened wreck of communities once prosperous before this or that marauding band of freebooters brought fire and slaughter, death to the man, slavery to the woman and the infant—much as our truculent barons, whose doughty deeds we are taught in childhood to admire, acted in their little day.   The motive and the immediate results differed not at all.   What the ultimate end may be here lies in the womb of the future, for at this point the roads diverge.   With us those dark hours vanished through the slow growth of indigenous evolution.   Here the strong hand of the alien has interposed, and, stretching at present the unbridged chasm of a thousand years, has enforced reform from without.

And what a weird thing it is when you come to worry it out, that this alien hand should have descended and compelled peace !   Viewed in the abstract, one feels it may be discussed as a problem of theory, for a second.   One feels it permissible to ask, will the people, or rather will the Governors of the people which has brought peace to this land, which has enabled the peasant to till the soil and reap his harvest in quietness, which has allowed the weaver to pursue and profit by his industry in safety which has established such security throughout the land, that you may see a woman and her child travelling alone and unprotected in the highways, carrying all their worldly possessions between them; will this people's ultimate action be as equally beneficial as the early stages have been, or will its interference be the medium through which evils, not of violence, but economic, and as great as the old, will slowly, but certainly and subtly, eat into the hearts of these Nigerian homes and destroy their happiness, not of set purpose, but automatically, inevitably so? I say that, approached as an abstract problem, it seems permissible to ask one's self that question as one wanders here and there over the face of the land, and one hears the necessity of commercially developing the country to save the British taxpayers' pockets, of the gentlemen who want to exploit the rubber forests of the Bauchi plateau, of the Chambers of Commerce that require the reservation of lands for British capitalists, and of those who argue that a native, who learned how to smelt tin before we knew there was tin in the country, should no longer be permitted to do so, now that we wish to smelt it ourselves, and of the railways and the roads which have to be built—yes, it seems permissible, though quite useless. But I confess that when one studies what is being done out here in the concrete, from the point of view of the men who are doing it, then it is no longer permissible to doubt. When one sees this man managing, almost single-handed, a country as large as Scotland; when one sees that man, living in a leaky mud hut, holding, by the sway of his personality, the balance even between fiercely antagonistic races, in a land which would cover half a dozen of the large English counties; when one sees the marvels accomplished by tact, passionate interest and self-control, with utterly inadequate means, in continuous personal discomfort, short-handed, on poor pay, out here in Northern Nigeria—

"THROUGH PLAIN AND VALLEY AND MOUNTAIN SIDE."

"WE HAVE TREKKED TOGETHER."

See p. 14.

then one feels that permanent evil cannot ultimately evolve from so much admirable work accomplished, and that the end must make for good.

And, thinking over this personal side of the matter as one jogs along up hill and down dale, through plain and valley and mountain side, through lands of plenty and lands of desolation, past carefully fenced-in fields of cotton and cassava, past the crumbling ruins of deserted habitations, along the great white dusty road through the heart of Hausaland, along the tortuous mountain track to the pagan stronghold, there keeps on murmuring in one's brain the refrain : " How is it done ? How is it done ? " Ten years ago, nay, but six, neither property nor life were safe. The peasant fled to the hills, or hurried at nightfall within the sheltering walls of the town. Now he is descending from the hills and abandoning the towns.

And the answer forced upon one, by one's own observations, is that the incredible has been wrought, primarily and fundamentally, not by this or that brilliant feat of arms, not by Britain's might or Britain's wealth, but by a handful of quiet men, enthusiastic in their appreciation of the opportunity, strong in their sense of duty, keen in their sense of right, firm in their sense of justice, who, working in an independence, and with a personal responsibility in respect to which, probably, no country now under the British flag can offer a parallel, whose deeds are unsung, and whose very names are unknown to their countrymen, have shown, and are every day showing, that, with all her faults, Britain does still breed sons worthy of the highest traditions of the race.

CHAPTER II

ON THE GREAT WHITE ROAD

You may fairly call it the Great White Road to Hausaland, although it does degenerate in places into a mere track where it pierces some belt of shea-wood or mixed trees, and you are reduced to Indian file. But elsewhere it merits its appellation, and it glimmers ghostly in the moonlight as it cuts the plain, cultivated to its very edge with guinea-corn and millet, cassava and cotton, beans and pepper. And you might add the adjective, dusty, to it. For dusty at this season of the year it certainly is. Dusty beyond imagination. Surely there is no dust like this dust as it sweeps up at you, impelled by the *harmattan* blowing from the north, into your eyes and mouth and nose and hair? Dust composed of unutterable things. Dust which countless bare human feet have tramped for months. Dust mingled with the manure of thousands of oxen, horses, sheep and goats. Dust which converts the glossy skin of the African into an unattractive drab, but which cannot impair his cheerfulness withal. Dust which eats its way into your boxes, and defies the brush applied to your clothes, and finds its way into your soup and all things edible and non-edible. Dust which gets between you and the sun, and spoils your view of the country, wrapping everything in a milky haze which distorts distances and lies thick upon the foliage. The morning up to nine, say, will be glorious and clear and crisp, and then, sure enough, as you halt for breakfast and with sharpened

A GROUP OF TUAREGS.

A BORNU OX.

appetite await the looked-for " chop," a puff of wind will spring up from nowhere and in its train will come the dust. The haze descends and for the rest of the day King Dust will reign supreme. It is responsible for much sickness, this Sahara dust, of that my African friends and myself are equally convinced. You may see the turbaned members of the party draw the lower end of that useful article of apparel right across the face up to the eyes when the wind begins to blow. The characteristic *litham* of the Tuareg, the men of the desert, may have had its origin in the necessity, taught by experience, of keeping the dust out of nose and mouth. I have been told by an officer of much Northern Nigerian experience, that that terrible disease, known as cerebo-spinal meningitis, whose characteristic feature is inflammation of the membranes of the brain, and which appears in epidemic form out here, is aggravated, if not induced, in his opinion—and he assures me in the opinion of many natives he has consulted—by this disease-carrying dust. In every town and village in the Northern Hausa States, you will see various diseases of the eye lamentably rife, and here, I am inclined to think, King Dust also plays an active and discreditable part.

The Great White Road. It thoroughly deserves that title from the point where one enters the Kano Province coming from Zaria. It is there not only a great white road but a very fine one, bordered on either side by a species of eucalyptus, and easily capable, so far as breadth is concerned, of allowing the passage of two large automobiles abreast. I, personally, should not care to own the automobile which undertook the journey, because the road is not exactly what we would call up-to-date. Thank Heaven that there is one part of the world, at least, to be found where neither roads, nor ladies' costumes are " up-to-date." If the Native Administration of the Kano Emirate had nothing else to be commended for, and under the tactful guidance of successive Residents it has an increasing account to its credit, the traveller would bear it in grateful recollection for its preservation of the trees in the immediate vicinity of, and sometimes actually on the Great White Road itself. It is difficult to over-estimate the value to man and beast, to the hot and dusty European, to the weary-footed carrier, to the patient pack-ox, and cruelly-bitted native horse, of the occasional shady tree at the edge of or on the road. And what magnificent specimens of the vegetable kingdom the fertile soil of Kano Province does carry—our New Forest giants, though holding their own for beauty and shape and, of course, clinging about our hearts with all their wealth of historical memories and inherited familiarity, would look puny in comparison. With one exception I do not think anything on the adverse side of trivialities has struck me more forcibly out here than the insane passion for destroying trees which seems to animate humanity, White and Black. In many parts of the country I have passed through the African does appear to appreciate his trees, both as shade for his ordinary crops and special crops (such as pepper, for instance, which you generally find planted under a great tree) and cattle. In Kano Province, for instance, this is very noticeable. But in other parts he will burn down his trees, or rather let them burn down, with absolute equanimity, making no effort to protect them (which on many occasions he could easily do) when he fires the grasses (which, *pace* many learned persons, it seems to me, he is compelled by his agricultural needs to do—I speak now of the regions I have seen). I have noticed quantities of splendid and valuable timber ruined in this way. The European — I should say some Europeans — appears to suffer from the same complaint. It is the fashion—if the word be not disrespectful, and Heaven forfend that the doctors should be spoken of disrespectfully in this part of the world, of all places—among the new school of tropical

"MAGNIFICENT SPECIMENS OF THE VEGETABLE KINGDOM."

medicine out here to condemn all growing things in a
wholesale manner. In the eyes of some, trees or plants
of any kind in the vicinity of a European station are
ruthlessly condemned. Others are specially incensed
against low shrubs. Some are even known to pronounce
the death-warrant of the pine-apple, and I met an official
at a place, which shall be nameless, who went near weeping
tears of distress over a fine row of this fruit which he had
himself planted, and which were threatened, as he put it,
by the ferocity of the local medical man. In another
place destruction hangs over a magnificent row of mango
trees—and for beauty and luxuriousness of foliage the
mango tree is hard to beat—planted many years ago by
the Roman Catholic Fathers near one of their mission
stations; and in still another, an official, recently returned
on leave, found to his disgust that a group of trees he
especially valued had been cut down during his absence by
a zealous reformer of the medical world.

In the southern portions of Southern Nigeria, where
Sir Walter Egerton is a resolute foe of medical vandalism,
I am inclined to think that the doctors will find it about
as easy to cope with plant growth as King Canute is
reputed to have found the waves of the seashore. But in
Northern Nigeria and in the northern regions of Southern
Nigeria it is a different matter, and one is tempted to
query whether the sacrifice of all umbrageous plants in
the neighbourhood of official and other residences because
they are supposed to harbour —and no doubt do harbour—
the *larvæ* of all sorts of objectionable winged insects, may
not constitute a remedy worse even than the disease. I
can imagine few things more distressing for a European in
Northern Nigeria, gasping in the mid-day heat of the
harmattan season, to have nothing between his eyes,
as he gazes out beyond his verandah, but the glare of
the red laterite soil and the parched-up grasses and little
pink flowers springing up amidst it ; and one feels disposed

to say to the devoted medicos, "*De grâce, Messieurs, pas de trop zèle.*"

In the particular part of the country of which I am now writing, another aspect of the case strikes you. In very many rest-camps, and mining camps one comes across, the ground is cleared of every particle of shade-giving tree—cleared as flat as a billiard table. There is no shade for man or beast. Now a grass-house is not the coolest place in the world with an African noon-day sun beating down upon it—I mean an all-grass-house, not the cool native house with clay walls and thatched roof, be it noted—and . . . well, I content myself with the remark that it would be much cooler than it is with the shade of a tree falling athwart it. Then they—the Public Works Department—have built a road from Riga-Chikum to Narraguta. I will say nothing about it except that it is, without exception, the hottest road and the one more abounding in flies that I have struck in this part of the world. And I assign a proper proportion of both pheno-mena to the—to me—inexplicable mania of the builders thereof to hew down the trees on the side of the road.

To come back to our Great White Road. What a history it might not tell! For how many centuries have not Black and Brown men pursued upon it the goal of their trade and their ambitions; have not fled in frantic terror from the pursuer, ankle deep in dust. What tragedies have not been hurried along its dusty whiteness. To-day you will meet upon it objects of interest almost every hour. Now, a herd of oxen on their way to doom, to feed the Southern Nigerian markets; now, a convoy of donkeys going south, in charge, maybe, of Tuareg slaves from far-distant Sokoto, or the Asben oases. These will be loaded with potash and tobacco. And even as you pass this one going south, another convoy of donkeys, going north, loaded with salt and kolas, will be trudging along behind you. Anon, some picturesquely-clothed and turbaned horseman will be seen approaching, who, with ceremonious politeness, will either dismount and salute, or throw up his right hand—doing the " jaffi," as it is termed.

The African is credited with utter callousness to human suffering. Like most generalities concerning him, it is exaggerated. Life in primitive communities (and to get a proper mental grasp of this country, and its people, you must turn up your Old Testament and read Exodus and Leviticus) is much cheaper and of less account than in more highly civilized ones. That is a commonplace too often forgotten by people who accuse the African of ingrained callousness. As a matter of fact, I have noticed many sights on the Great White Road which show how rash such generalities can be. I have seen water handed from one party to another under circumstances which spoke of kindly appreciation of a want. I have frequently seen fathers, or elder brothers, carrying small children on their backs. The Residents have known cases of men found injured on the road who have been tended and taken home by utter strangers ; the Good Samaritan over again, and in his old-world setting.

CHAPTER III

ON THE CARRIER

" SOME Africans I have met "—the words conjure up a series of powerful chiefs, or fantastic " witch doctors," or faultlessly-attired barristers from some centre of light and learning on the Coast. I shall be content—if only by recording my gratitude for much amusement and no little instruction—with jotting down a brief line or two which shall be wholly concerned with a type of African to whom not the greatest Negrophile that ever lived would dream of applying the epithet distinguished. I refer to the carrier.

To-morrow I part with my carriers. We have trekked together for exactly four weeks—one little man, indeed, with a goatee beard and a comical grin, has been with me six weeks, having rejoined from my original lot. And at the end of four weeks one gets to know something of one's carriers. Presumably, by that time they have their own opinions of you.

Whence do they come, and whither do they go, these vagrants of the road, flotsam and jetsam that we create ? Runaway slaves, ne'er-do-weels, criminals, driven from their respective folds, unsuccessful farmers, or restless spirits animated by a love of travel and adventure—*la vie des grands chemins*. Reckless, improvident, gamblers, wastrels ; they are altogether delightful people. As an ecclesiastical friend invariably winds up with a description of the man (or woman) he is interested in, who has broken most of the commandments, and would have broken the

14

others had circumstances allowed : " X—— is the very best of creatures really, and I love him (or her) "—so it is impossible not to like the carrier. For with all his faults, he attracts. His spirit of independence appeals somehow. Here to-day, gone to-morrow. And, like the sailor, with a sweetheart at every port, somebody else's sweetheart will do quite as well at a pinch. Then consider his cheeriness. Be the load heavy or light, be the march long or short, he has always a smile and a salute for you as you pass along the line. I speak as I have found, and many men will bear me out. Some men may have a different tale to tell, sometimes with justification, sometimes, I think, without. For if there is the bad type of carrier— and there is : I have found two in my crowd, but their " little games " have fallen foul of the views of the majority —there is also the type of European who, shall we say, forgets. He gets into camp a long way ahead of his men, tired and hungry maybe, and curses them for a pack of lazy scoundrels. He forgets, or long custom has blunted perception, the potency of that sixty-pound load. Think of it ! Sixty pounds—the regulation load. Sixty pounds on your head for anything from fifteen to thirty miles.

I say consider that under these conditions the man is cheerful. Nay, he is more. He is full of quips and jokes . . . at the expense of his companions, and quite as much at the expense of himself. If you have a special peculiarity about you, ten to one he crystallises it into a name, and henceforth you are spoken of not as the " Baturi " the White man, but as " the man with a back like a camel," or " white hair," or the " hump-backed man of war," or " red pepper," or " hot water," or as the " man with a face like a woman," and so on. It is this extraordinary cheeriness which appeals to the average white human. That a creature of flesh and blood like yourself, carrying sixty pounds on his head for hours and hours in the blazing sun, dripping with perspiration, pestered by flies, and earning sixpence a day—threepence of which is supposed to be spent in " chop "—and doing this not for one day, but for day after day, sometimes for over a week without a sit-down, can remain cheerful—that is the incredible thing. One hopes that it is a lesson. Assuredly it ought to be an inspiration. These votaries of Mark Tapley are severely tried at times. Yesterday, after a tramp from six-thirty to half-past twelve, the camp aimed for was found to be tenanted by other white men and their carriers. There was nothing for it but to push on another eleven miles to the nearest village and stream. Just as dusk began to sweep down upon the land, the first carrier straggled in—smiling. " No. 1," a long-limbed man with the stride of an ostrich, who always goes by that name because he is always the first to arrive, delighted at having kept up his reputation ; " Nos. 2 " and " 3 " equally pleased with themselves for being close at his heels, and coming in for their share of the prize money in consequence. And then, in twos and threes, dribbling up, some un-utterably weary, others less so, all galvanised into new life by a chance joke, generally at their own expense ; joining in the acclamation which invariably greets the strong man of the party—the mighty Maiduguli, to wit— who, because of his muscles, carries the heaviest load, and whom Fate decrees, owing to that load's contents, shall be the last to start, both at the opening of the day and after the breakfast halt, but who manages to forge ahead, and to turn up among the first six, chaffing the tired ones on their way, and stimulating them to fresh exertions. And when all had reached their destination they had to stick up a tent by the light of the moon.

I have asked you to consider the carrier's cheeriness and powers of endurance—and my lot at least are not, with the exception of the mighty man of valour already mentioned, big men physically. I ask you now to consider his honesty—honesty in the literal sense and honesty in

16

the fulfilment of a bargain. For hours this man is alone
—so far as you are concerned—with your goods. You
may, you probably are, either miles ahead of him, or miles
behind him. The headman—"Helleman," as he is
termed by the rank and file—is at the rear of the column.
Between the first man and the "Helleman" several miles
may intervene, and so on, proportionately. During these
hours of total lack of supervision, your property is absolutely at the carrier's mercy. Your effects. The uniform
case in which, he knows, you keep your money. The
uniform case, of which he knows the lock is broken. The
"chop-box," of which he knows the padlock is missing.
But at the end of every day your things are intact. I
have not lost a matchbox, except a few dozen or so that
white men have stolen (I may say it is the local fashion—
I have caught it myself, and steal matches regularly whenever I get the chance). The only thing I have lost is
something I lost myself. You may say "Yes, but think
of the risk and the difficulty of breaking open a uniform
case on the road." As for the difficulty, there is little or
none. A vigorous fling upon one of these granitic boulders,
and there would be precious little left of your uniform case.
As for the risk, well, in many parts of the country I have
traversed, a carrier could get clear away with his loot, and
not all the *Sarikuna* and *dogari* in the country would set
hands on him. Faithfulness to the bargain struck. Well,
I have passed through the mining country. Some of the
mines declare they are short of labour—those that do not
suffer from that complaint declare that those that do have
themselves to thank for it—and the mines pay ninepence
a day for work which is much lighter than that of a carrier,
who gets sixpence. The few shillings a carrier would
sacrifice by deserting, he would recoup at the mines in ten
days, or less. I have not had a desertion. The only man
of the crowd who has absconded, did so openly. On a
certain spot on the line of march he suddenly got a fit of

17

fanaticism, or something unhealthy of that kind, and declared himself to be proof against sword cuts. Whereupon, being laughed at, he " gat unto himself " a sword and smote himself with much vigour upon the head, with the natural result of inflicting a deep scalp wound nearly seven inches long. The next morning, finding his load incommoded him in consequence, he returned homewards, a sadder, and, presumably, a wiser man.

If I were a poet I would write an ode to the African carrier. I cannot do justice to him in prose. But I place on record this inadequate tribute to the reckless, cheery, loyal rascal, who seems to me a mixture of the knight of the road and the poacher—-for both of whom I have ever conceived a warm affection . . . in books—and with whom I shall part to-morrow with regret, remembering oft in days to come that cheery " *Sanu zāki* " as I passed him, footsore, weary and perspiring, on the road.

CHAPTER IV

ON AFRICAN MODESTY AND AFRICAN COURTESY

EACH twenty-four hours brings its own series of events and its own train of thoughts following upon them. A new incident, it may be of the most trivial kind, sets the mind working like an alarum; a petty act, a passing word, have in them revealing depths of character. Nature seems such an open book here. She does not hide her secrets. She displays them; which means that she has none; and, in consequence, that she is as she was meant to be, moral. The trappings of hide-bound convention do not trammel her every stride like the hobble skirts of the foolish women who parade their shapes along the fashionable thoroughfares of London. What quagmires of error we sink into when we weigh out our ideas of morality to the African standard—such a very low one it is said.

Well, I have covered a good deal of ground in this country—although I have not been in it very long, measured in time—and I have seen many thousands of human beings. I have seen the Hausa woman and the bush Fulani woman in their classical robes. I have seen the Yoruba woman bathing in the Ogun, clad only in the natural clothing of her own dusky skin. I have seen the scantily-attired Gwarri and Ibo woman, and the woman of the Bauchi highlands with her bunch of broad green leaves " behind and before," and nothing else, save a bundle of wood or load of sorts on her head, or a hoe in her hand. I have visited many African homes, sometimes announced, sometimes not, at all hours of the day, and sometimes of the night. I have passed the people on the beaten track, and sought and found them off the beaten track. I have yet to see outside our cantonments—where the wastrels drift—a single immodest gesture on the part of man or woman. Humanity which is of Nature is, as Nature herself, moral. There is no immodesty in nakedness which " knows not that it is naked." The Kukuruku girl, whose only garment is a single string of beads round neck and waist, is more modest than your Bond Street dame clad in the prevailing fashion, suggesting nakedness. Break up the family life of Africa, undermine the home, weaken social ties, subvert African authority over Africans, and you dig the grave of African morality. It is easy, nothing is easier, and it may be accomplished with the best intentions, the worthiest motives, the most abysmal ignorance of doing harm. Preserve these things, strengthen them, and you safeguard the decencies and refinements of African life.

Here is a homily ! Its origin one of those trivialities of which I have spoken. One had pushed on ahead, desiring to be alone. With that curious intuition which the African seems to possess, one's mounted escort had, somehow, gathered that, and a good half-mile separated one from one's followers. The sun was at its zenith, and danced over the dusky track. But there were broad grateful trees on either side, and low bushes with white sweet-scented flowers. A bend in the road brought into view a little cameo of natural life. By a tree, straight-backed and grave-faced, an elderly Fulani woman, supporting on her lap the head and shoulders of a younger woman, who lay outstretched. At her feet a small child trying to stand upright, with but indifferent success. For a moment one was not perceived, both women's eyes being fixed on the infant's resolute efforts, and one's approach being quietened by the deadening dust under foot. For a moment only. Then all three looked up. From her position the younger woman's limbs were more uncovered than a Hausa or Fulani woman considers compatible with modesty before a stranger, and, with a sight of that stranger, the instinctive movement came —the position was slightly shifted, the robe drawn down, with no fuss or precipitancy, but calmly, with dignity and decision.

We strayed yesterday. Starting off early we struck across country, leaving the road, the red-and-green dressed gentleman and I; having arranged to meet the rest . . . somewhere. It does not matter where, because, as a matter of fact, we didn't. An imposing person the aforesaid *dogari*, with a full black beard and fierce sword. It was good to get away from the road, despite its varied interests, and for a couple of hours one gave one's self wholly up to the charms of the crispness of the morning, the timid but sweet song of the birds, the whiffs of scent from the mimosa bushes, the glimpse of some homestead farm in the distance, the sight of a group of blue-robed women with biblical earthenware pitchers on their heads issuing from a neatly thatched village, or congregated in a circle round one of the wells whose inner rim is lined and rendered solid by thick branches to prevent earth from falling in and fouling the water. Their laughing voices were wafted across the cultivated fields towards us, as cheery as the antics of the little brown goats skipping over the ground. What a world of simple happiness in this agricultural life of the *talakawa*—the common people—of Hausaland. And then, well we were clearly at fault. No signs of any of the men. No signs of breakfast, I mean of the person by whom breakfast is supposed to be produced—and nearly eight o'clock. The gentleman in red and green twisted his turbaned and bearded visage to right and left. He looked at me expressively, which look I returned—with equal gravity,

the substance of our power of communicativeness. Then
he turned his broad back and his white horse's head, and
ambled on, and I followed. It is queer how you accom-
modate yourself to philosophy, or how philosophy
accommodates itself to you. After all, every road leads
to Rome ; and there is a certain amount of exhilaration
in not knowing what particular Rome it may be, or
through what twists and turns the track may lead you
on the way thither. No homesteads now, and the risen
sun had warmed the birds into silence. One notices that,
by the way. In the early mornings the timid notes are
heard, and as the sun's rays pierce through the mists
and burn them up, they cease. It is a melodious little
ode to the great Life-giver, and when it has served its
purpose it quavers, quivers, and is no more.

On a sudden the thunder of hoofs behind us, and an
elderly, aristocratic-looking horseman with an aquiline
nose, short grey beard and piercing eyes, gallops up over
the deep furrows, followed by three attendants also on
horseback. An imposing figure of a man he is, splendidly
mounted on a chestnut stallion, with a heavy cloak of
dark blue cloth flung across his shoulders, the red crest
of a fez just showing through the top of his dark blue
turban. An animated conversation ensues between him
and the gentleman in red and green. The Chief—for
one knows he must be such from his bearing and the
sharp ring of his tones—waves a long, thin hand
to right and left. The *dogari* listens respectfully, somewhat crestfallen in appearance (perhaps he was hungry
too !). The mounted attendants career away in different
directions, one, I learn afterwards, to trace the main
body of carriers, the other to find the cook, the third
to call for milk and firewood from some neighbouring
village. Then the Chief bows low over his horse's neck,
places himself between the *dogari* and myself, and we proceed once more along the narrow pathway, cut at frequent

intervals by small streams, now mostly dry, with precipitous banks that need some negotiating. The courtesy of that grey-bearded old aristocrat—every inch a ruler of men—the Fulani who has become the statesman and the lord over many! He is the Governor, I learn later, of one of the principal districts of Kano province, and he looks it from head to foot. At the approach of every stream, half hidden with tangled creepers, wherever the path is broken or impeded by some natural obstacle, he half turns his horse towards one in warning, then waits on the other side until he is satisfied that the difficulty is overcome. Does the over-hanging branch of some tree threaten a blow to the careless rider? He either breaks it off short in its passage, or, if it be too formidable for that, points with uplifted finger. And when, at last, in an open space a small group under a tree proclaims the much perturbed — his usual condition — cook, busy boiling milk and cocoa, another low bow, and the old gentleman retires at an appropriate distance, turning his back with the politeness required of tradition and custom, but not before another rapid order has been given, and the quite unnecessary attention of clearing a piece of ground where you may conveniently partake of your meal is in process of accomplishment.

And soon from out of nowhere come shouts and laughter, and the jangle of bits and the confused hum of approaching men and horses. The bush and the grasses cave outwards and your people appear, a little wondering whether the white man is grumpy or not; very pleased to know they have pitched on the right road at last; rather enjoying the adventure and thoroughly happy with themselves and the world in general. Off-saddle and hobble the beasts! Down with the loads! Out with the " chop! " And all as merry as a marriage bell. So another morn has dawned and gone, bringing with it its lessons and its thoughts.

CHAPTER V

IT was dusk, dark almost. The road glimmered dimly in the distance. Over the deep furrows the shadows crept, and the little path between them mingled with the gathering gloom.

I became aware of a vague white figure standing out from the sombre background some little distance off. Presently it seemed to sink downwards and assume formlessness. My route back to the camp took me within perhaps a dozen yards of it. A nearer view disclosed a man, whose bent back was turned to me, making his solitary evening prayer to God. Alone. Yet not alone, perhaps.

That night I passed through my sleeping camp at the foot of the giant *bombax*, bathed in the silvery beams of a full moon shining out of a velvet sky ; and trod the road again, trying to puzzle it out.

What does the word " religious " mean, I wonder ? This white-robed figure of a man was religious as one generally interprets the word. Yet we are to suppose that he really wasn't, because his religion is not the religion we, in Europe, practise. But is that what " religious " infers ? One kind of religion ?

What a queer mixture the Anglo-Saxon is. Probably it would be impossible to convince the average Englishman that the African is a more religious being than himself ; or that there is anything - incongruous in himself, the Englishman, being at one and the same

24

time the Imperialist ruler of these dark races and their spiritual uplifter. And yet, to what vital extent do spiritual influences mould the society or the policy of Europe ? Has not religion—official religion—there taken upon itself very largely the character of a social force, and lost its spiritual significance ? Is not its whole trend social rather than spiritual ? Has Europe, in any racial sense, an inner spiritual life, as has the East ? The " law of Christ," says the Church, in the matter of relations between the sexes *everywhere*, commands monogamy. But the law of Christ commands, in a far more definite manner than any words that may be culled from His sayings in regard to this, many other things which the religion of Europe absolutely, entirely, and wholly ignores, because the customs of Europe and the laws of Europe, and the social life of Europe do not square with it.

I was told the other day that a great Emir in these parts was informed of the intended visit—this happened some years ago—of a great White *Mallam* who was coming to uplift the spiritual life of the people. The Emir and his councillors looked over the wide plain. " Surely," they said to one another, " as the White man is so strong in war, so cunning in invention, so mighty in knowledge, then the White man's *Mallam* must be very, very near to *Allah*." Soon they saw a cloud of dust. Marvelling somewhat, the Emir, nevertheless, sent out messengers. The messengers sped swiftly onwards. They looked for a solitary figure, the figure of an ascetic, bearing stamped upon features, lined and worn with thought, and in gaunt form, the imprint of holiness ; in whose eye, illumined with the fire of inspiration, they would read intimate communing with God. What they saw was a long file of weary carriers, conveying boxes full of food, drink, apparel, and camp furniture. Behind them, quite an ordinary looking White man on horseback. " Is this the great White preacher ? " they asked the interpreter, who headed the caravan. " Is this the *Mallam* who is to uplift our souls ? " " Even so," replied the inter-preter. So two of the Emir's messengers off-saddled, and when the preacher came along they bowed low, as is the custom of the country. But the third messenger had turned back. He prostrated himself before the Emir, and he told what he had seen.

The Emir drew his flowing cloak a little closer round him, for the sun was about to set, and the air grew chill. Then he turned himself towards Mecca, and lowered his forehead in the dust, followed by his councillors.

It is difficult to write plainly of Christian missionary effort in West Africa. The individual missionary may be an influence for good in the best sense. He may not be. He does not go into the country to make money. He is, as a rule, singularly selfless. His life is often, perhaps generally, a work of essential self-sacrifice. In the category of human motives gravitating towards West Africa, his, it must be conceded, takes front rank. Than the apostolic missionary there is no grander figure, whether in West Africa or elsewhere. But it is the genesis of the effort, not the man, that most counts fundamentally. If the effort itself is out of perspective the work of the individual must feel the effect. I say it is difficult to write about missionary effort. It seems to be regarded as taboo. You must not touch it lest you hurt people's feelings. But nowadays, one sphere of human activity cannot be ruled out of discussion. Christian effort out here seems to me to have forgotten in many cases that Christ was the servant of the people, not their master. It is intolerant of native customs; native religions irritate it ; native law it regards with contempt. I walked one evening along the Niger banks with a missionary. We passed some native huts. In one was a fetish with a votive offering at its feet. My companion jerked his stick disdainfully towards the object, and with scorn in his voice declaimed against the "idol." Yet he knew, or ought to have known, that it was not the thing of wood that was worshipped, but its indwelling spirit. That gesture was so characteristic of much one sees and hears out here. I exclude the Roman Catholics from that remark. Amongst them I have met the broad, tolerant spirit of generosity and true kindliness of heart. I can hear now the cheery, warm-hearted, jovial laughter of the Onitsha priests, their sunniness, their infecting optimism.

There is so much that is dark and dismal about this missionary effort, inwardly I mean. All the African world is black to it, black with sin, black with lust, black with cruelty. And there is its besetting misfortune— it is alien. It preaches an alien God ; a White God, not a Black God. The God that is imported here has nothing African about Him. How can He appeal to Africa ?

I saw a week ago in an English paper (about two months old) that there is to be a crusade against Islam in Nigeria. Emissaries are to come out and check this poisonous growth. That, too, is very strange to read . . . out here, as one listens to the call to God in the evening, and in the morning, pealing out to the stars. These people are worshipping the God of Africa. It seems they ought to worship the God of Europe ; and yet there is more evidence of spiritual influence out here, than in our great congested cities. With the cry of the African priest, the faithful bows his body to the earth—out here. The day before I left England, I heard the bells ringing out in an old cathedral city. Their note was both beautiful and sad. It was a spacious building, arched and vaulted, noble in proportions. It might easily have held seven hundred worshippers. There were many people in the streets. Yet, when the bells had ceased to ring, there were less than a dozen worshippers within.

Yes, it is a great puzzle.

All is silent in the camp. The fires have gone out. Over the thatched roofs the *bombax* towers upwards to the majestic heavens. The whole countryside is flooded with a soft, delicate effulgence, and the Great White Road appears as a broad ribbon of intenser light, winding away, away into the infinite beyond.

It is eleven o'clock. One wonders if London is looking quite so spiritual just now, with its flaming lights, its emptying theatres, its streets thronged with jostling, restless crowds.

CHAPTER VI

A RAGÔUT OF THINGS SEEN AND FELT

SOME things detach themselves, as it were, from the general background, rooting themselves in memory. Such, the rise in the road beyond which the first of the great Mohammedan towns of the north lay concealed. Bida, the capital of the Nupes, the centre of an active trade, known for its handsomely embossed, if unsubstantial, brassware ; known, too, for its rough glass bangles of black or dull blue, made out of nothing more romantic than old bottles melted in native furnaces kept going by the blowers who, when the stuff is sufficiently liquid, twirl it round a stick until the desired shape is attained ; known, too, for its special species of kola—the *labozhi*, highly esteemed throughout Nigeria, requiring shade and a rich, deep loamy soil to bring it to perfection. Until the British occupation the cultivation and sale of the *labozhi* kola were the prerogative of the ruler, the Emir, who must now be content with a tenth of the crop, and let his subjects have a chance. Past a Fulani cattle encampment ; past flat country covered with rice fields ; past rustling fields of guinea corn ready for the cutter, with heads towering eleven feet in height ; past clumps and dotted specimens of shea butter trees, in the branches of many of which are fixed calabashes for the bees ; past the weird red clay monuments of the white ants dotting the plain ; along the rough pitted, red dusty road, and so on until the rise. And then, between us and the rambling

29

city, with its decaying walls, its wide central avenue, and its umbrageous trees, its masses of blue robed men and women with their henna-dyed teeth and picturesque head-dress, a cloud of dust, and borne down the wind blowing towards us the blare of trumpets and the rattle of drums.

The great Mamodu himself, once a notorious slave raider and the perpetrator of innumerable infamies, has elected to ride out and meet us. Surrounded by two or three dozen notables and officers of his household, by a scarlet and green robed bodyguard, by four mounted drummers and two mounted trumpeters; ambling gently beneath a large umbrella of many colours held over his head by an attendant, and clad from head to foot in green-grey robes, with a turban of the same colour, Mamodu's tall, powerful figure and olive complexion— a Nupe with Fulani blood—emerges from the crowd. Trumpets—long thin trumpets blown lustily and not inharmoniously—blare, drums beat, horses curvet and try to bite one another's necks. Mamodu and his escort dismount and do their *gaisua* (salutation). We dismount also, advance, shake hands, and become the target for a hundred pairs of dark pupils in bloodshot, whitish-yellow balls, which glare at us over the lower part of dark blue turbans swathed across chin and mouth and nose, while the introduction formally proceeds to the accompaniment of many a guttural "*Ah! Um, Um, Um!*" At a word from the stalwart gentleman in grey we could be cut down in a couple of minutes with these long, fierce, leather-sheathed swords which hang at every hip. In point of fact, we are a great deal safer on this African road than we should be crossing Trafalgar Square. Presently we shall see the process, here conducted by one Englishman—trusted, and even liked for his own sake, by the people—aided by an assistant, of turning *ci-devant* slavers and warriors into administrators. In his work

DUG-OUT ON THE KADUNA MANNED BY NUPES.

"SILHOUETTING PERCHANCE A GROUP OF PALMS."

See p. 4.

this Englishman relies for the pomp and panoply of power upon three policemen, one of whom is old and decrepit. The Bida division covers 5,000 square miles, and Bida itself counts 35,000 souls. The facts suggest a thought or two.

A long, broad stretch of golden sands. Winding through them the clear green water of the reduced Kaduna. Several dug-outs, manned by Nupes, magnificent specimens of muscular development, cross backwards and forwards with men, women, and children conveying wares to market. Small mites, naked and tubby, splash and rollick about on the water's edge. Lower down stream fishermen are getting out their nets, and, at a shallow ford, shepherds are piloting a flock of sheep across, from whose scattered ranks a chorus of loud bleating arises. A file of pack donkeys stream across the sands to the village on the opposite bank. We watch the sight from the foot of a great tree, from which hang sundry charms, and as we sit there—it is a rendezvous, it seems, and a small market-place in its way—several young women stroll towards us bearing wares in grass platters which they spread close to us on the ground, conversing in low tones broken now and again by the jolly African laughter—the mirth of the child of nature with few cares and fewer responsibilities. The winding river, the golden sands, the blue sky, the two villages— one on either side of the crossing—with their conical thatched roofs, the green of the trees and of the water, the peaceful, quiet human life, combine to make as pretty and as harmonious a picture as you would wish to see.

Tramp, tramp, tramp! The stamping of innumerable feet. The murmur of innumerable voices. The waving of arms, the jangle of iron anklets, and the rising cloud of dust beneath the trampling of bare toes. The dancers range themselves in a wide circle, which slowly revolves in the light of the moon, now lighting up this part, anon the other part, giving a grey and ghostly look to the naked shoulders and close-cropped heads. *Aah!* *Aah! Aah!* The chant rises and falls, monotonous, barbaric. Bracelets and anklets, amulets and charms clash and clang again as the wearers thereof bend this way and that, crouching, stooping, flinging the upper part of their bodies backwards, raising high the knee and bringing down the leg with thunderous stamp, shaking themselves from head to foot like a dog emerging from his bath Naked bodies, but for a strip of jagged leather falling athwart the hips ; naked, lithe bodies on which the moon sheds her beams. *Aah! Aah! Aah!*

And with it the sound of the drum, the everlasting drum ; stimulus to labour, spirit of the dance, dirge at the death-bed, call to the feast, frenzy-lasher at the religious ceremonial, medium of converse, warner of peril, bearer of news, telephone and telegraph in one. Go where you will, you cannot escape the drum—where human life is. The everlasting drum which heralds the setting sun, which ushers in the morn, which troubles your sleep and haunts your dreams. Borne across the silent waters, booming through the sombre forest, rising from the murmuring town, cheering on the railway cutters—the fascinating, tedious, mysterious, maddening, attractive, symbolic, inevitable, everlasting African drum.

I suppose they must be thirsty like every other living thing in the glare of the sun and the heat of the sky and the dust of the track, for they crowd thick and fast about the *kurimi*, the narrow belt of vegetation (a blessed sight in the " dries ") where the stream cuts the road. *Pieridæ* with white and yellow wings ; *Lycaenæ* shot with amethyst and azure ; *Theklas*, too, or what I take for such, with long, fragile, waving extremities, infinitely beautiful.

A RAGÔUT OF THINGS SEEN AND FELT

Now and then a black and green *Papilio*, flashing silver from his under wing, harbinger of spring. Or some majestic, swift-flying *Charaxes* with broad and white band on a centre of russet brown—not the *castor*, alas! nor yet the *pollux*—I have yet to live to see *them* afloat 'neath the African sun. Narrow veins of muddy ooze trickle from the well-nigh dried-up bed. And here they congregate in swarms, proboscis thrust into the nectar, pumping, pumping up the liquid, fluttering and jostling one another for preferential places even as you may see the moths do on the " treacles " at home. The butterfly world is much like the human world after all in its egotism.

But if you want to see it at its best, plunge into the cool forest glades before the sun has attained his *maximum* (when even the butterflies rest) and watch the green and gold *Euphædra* dodging in and about the broad green leaves or tangled creepers. See him spread his glorious panoply where that fitful sunbeam has somehow managed to pierce the vault. A sight for the dear gods, I tell you— is the *Euphædra* sunning himself on a Niger forest path. Men and politics become as small fry. The right perspective asserts itself. You almost forget the beastly, clogging, mentally muddling helmet (how the Almighty has blessed the African by granting him a thick skull which he can carry on his neck, shaved—shaved, mind you (the bliss of it even in thought !),—and as clean as a billiard ball at that) as you watch the *Euphædra*, and absorb the countless other delights the forest contains, foremost amongst them silence, silence from humans at least. " These are the best days of my life. These are my golden days."

The floods have fallen and a thousand dark forms are building up the muddy, slippery banks against the next invasion, with saplings rough hewn in the forest ; the men chopping and adjusting these defences, the women

carrying up earth from below in baskets.   Beneath, the
fishermen are making fast their canoes and spreading
out their nets to dry—all kinds of nets, ordinary cast
nets, nets resembling gigantic hoops, stiff nets encased
in wood somewhat after the pattern of the coracle.   The
broad river fades away into the evening haze.   For the
swift wings of night are already felt, and the sun has just
dropped behind the curtain of implacable forest.

One by one, in twos and threes, in struggling groups,
the workers scramble up the slope on to the path—or
what remains of it from the floods—which skirts the village.
It grows dark.   One is vaguely aware of many naked,
shadowy, mostly silent figures on every side of one ;
wending their way along the path, or flitting in and out
among the houses.   Eyes flash out of the semi-obscurity
which is replete with the heavy, dank odour of African
humanity when African humanity has been busily at
work.   In the open doorways a multitude of little fires
spring into life, and with them the smell of aromatic wood.
The evening meal is in preparation, and presently tired
and naked limbs will stretch themselves to the warmth
with a sense of comfort.   The lament of a child serves
to remind you how seldom these Niger babies cry.

And now it is the turn of the fireflies to glow forth.
Thick as bees, they carpet the ground on every marshy
spot where the reeds grow—vivid, sentient gems.   Patches
of emeralds : but emeralds endowed with life ; emeralds
with an ambient flame lighting them from within.   They
hover above the ground like delicate will-o'-the-wisps.
They float impalpable, illusive, unearthly beautiful in
the still night air, as some rare and fleeting dream of
immortality, some incarnation of transcendent joy towards which dull clay stretches forth arms everlastingly
impotent.

THE HOE-DANCERS. [THE HOE-DANCE IS A HAUSA AGRICULTURAL DANCE OF GREAT ANTIQUITY.]

CHAPTER VII

ALL Zaria is astir, for this is December, the sacred month,
the month when the pilgrims to Mecca are offering sacri-
fices, and to-day the Sallah celebrations begin. At an
early hour masses of men began to swarm out of the
great Hausa city, dressed in their best gowns, driving
before them bullocks, sheep, and goats to be sacrificed
on the hill—even Kofena, the hill of many legends, the
old centre of Hausa " rock worship," beyond the city
walls—to the sound of invocations to Almighty God.
For days beforehand people have been pouring in from
the villages in the surrounding plain. Long files of oxen,
sheep, and goats have been passing through the gates.
Every household has been busy getting together presents
for friends, making provision for poor relations, bringing
forth the finest contents of their wardrobes, preparing
succulent dishes for entertainment. Every class of the
population has been filled with eager anticipation, agriculturists and weavers, blacksmiths and tanners, dyers
and shoemakers. The barbers have plied an active
trade, and the butchers likewise. Every face has worn
a smile, and the hum of human life has been more insistent than usual. A city of great antiquity this, boasting
a long line of fifty-eight Hausa kings before the Fulani
dynasty arose, and thirteen since that event early in last
century. It rises out of an enormous plain, cultivated
for many miles around, dotted here and there with

fantastic piles of granite, resembling mediæval castles. Its reddish clay walls, crumbling in parts, twenty to thirty feet high in others, and many feet in thickness at the base, enclose a sea of compounds and tortuous picturesque streets, above which wave the fan-palms, the paw-paw, the beautiful locust-bean tree, and the graceful tamarind. In the plain itself the gigantic *rimi*, or cotton tree, is a conspicuous landmark, and its rugged staunchness is the subject of a legend uncomplimentary to the ladies of Zaria : *Rimayin Zaria sun fi matan Zaria alkawali*, meaning that the old *rimi* trees are more dependable than the fickle beauties of the town.

But the outstanding feature of the day approaches. It is ten o'clock, and the procession from Kofena hill is winding its way back again to the city. Here the Emir will arrive in state after the performance of his religious devoirs, and will address his people. Here, in the great open square flanking the mosque, the district chiefs and notables will charge down upon him in the traditional " jaffi," or mounted salute. As we enter the gates of the city, after a two miles canter from the Residency down a long and dusty road, we find almost deserted streets. Every one is congregating in the square. Soon we enter into it, to see a vast concourse of people clothed in white and blue. They form a living foreground to the walls on either side of the Emir's residence, which stands at one extremity of the square. Around the mosque, on the left, they are as thick as bees, and, opposite the mosque, some broken hillocky ground is covered with a multitude. At its further extremity the square narrows into the road leading through the city to Kofena, and towards the opening of this road as it debouches into the square all eyes are directed. The brilliant sun of tropical Africa smites downwards, giving a hard line to lights and shadows, and throwing everything into bold relief. With the exception of a few

THE "JAFFI," OR MOUNTED SALUTE.

denationalised Hausa wives of our own soldiers, the crowd is exclusively one of men and youths, for, according to custom, the women will not put in an appearance until later in the day. We three White men,—the Resident, much respected, and wise with the wisdom which comes of long years of experience of this fascinating country, and with a knowledge of Mohammedan law which fills the wisest *mallams* with astonishment—his assistant, and the writer take our stand on the right of the Emir's residence. Behind us a few mounted men in gallant array, and immediately on our left a charming group of the Emir's sons, or some of them, in costly robes of satin. One little fellow, eight years old, perhaps, with a light olive complexion, glances rather bored looks from under a snow-white turban. Another rather bigger boy, clad in dark yellow satin, is an imposing figure.

A deep " Ah " comes from the throats of the assembled thousands as the blare of trumpets resounds faintly in the distance, and a cloud of dust rises from the road. From out of it there emerge a dozen horsemen charging down the square at break-neck speed, their right arms raised, their multi-coloured robes flying out behind them. With a shout they rein up their steeds in front of the Emir's residence, then wheel swiftly, and are off again whence they came—the *avant-garde* of the procession. The sound of drums and trumpets gets louder. The head of the procession comes in sight, or, to be more accurate, the dust solidifies itself into a compact mass, flashing and glittering with a thousand shades. First, many hundreds walking on foot, who, as they enter the square, deploy right and left and mingle with the waiting crowd. Behind them more horsemen detach themselves and gallop towards us, backwards and forwards. Each man is dressed according to his own particular fancy. Some in red, some in blue, some in white, some in green, others in vivid yellows, but most of them, it would seem, wearing half a dozen different colours at the same time, both as to robes and turbans. Their leather boots, thrust into shovel-headed stirrups, are embroidered with red and green ; their saddle-cloths and bridles are also richly embroidered and tasselled. The majority, we observe, wear long cross-handled swords in leather scabbards. Some carry thin spears in their hands ; one fierce-looking warrior a battle-axe. He seems to have stepped out of the Middle Ages does this particular chief, his horse wearing a metalled protection as in the old days of the Crusaders. But the heart of the procession, moving up slowly, puts an end to these evolutions, and the horsemen range themselves up on either side of the Emir's residence, their gallant beasts, curvetting and prancing as the " Ah " of the crowd changes into a great roar of sound. As a trial of patience I commend the effort to take a photograph over the ears of a horse who is making strenuous efforts to stand up on its hind legs, while a fine and smarting white dust rises in clouds, entering eyes and mouth, and all round you are people in a fine frenzy of excitement, mingled with apprehension, lest your mount takes it into his head to ride amuck in the midst of them, which he has every appearance of wishing to do.

Rattle, rattle, come the drums, mingled with the long-drawn-out notes of the tin or silver trumpets. Suddenly a loud shout arises, a shout of merriment, as a monstrous figure, clad in skins of beasts, and, apparently, hung round with bladders, in his hand a long stick, dashes out of the advancing throng, clearing the intervening space between it and the Emir's residence in a succession of frantic bounds. This is the Court fool, and his appearance is quite in setting with the piece. For this whole scene is a scene out of the Arabian Nights, and, really, one would hardly be astonished at the appearance of Jins, or even of Eblis himself. At last, here is the Emir and his immediate bodyguard, and the drummers and the

THE EMIR OF ZARIA.

THE EMIR OF KATSINA.

See p. 146.

trumpeters. The air resounds with prolonged " Ah ! Ah ! Ahs." There is a vast tossing of arms, and prancing of horses, and glittering of spears, a climax of sound and colour—and dust.

The Emir Aliu is a fine looking man, with a good straight nose, intelligent, rather cruel-looking eyes. His mouth we cannot see, for the folds of the turban are drawn across the lower part of his face. A dark, indigo-dyed purple turban and under-cloak ; over it a snow-white robe of silk with a tasselled cape which half hides the turban—these are the principal coverings to volu-minous robes of many tints. His feet are encased in beautifully embroidered boots, and his saddle is richly ornamented. On the forefinger of his left hand is a heavy silver ring. Halting, he turns and faces the multitude. His attendants, one on either side, wave the dust away from his face with ostrich feather fans. Others, dressed in red and green, and carrying long staves, range them-selves in front of him and shout his praises in stentorian tones. Four figures on foot advance, three of them are clad in skins and carry drums. The fourth is a crouching creature with a curious wizened face bearing a drawn sword in his hand. A sword dance ensues, the four going round and round in a circle. The gentleman with a sword contorts himself, prods viciously at imaginary foes, and every now and then makes a playful attempt to smite off one of the drummers' legs. This performance being terminated—accompanied the while by incessant shouting on the part of every one in general—the actors retire, and the Emir holds up his thin aristocratic hand.

Instantly a silence falls. The change is singularly impressive. The Emir begins to speak in a low voice to a herald mounted on a raised platform at his side. The herald, the perspiration pouring down his face, shouts out each sentence as it falls from the Emir's lips. As the speech proceeds the Emir becomes more animated. He waves his arm with a gesture full of dignity and command. And now the silence is occasionally broken with sounds of approval. Finally he stops, and it is the turn of the Resident who smilingly delivers himself of a much shorter oration which, as in the previous case, is shouted to the assemblage by the herald. I was able to obtain, through the courtesy of the Resident, from the Emir's *Waziri* a rendering of the speech of which the following is a translation—

" The Emir greets you all with thanks to God. He thanks God's messenger (Mohammed). He gives thanks for the blessings of his parents and his ancestors. He gives thanks to the Europeans who are the gates of his town. He thanks all White men. Next—you must attend to the orders which the Emir gives you every year. I say unto you leave off double dealing. Remove your hand from the people. Let them follow their own courses. Separate yourselves from injustice. Why do I say 'Give up injustice'? You know how we were in former days and you see how we are now. Are we not better off than formerly? Next—I thank my headmen who assist me in my work. I thank my servants who are fellow workers. I thank my young chiefs who are fellow workers. I thank the men of my town who are fellow workers. I thank my followers in the town. I thank the village heads. I thank all the people of the land of Zaria who are helping me in my work. Next—I wish you to pay attention to the commands of the English. And I say unto you that all who see them should pay them respect. He who is careless of the orders of the White man does not show them respect. Though nothing happens to him he cries on his own account (*i.e.* his stupidity is his punishment), for it is his ignorance that moves him. Next—every one who farms let him pay his tax. Every one who says this man is my slave, or this woman is my slave, or these people are my slaves, and uses force against them, let judgment fall upon him. What I say is this—may God reward us! May God give us peace in our land! May God give us the abundance of the earth! Amen. Those who feel joyful can say—' This is our desire! this is our desire! ' "

After a vain attempt to shake hands with the Emir, our respective mounts altogether declining to assist, we ride out of the town escorted by a couple of hundred horsemen. A little way past the gates we halt while they, riding forward a hundred yards or so, wheel, and charge down upon us with a shout, reining their horses with a sudden jerk, so near to us that the ensanguined foam from the cruel bits bespatters us.

As we ride home to the Residency two miles out of the town, uppermost in the mind at least of one of us is the fascination of this strange land, with its blending of Africa and the East, its barbaric displays, its industrial life, its wonderful agricultural development—above all, perhaps, the *tour de force* of governing it with a handful of White officials and a handful of native troops.

PART II
SOUTHERN NIGERIA

CHAPTER I

NIGERIA is a geographical expression applied to a territory in West Africa which by successive stages, covering a period of more than one hundred years, under circumstances widely differing in character and incentive, and almost wholly as the result of the initial enterprise of British explorers and merchants, has passed under the protection of Britain. With the discovery of Nigeria are associated exploits which for romantic interest and personal achievements hold a prominent place in British exploring records. The angry swirl of the Bussa rapids must ever recall the well-nigh superhuman achievements of Mungo Park, as the marvellous creeks and channels of the Niger Delta evoke the memory of Richard Lander * and John Beecroft.

You cannot visit the Court of the Emir of Kano without remembering Clapperton's account of the awkward religious conundrums with which the gallant sailor, the first European to enter that fascinating African city, was amazed and confounded by one of the present Emir's predecessors ; nor ride over the wide and dusty road into the heart of Hausaland without thinking that but for Joseph Thomson's diplomatic tact in negotiating the early treaties with its potentates, which were to pave

---

* Lord Scarborough, I am glad to know, is instituting a movement designed to put up a monument to Richard Lander and Mungo Park at Forcados, one of the mouths of the Niger. The suggestion that a monument should be erected to the memory of Richard Lander at the mouth of the Niger was made last year in the *Times* by the writer, who had the honour of reporting to Lord Scarborough upon various sites examined in the course of this year, and recommending Forcados as the most appropriate.

the way for the statesmanship of a Taubman-Goldie and the organising genius of a Lugard, Nigeria would to-day be the brightest jewel in the West African Empire of the French. The spirit of MacGregor Laird, the hardy pioneer who laid the first foundations of British commerce in this country seems to hover over the broad bosom of the Niger. The marvellous panorama that unfolds itself before your eyes at Lokoja (the confluence of the Niger with its tributary the Benue) conjures up the heroism and tragedy of the Allan-Trotter expedition ; while to negotiate in a dug-out the currents that eddy round the famous *ju-ju* rock—still termed Baikie's Seat—is a reminder that somewhere in the blue depths below lie the remains of Dr. Baikie's ill-fated *Day-spring*.

This land is, indeed, a land rich in heroic memories to men of British blood. It is the more astonishing that so little appears to be known by the general public either of its past or, what is much more important, of the many complex problems connected with its administration.

Nigeria is, at present, arbitrarily divided into two units, " Southern " and " Northern ; " the division corresponds with the historical events which have distinguished the assumption of British control, and is to that extent inevitable. But to-day, with internal communications and administrative control rapidly extending, this situation presents many drawbacks. In the absence of any considered scheme of general constructive policy laid down at home, the existence of two separate Governments with ideals necessarily influenced by the personal idiosyncrasies of frequently changing heads in a territory geographically united, through which the channels of a singularly intensive internal trade have flowed for centuries, must of necessity tend to promote divergencies in the treatment of public questions, and, therefore,

JU-JU ISLAND NEAR JEBBA.
(Photo by Mr. E. Firmin.)

SHIPPING PALM-OIL ON THE NIGER AT HIGH WATER.

See p. 52.

create numerous difficulties for the future. I propose to deal with this subject in greater detail later on.

Meantime it would seem necessary at the outset to emphasize two facts which the public mind does not appear to have realized. The first is that Nigeria, both in size and in population, is not only the most considerable of our tropical dependencies in Africa, but is the most considerable and the wealthiest of all our tropical dependencies (India, of course, excepted). Embracing an area of 332,960 square miles, Nigeria is thus equal in size to the German Empire, Italy and Holland, while its population, though not yet ascertained with accuracy, can hardly amount to less than fifteen millions, being double that of British East Africa and Uganda with Nyassaland thrown in, and nearly three times as numerous as the native population comprised in the South African Union. The second is that nowhere else in tropical or sub-tropical Africa is the British administrator faced, at least on a large scale, with a Mohammedan population, already to be counted in millions and increasing year by year with significant rapidity. Until a few years ago the work of Great Britain in West Africa, apart from a few trifling ex ceptions, was confined to the administration of the Pagan Negro. The position is very different now. In the southern regions of the Protectorate, where its progression is a modern phenomenon, Islam is, from the administrative point of view, a purely social factor. But in the northern regions, where Mohammedan rule has been established for centuries, under the Hausas, and in more recent times under the Fulani, Islam has brought its laws, its taxation, its schools and its learning. It is there a political as well as a religious and social force, solidly entrenched. This fact which, administratively speaking, need not alarm us—unless the Administration is goaded into adopting a hostile attitude towards its

Mohammedan subjects—does, however, invest Nigeria with an additional interest of its own and does supply a further reason why the affairs of this greatest of our African protectorates should receive more intelligent consideration and study at the hands of the public than it has enjoyed hitherto.

CHAPTER II

THE NIGER DELTA

WHAT is now known as Southern Nigeria comprises 77,200 square miles, and includes the whole seaboard of the Nigerian Protectorate, some 450 miles long, and the marvellous delta region whose network of waterways and surpassing wealth in economic products must be seen to be realized. Pursuing its southward course, the Niger, after its journey of 2,550 miles across the continent from west to east, bifurcates just below Abo into the Forcados and the Nun. This is the apex of the delta. and here the Niger is, indeed, majestic. From each of these main channels of discharge spring countless others, turning and twisting in fantastic contours until the whole country is honeycombed to such an extent as to become converted into an interminable series of islands. The vastness of the horizon, the maze of interlacing streams and creeks, winding away into infinity, the sombre-coloured waters, the still more sombre impenetrable mangrove forests—here and there relieved by taller growth—impress one with a sense of awe. There is something mysterious, unfathomable, almost terrifying in the boundless prospect, the dead uniformity of colour, the silence of it all. It is the primeval world, and man seems to have no place therein.

Small wonder that amidst such natural phenomena, where in the tornado season which presages the rains the sky is rent with flashes only less terrific than the echoing peals of thunder, where the rushing wind hurls forest giants to earth and lashes the waters into fury, where for months on end torrential downpours fall until man has no dry spot upon which he can place his foot ; where nature in its most savage mood wages one long relentless war with man, racking his body with fevers and with ague, now invading his farms with furious spreading plant life, now swamping his dwelling-place—small wonder the inhabitants of this country have not kept pace with the progression of more favoured sections of the human race. It is, on the contrary, astonishing, his circumstances being what they are, that the native of the Niger delta should have developed as keen a commercial instinct as can be met with anywhere on the globe, and that through his voluntary labours, inspired by the necessities and luxuries of barter, he should be contributing so largely to supply the oils, fats, and other tropical products which Western industrialism requires. Trade with the outer world which the merchant—himself working under conditions of supreme discomfort, and in constant ill-health—has brought ; improved means of communication through the clearing and mapping of creeks and channels, thereby giving accessibility to new markets which the Administration is yearly creating—these are the civilizing agents of the Niger delta, the only *media* whereby its inhabitants can hope to attain to a greater degree of ease and a wider outlook.

The outer fringe of the delta is composed entirely of mangrove swamps, whose skeleton-like roots rise up from the mud as the tide recedes, and from whose bark the natives obtain, by burning, a substitute for salt. For untold centuries the mangrove would appear to have been encroaching upon the sea, the advance guard of more substantial vegetation springing up behind it with the gradual increase of deposits affording root-depth. Apart from the deltaic system proper, produced by the bifurcation of the Niger and its subsequent efforts to reach the ocean, the seaboard is pierced by several rivers, of which the Cross, navigable for stern wheelers of light draught in the wet season for 240 miles and in the dry for forty, is the most important. The Benin River links up with the deltaic system on the east, and on the west with the lagoon system of Lagos, into which several rivers of no great volume, such as the Ogun and Oshun, discharge themselves. So continuous and extensive are these interior waterways that communication by canoe, and even by light-draught launches, is possible from one end of the seaboard to the other—*i.e.*, from Lagos to Old Calabar.

The mangrove region is sparsely populated by fishing and trading tribes. It is curious to come across signs of human life when you would hardly suspect its possible presence. A gap in the whitened, spreading roots, a tunnelled passage beyond, a canoe or two at the opening; or, resting upon sticks and carefully roofed, a miniature hut open on all sides, in which reposes some votive offering, such are the only indications that somewhere in the vicinity a village lies hidden. A visit to some such village holds much to surprise. Diligent search has revealed to the intending settler that the particular spot selected contains, it may be a hundred yards or so from the water, a patch of firm land where, doubtless with much difficulty, a crop of foodstuffs can be raised, and here he and his family will lead their primitive existence isolated from the outer world, except when they choose to enter it on some trading expedition. Further inland somewhat, as for instance, near the opening of the Warri creek (whose upper reaches, bordered with cocoanut palms, oil palms, and ferns, are a dream of beauty), one of the many off-shoots of the Forcados, where behind the fringe of mangroves the forest has begun to secure a steady grip, neatly kept and prosperous villages are more numerous. Their denizens are busy traders and there are plentiful signs of surface civilization. An expedition in canoes to the chief of one of these Jekri villages led us from a little landing stage cut out of the mangroves and cleverly timbered along a beaten path through smelling mud, alive with tiny crabs and insect life of strange and repulsive form, into a clearing scrupulously clean, bordered with paw-paw trees and containing some twenty well-built huts. A large dug-out was in process of completion beneath a shed ; fishing-nets were hanging out to dry ; a small *ju-ju* house with votive offerings ornamented the centre of the village green, as one might say ; a few goats wandered aimlessly about, and a score of naked tubby children gazed open-eyed or clung round their mothers' knees in affected panic. Beyond the *ju-ju* house a one-storeyed bungalow with corrugated iron roof and verandah unexpectedly reared its ugly proportions, and before long we were discussing the much vexed question of the liquor traffic over a bottle of ginger ale across a table covered by a European cloth, with an intelligent Jekri host, whose glistening muscular body, naked to the waist, contrasted oddly with the surroundings. These included a coloured print of the late King Edward hanging upon the walls in company with sundry illustrated advertisements all rejoicing in gorgeous frames. The walls of the vestibule below were similarly adorned, and through a half-open door one perceived a ponderous wooden bed with mattress, sheets, pillows, and gaudy quilt (in such a climate !) complete.

The deltaic region is the real home of the oil palm with its numerous and still unclassified varieties, although it extends some distance beyond in proportionately lessening quantities as you push north. No other tree in the world can compare with the oil palm in the manifold benefits it confers upon masses of men. Occurring in tens of millions, reproducing itself so freely that the natives often find it necessary to thin out the youngest trees, it is a source of inexhaustible wealth to the people, to the country, to commerce, and to the Administration. The collection, preparation, transport, and sale of its fruit, both oil and kernels for the export trade is the paramount national industry of Southern Nigeria, in which men, women, and children play their allotted parts. Beautiful to look upon, hoary with antiquity (its sap was used in ancient Egypt for cleansing the body before embalment), the oil palm is put to endless uses by the natives—its leaves and branches as roofing material, for clothing, for the manufacture of nets, mats, and baskets ; its fruit and covering fibre in various forms for food (not disdained by the resident European in the famous palm oil chop), for light, for fuel. To the Southern Nigerian native inhabiting the oil-palm area the tree is, indeed, domestically indispensable, while its product represents something like 90 per cent. of his purchasing capacity in trade. How entirely wrong would be any attempt at restricting his free enjoyment of its bounties needs no emphasizing. The importance of the export trade in the products of the oil palm may be gauged by the returns for 1910, which show that Southern Nigeria exported 172,998 tons of kernels and 76,850 tons of oil, of a total value of no less than £4,193,049 ; and yet the capacities of the trade, especially in kernels, are only in their infancy.* Many districts, rich in oil palms are unproductive owing to inaccessibility of markets or lack of transport ; in others which supply oil, the kernels, for sundry reasons, among which insufficiency of labour to spare from farming operations no doubt predominates, are not collected, although it is commonly reckoned that three tons of

* The total value of the nett commercial trade of Southern Nigeria amounted to £9,288,000 in 1910, viz. imports £4,320,000, exports £4,968,000. Among the imports, cotton goods amounted to £1,306,812. Ten years ago the total import of the latter was only £605,146. The whole commercial movement has grown enormously in the last few years, the total nett turnover in 1907 amounting only to £6,974,000.

kernels should be available for every ton of oil. In considering these figures, realizing the future potentialities of the trade, and realizing, too, the truly enormous sum of African labour which it represents (every nut is cracked by hand to extract the kernel), one cannot but reflect upon the foolish generalities which ascribe "idleness" to the West African negro, whose free labour in this trade alone gives employment directly and indirectly to tens of thousands in England and in Europe, from the merchant and his clerks, from the steamship owner and his *employés* on land and sea, to the manufacturer of soap and candles and their allied trades ; from the coopers who turn out the casks sent out from England in staves for the conveyance of the oil, to the Irish peasants who collect the stems of the common sedge shipped out to Nigeria from Liverpool for caulking these casks.

The bulk of the oil is exported to England (£1,191,000 value in 1909), but nearly the entire kernel crop goes to Germany, where it is treated by the big crushing mills. It is possible that this state of affairs may undergo considerable change within the next decade, and the reason for it is, incidentally, of considerable economic interest, as it is of moment to Nigeria. Up to within three or four years ago palm kernels were crushed and the oil almost entirely used by the soap trade, but chemistry has now found a process of refining and making palm-*kernel* oil edible, as it may, perhaps, do some day for palm oil itself, as a base for margarine, for which coprah and ground-nut oil were formerly employed. This has had as a consequence an enormous widening of the home market, and the soap trade has now to contend with keen competition for the supply of one of its staples. The resultant effect is the initiative of Lever Brothers (Limited), who, finding the need of enlarging and giving increased security to their supplies of the raw material, are, with commendable enterprise, erecting three large crushing mills in

Southern Nigeria, the one at Lagos being already in a fair way to completion. If the numerous difficulties they will have to face are successfully negotiated, the ultimate result can hardly fail to be that of transferring the considerable palm kernel crushing industry from the banks of the Rhine to those of the Niger, besides creating a new export trade in oil cake from the Niger to England and the Continent.

CHAPTER III

BEYOND the deltaic region proper lies the vast belt of primeval and secondary forest of luxurious growth, giant trees, tangled vines and creepers, glorious flowering bushes, gaudy butterflies, moist atmosphere, and suffocating heat. Beyond the forest belt again lies, with recurrent stretches of forest, the more open hilly country, the beginning of the uplands of the North. When an authority on forestry recently wrote that "British Columbia is the last great forest reserve left," he forgot West Africa. That is what West Africa has continually suffered from—forgetfulness. The resources of the Nigerian forest belt are as yet far from being fully determined, but sufficient is now known of them to show that they are enormously rich. Besides the oil palm and the wine palm (which produces the *piassava* of commerce) the forest belt contains large quantities of valuable mahoganies, together with ebony, walnut, satin, rose, and pear woods, barwood, and other dye-woods, several species of rubber, African oak, gums (copal), kola, and numerous trees suitable to the manufacture of wood-pulp. Oil-bearing plants abound in great quantities, as do also fibres, several of which have been favourably reported upon by the Imperial Institute. The shea-butter tree, to which I shall have occasion again to refer, is an inhabitant of the dry zone.

The soil of this forest region is wonderfully fertile, and forest products apart, the possibilities of agricultural

56

THE TROPICAL BUSH.

development are considerable. The three articles under cultivation by the natives the Administration has of late years done its best to popularize have been cotton, cocoa, and maize. For several reasons maize is an uncertain quantity. The land bears two crops a year, the larger crops ripening in July, but a wet August will play havoc with harvesting and storing arrangements, while the amount available for export must always depend upon local food requirements and available labour. The cultivation of cocoa, for which the humid atmosphere, rich alluvial soil, and abundant shade of the forest region seem peculiarly suitable, has, on the other hand, steadily, if slowly, increased since it was started fifteen years ago. In 1900 the quantity of cocoa exported was valued at £8,622. It had risen in 1910 to £101,151. The efforts made within the last few years by the British Cotton Growing Association, supplemented by those of the Administration, to revive on a large scale the export trade in raw cotton started by the Manchester manufacturer, Mr. Clegg, at the time of the American Civil War, has so far been partially, but only partially, successful. The industry has progressed, but far less rapidly than its promoters hoped.* Things do not move quickly in West Africa. In all these questions several factors have to be taken into account, for which sufficient allowance is not made in Europe. For one thing, the really immense amount of labour which the Nigerian population is already required to put forth in order to feed itself and to sustain the existing export trade is not appreciated.

The idea that the native has merely to scratch the earth or watch the fruit ripening on the trees in order to sustain himself and his family is, speaking generally, as grotesque an illusion as that he is a helpless, plastic creature with no will of his own. The native is on the whole an active, hard-working individual, the ramifications

* Vide Part IV.

of whose domestic and social needs involve him in constant journeyings which absorb much time, and if his soil is prolific in the bearing of crops, it is equally so in invading vegetation, which has constantly to be checked. He is also a keen business man and a born trader, as any European merchant who has dealings with him will bear witness, and he will turn his attention to producing what pays him best. In that respect he differs not at all from other sections of the human race amongst whom the economic sense has been developed, and he cannot be fairly expected to devote his attention to raising one particular raw material which a certain home industry may desire, if he can make larger profits in another direction. The opening up of the country, the increasing dearness of food supplies in the neighbourhood of all the great centres, the intensifying commercial activity and economic pressure so visible on every side, the growth of population, and the enlargement of the horizon of ideas must necessarily lead to a steady development in all branches of production. But the native must be given time, and the country is one which cannot be rushed either economically or politically.

No sketch, however brief, of the potentialities of the Nigerian forest belt would be complete without a reference to the labours of the Forestry Department, which owes its initiation to the foresight and statesmanship of the late Sir Ralph Moor. Such reference is the more necessary since the work of the department crystallizes, so to speak, the conception of its duties towards the native population which guides the Administration's policy. No other department of the Administration reveals so clearly by its whole programme and its daily practice what the fundamental object of British policy in Nigeria really is, and in view of the increasing assaults upon that policy by company promoters at home, on the one hand, and the obstacles to which its complete realization is subjected in Africa on the other, it is absolutely essential that public opinion in Britain should become acquainted with the facts and be in a position to support the Colonial Office and the Administration in combining equity with commonsense.

Briefly stated, the Forestry Department is designed to conserve forest resources for the benefit of the State— the State meaning, in practice, the native communities owning the land and their descendants, and the Administration charged with their guardianship, and while encouraging any legitimate private enterprise, whether European or native, to oppose the wholesale exploitation of those resources for the benefit of individuals, white or black. It aims at impressing the native with the economic value of his forests as a source of present and continual revenue for himself and his children ; at inducing native communities to give the force of native law to its regulations and by their assistance in applying them, to prevent destruction through indiscriminate farming operations and bush fires, to prevent the felling of immature trees, to replant and to start communal plantations. It aims at the setting aside, with the consent of the native owners, of Government reserves and native reserves, and at furthering industrial development by private enterprise under conditions which shall not interfere with the general welfare of the country. In a word, the Forestry Department seeks to associate the native communities with the expanding values of the land in which they dwell, so that for them the future will mean increasing prosperity and wealth, the essence of the policy being that these communities are not only by law and equity entitled to such treatment, but that any other would be unworthy of British traditions. It is what some persons call maudlin sentiment, the sort of " maudlin sentiment " which stands in the way of the Nigerian native being expropriated and reduced to the position of a hired labourer on the properties of *concessionnaires* under whose patriotic activities the Nigerian forest would be exploited until it had disappeared from the face of the earth like the forests of Wisconsin, Michigan, Minnesota, and Eastern Canada.

Apart from the question of safeguarding the rights of the people of the land, our wards, the necessity of forest conservation in the interest of the public weal has been taught by bitter experience, and experience has also shown that scientific forestry can only be profitably undertaken by the Government or by bodies whose first obligation is the interest and protection of the community. The Forestry Department of Southern Nigeria, short as its existence has been, is already a revenue-making Department, for in the last ten years it has either planted, or induced the natives to plant, trees (some of which, like the rubber trees in Benin, are now beginning to bear) whose present estimated value is £287,526, and has thus added over a quarter of a million to the value of the capital stock of the forests without taking into account the indirect effects of the steps taken to help their natural regeneration. The Department has many local difficulties to contend with, especially in the Western province, which I shall have occasion to discuss in connection with the general administrative problem facing the administration in that section of the Protectorate.

The character of its work necessitates that, in addition to scientific training in forest lore, those responsible for its direction shall be possessed of knowledge of native customs and of considerable tact in conducting negotiations with native authorities, always suspicious of European interference in anything which touches the question of tenure and use of land. The Administration is fortunate in possessing in the Conservator and Deputy-Conservator two men who combine in a rare degree these dual qualifications. It is but the barest statement of

60

fact to say that Mr. H. N. Thompson, the Conservator who went to Southern Nigeria after many years in Burma, enjoys an international reputation. As an expert in tropical forestry he stands second to none in the world. His colleague, Mr. R. E. Dennett, has contributed more than any other European living to our knowledge of Nigerian folklore, and he understands the native mind as few men of his generation do. In view of its immense importance to the future of the country it is very regrettable to have to state that the Forestry Department is greatly undermanned and its labours curtailed in many directions by the insufficiency of the funds at its disposal. No wiser course could be taken by the administration than that of setting aside a sum of borrowed money to be used, as in the case of the railways, as capital expenditure on productive forestry work.

CHAPTER IV

IN connection with the internal government of the Protectorate it may be advisable to refer briefly to the House Rule Ordinance of 1901 which has recently given rise to some controversy. The House Rule Ordinance is a measure designed by the late Sir Ralph Moor to prevent social anarchy from ensuing when slavery was abolished by the British Government. It gives force of Law to House Rule. House Rule is, in reality, the native form of government, which has existed in Southern Nigeria for many centuries. In recognizing the former the Administration acknowledges the existence of the latter for which it can provide no substitute. Native society, as already stated, is in the patriarchal state. The foundation of it is the " Father," whether of the family, of the community, or of the tribe. The members of the House are, in a measure, apprentices. Under native law there are obligations on both sides. It is a transitional stage, and should be regarded as such, and allowed to reform itself from within. The one difficulty, in this respect, is lest the Ordinance should tend to prevent a gradual internal evolution towards a higher state by sterilizing any healthy influences making for modification. A much greater danger would be any sudden change which would throw the whole country into absolute confusion. In the Western Province and in the Bini district, where native rule has developed more rapidly than in the Eastern and Central, the Father of the House is subject to the Father of the district, and he in turn is subject to the Paramount Chief of the whole tribe—the Supreme Father. There is, therefore, a check upon despotic abuses by the head of the House. In the bulk of the Central Province and in the whole of the Eastern Province, the head of the House is virtually the head of the community, the higher forms of internal control not having evolved. Any hasty and violent interference which domestic " slavery," as it is termed, in a country like the Central and Eastern Provinces should be strenuously opposed. It would be an act of monstrous injustice, in the first place, if unaccompanied by monetary compensation, and it would produce social chaos. But there seems to be no reason why the House Rule Ordinance should not be amended in the sense of substituting for Paramount Chieftainship therein—which is virtually non-existent—the District Commissioners, *aided by the Native Councils*, as a check upon the now unfettered action of the heads of Houses. To destroy the authority of the heads would be to create an army of wastrels and ne'er-do-weels. Native society would fall to pieces, and endless "punitive expeditions" would be the result.*

For purposes of administration Southern Nigeria is divided into three Provinces, the Eastern (29,056 square miles), with headquarters at Old Calabar ; the Central (20,564 square miles) with headquarters at Warri ; and the Western (27,644 square miles), with headquarters at Lagos, the seat of Government of the Protectorate. To the Western Province is attached, as distinct from the Protectorate, what is termed the " Colony of Lagos," comprising the capital and a small area on the mainland —Lagos itself is an island—amounting altogether to 3,420 square miles. The supreme government of the three Provinces is carried on from Lagos by the Governor,

* In this connection Mr. Dennett's paper in the September issue of the journal of the Colonial Institute is very valuable.

assisted by an Executive Council and by a Legislative Council composed of nine officials and six unofficial members selected by the Governor and approved by the Secretary of State. Each Province is in charge of a Provincial Commissioner, although in the Western Province his duties are more nominal than real. In none of the Provinces is there a Provincial Council. The Central and Eastern Provinces are sub-divided into districts in charge of a District Commissioner and Assistant Commissioner, who govern the country through the recognized Chiefs and their councillors by the medium of Native Councils which meet periodically and over which the District Commissioner or his assistant presides. These Native Councils or Courts constitute the real administrative machinery of the country. They administer native law in civil and criminal cases between natives. They may not, however, except by special provision, deal with civil cases in which more than £200 is involved, or with criminal cases of a nature which, under native law, would involve a fine exceeding £100 or a sentence of imprisonment exceeding ten years with or without hard labour, or a flogging exceeding fifteen strokes. Appeal from the Native Courts to the Supreme Court can be made through the District Commissioners, who have the powers of a Judge of the Supreme Court with powers of jurisdiction limited by law. The District Commissioner's Court is virtually a branch of the Supreme Court, and deals almost entirely with cases in which non-natives are concerned.

The Central and Eastern Provinces, which include the deltaic and the larger part of the forest region, are inhabited by Pagan tribes, among whom Mohammedanism is at present making but relatively slow progress (none at all in many districts) and Christianity, which by fits and starts and with long intervals has been at them since the fifteenth century, still less. These tribes are of an

64

independent, sturdy temperament, and in the remoter parts of both Provinces still uncontrolled, or virtually so. They are, almost without exception, great traders, and the British merchants who know them best speak highly of their honesty in commercial transactions.

The problem of governing these peoples offers no complications, which may be called political, of a serious character. It is rendered easier in the Central Province, where the authority of the Benin Kingdom, exercised for so many centuries, has led to the centralization of a strong native authority ; and proportionately less so in the Eastern Province, where no considerable native power was ever evolved. The Administration levies no direct tax, and its chief concern is to keep the peace, to open up the country, and to check barbarous customs. Astonishing progress has been effected in these respects during the past decade, nor must it be supposed that because there is an absence of complex political questions, progress has not been attended with complexities of a different order. Indeed, people at home can have no conception of the natural difficulties under which the administrator, the merchant, and, for that matter, the native also, labour in carrying out their respective tasks and avocations in the deltaic and forest regions of Nigeria. For six months in the year a very large portion of the Central and Eastern Provinces is partially submerged. The Niger overflows its banks, every forest rivulet becomes a river, the creeks and channels spread their waters upon the land, the forest is flooded over an enormous area, and the pathways intersecting it are impassable.

It is in circumstances such as these that District Commissioners have to keep in touch with their districts, not infrequently spending days and even nights in dugouts under conditions which may be better imagined than described ; marching in the rear of weary carriers through reeking, soaking, steaming forest ; negotiating streams swollen into torrents ; camping where and when they can, the boots they remove getting mouldy in a night, the clothes they hang up wringing wet when they come to put them on again ; add to this a body often plagued with malaria and rheumatism, poorly nourished with sometimes insufficient and usually untempting diet, tormented by stinging insects, and a faint idea can be formed of conditions, during the rainy season, of a life which even in the dry season calls upon the utmost reserves of a man's moral fibre, to say nothing of his physical powers. That the latter give way does not, alas! need demonstration, for while a favoured few resist, the roll of deaths and invaliding tells its own tale ; and it would not be surprising if the former proved itself frequently unequal to the strain. Such cases are, however, extremely rare, and it is but natural if men labouring for their country under the conditions of hardship I have inadequately sketched should bitterly resent being portrayed on public platforms at home in the light of rivets in an administrative machine cynically demoralizing the natives of the country with drink in order to raise revenue.* Assuredly it is necessary, as a prominent statesman addressing the House of Commons declared some years ago, that "the more you extend your Empire the more imperative it is that this House should extract from its agents abroad the same standard of conduct which we exact at home." But it is also necessary that public opinion in Britain should take more trouble than it does to realize something of the conditions under which its agents in the most unhealthy tropical regions of the Empire have to spend their lives, and should extend to them more sympathy than, at present, it seems often inclined to do.

It is in this part of Nigeria, where natural man is perpetually in conflict with his environment, that you

* Vide Part IV.

A SCENE IN YORUBALAND.

See p. 77.

ONE OF THE COMMUNAL RUBBER PLANTATIONS
[FUNTUMIA ELASTICA], BENIN CITY.

would expect to find those darker customs and practices connected with the spiritual side of life, whereby humanity has in all ages sought to propitiate the forces of Nature ; customs which under the modern form of sword-dances, Morris dances, and the like attest to their former existence in Europe. If we are honest with ourselves we must admit that the inspiration which has evolved a sort of misty horror around the peoples of the West Coast of Africa, has been largely drawn from the setting of swamp and forest where the sacrificial rites associated with them, more prominently, perhaps, than they deserve, have been performed. In themselves these rites differ in no way from those we are familiar with in the records of white peoples when they had reached a stage of intellectual advancement which the Nigerian negro has certainly never attained, and which it is doubtful if any human stock could, or can ever, attain, in such an environment. Owing to the unconquered and, I think, unconquerable natural forces surrounding him, the Nigerian of the delta is still in the stage " to listen to the will of Jove which comes forth from the lofty and verdant oak " ; to seek as the load-star of his spiritual necessities and in his ceaseless struggle against implacable odds, the conciliation of the fertilizing spirit through whose assistance alone he can hope to subject them ; to incorporate the personality of protecting deities into man by oblation and by human or animal sacrifice, the shedding of blood being the mystic symbol of established contact with the protecting spiritual elements (the same prompting animates the most sacred of Christian rites) as it remains the tangible and most potent symbol of human brotherhood. The sacrificial knife of the Nigerian negro may seem more repulsive to the modern eye from the setting of black forms framed in the deep shadows of primeval forest and fœtid swamp, and a double dose of original sin may with complacency be assigned to him by the superficial. But in itself and in the motive which raises it quivering over the bound and helpless victim, it differentiates not at all from the story of Abraham and Isaac handed down to us in the sacred writings and not, certainly, in a light other than commendable, given the setting. If some of those who are so ready to pass shallow judgment upon the social and spiritual habits of the West African *chez lui* and who are responsible for so much misapprehension in the public mind as to his true character, would study the book of Genesis, they might approach the subject with an exacter sense of proportion. For a cessation of these practices in their most repellant forms—already much curtailed, openly at least —time must be relied upon and the most powerful element in hastening the process is not the punitive expedition, but increased facility for inter-communication which trade expansion generates and entails upon Government to provide. It may be safely predicted that the process will be far more rapid than it was in Europe.

No more striking object lesson in the capacity for real progress along indigenous lines possessed by the Southern Nigerian pagan could be sought than a comparison between the Bini people of 1897 and the Bini people of to-day. A powerful tribe now numbering some 150,000 and inhabiting the Central Province, the Binis had long been the slaves, so to speak, of a theocracy which had succeeded in denaturalizing the original native state-form and in obtaining an over-mastering hold over the people. The King's superstitions made him a puppet in its hands. The murder of several British officials was followed by the capture of the city, and the occupation of the country. Though mild in comparison with the *autodafés* and kindred pursuits of the Spanish Inquisition and the long persecution of the Jews which have distinguished other priesthoods in cultured surroundings that call for a certain sobriety of judgment in discussing

BENIN CITY TO-DAY.   BINI CHIEFS SITTING OUTSIDE THEIR NEW COURT HOUSE.

(Photo by Sir Walter Egerton.)

the priesthood of primitive Benin, the latter had succeeded in inspiring a reign of terror throughout the country. No man's life was safe, and Benin city, the capital, was a place of abominations. The priesthood were rightly broken, but the authority of the chiefs maintained, and despite one single administrative error, which, if not repaired, may occasion trouble later on, the Binis have become one of the most prosperous and law-abiding people in the Protectorate. They have co-operated so efficiently with the Forestry Department that throughout the Benin territory no tree can be unlawfully felled without the Forest Officer being informed. They are planting up their forest land with valuable timber trees. Supplied by the department with seeds, shown how to make nurseries and to supervise transplanting, but doing their own clearing, planting, and upkeep, no fewer than 700 villages have established communal rubber plantations of *Funtamia elastica* which they are increasing year by year. Many of the trees—of which there are one and a quarter millions whose present estimated value at a low computation is £165,000—are now of tappable size. Their share in the licence fees paid by European lease-holders engaged in the timber and rubber industry in Bini territory supplies the Bini communities with a further source of income. So greatly do these intelligent people appreciate the efforts of the Administration to enrich their country that when a little while ago they started tapping operations in their rubber plantations under the supervision of the Forestry Officer, the chiefs and villagers insisted that a third share should go to Government, and, despite the Governor's objections, they would consent to no other arrangement. This has now become embodied in law. The Forestry Department undertakes to dispose of the rubber from the communal plantations, the profits being divided as to one-third for the paramount chiefs, one-third for the village community, and one-third for the Administration. From their increased revenues the chiefs of Benin city, " the city of blood," as it used to be termed, have already built for themselves a substantial court-house of stone and brick and furnished their capital with a proper water-supply, putting down four miles of piping—thus saving the labour of thousands of persons who had daily to trudge to and from the river—and finding the money for a reservoir, a pumping station, and public hydrants.

Such surprising results in the short space of fourteen years are at once a tribute to British rule and to the negro of the Nigerian forests. Many obvious morals suggest themselves.

CHAPTER V

EARLY in the seventies, a decade after the British occupation, Lagos, for more years than one cares to remember an important export centre of the slave trade, was a small settlement inhabited by Yoruba and Bini agriculturists and traders. The Hinterland, threatened by Dahomeyan invasions from the west and Fulani inroads from the north, distressed by internal struggles between various sections of the Yoruba people rebelling against the central authority, was in a state of perpetual ferment. Severed from the mainland, maintaining themselves from hand to mouth, and swept by disease, the few British officials led an unenviable existence. A small three-roomed house protected from the rains by an iron roof harboured the Governor, and the members of his staff were glad to accept the hospitality of European merchants earning a precarious if lucrative livelihood by trading with the natives in palm oil, kernels, ivory, and cotton.

To-day Lagos is a picturesque, congested town of some 80,000 inhabitants, boasting many fine public buildings and official and European and native merchants' residences, churches, wharves, a hospital, a tramway, a bacteriological institute, a marine engineering establishment, to say nothing of cold storage and electric light plant, hotels, a racecourse, and other appurtenances of advanced civilization. Like every other part of West Africa

71

that I have seen, Lagos is full of violent contrasts. Every variety of craft—the tonnage of the place is something like 250,000 tons per annum—is to be observed in the water and every variety of dress in the busy streets, from the voluminous robes of the turbaned Mohammedan to the latest tailoring monstrosities of Western Europe. The Yoruba lady with a Bond Street hat and hobble skirt ; her sister in the infinitely more graceful enfolding cloths of blue or terra-cotta, with the bandanna kerchief for head-gear ; opulent resident native merchants or Government clerks in ordinary English costume ; keen-featured " uneducated " traders from whose shoulders hang the African *riga*—a cosmopolitan crowd which includes Sierra Leonean, Cape Coast, and Accra men, attracted by the many prospects of labour an ever-increasing commercial and industrial activity offers to carpenters, mechanics, traders' assistants, and the like. Here a church thronged on Sundays with African ladies and gentlemen in their finest array ; here a mosque built by the local and rapidly increasing Yoruba Muslims at a cost of £5,000. Here a happy African family laughing and chattering in a tumble-down old shanty within close proximity to a " swagger " bungalow gay with brilliant creepers ; there a seminary where a number of young ladies, looking supremely uncomfortable in their European frocks, supplemented by all the etceteras of Western feminine wardrobes, their short hair frizzled out into weird contortions, are learning as fast as their teachers can make them those hundred and one inutilities which widen the breach between them and their own beautiful, interesting land. A certain kind of prosperity is writ large over the place, but there is good reason to believe that economic pressure in its different forms, none more acutely felt than the ascending price of foodstuffs, is beginning to bear hardly upon the poorer classes, and the political and social atmosphere of the town is not altogether healthy.

LAGOS AND ITS PORT

Historical circumstances rather than natural advantages have made Lagos the most important commercial emporium of British West Africa and the starting-point of a railway into the interior. It is difficult to see, if the traffic of this railway and its future feeders develops, as there is every reason to believe it will, how the already crowded and circumscribed area of Lagos can possibly prove equal to the demands upon it. Indeed, its physical features are in many respects most disadvantageous for the *rôle* of the West African Bombay it appears called upon to bear, and it is only by the expenditure of millions which, spread over the Protectorate, would have achieved results of much greater fruitfulness, that Lagos can be converted into a harbour worthy of the name. For Lagos is cursed with a bar which vessels drawing more than fourteen feet cannot cross, and the absurd anomaly, to say nothing of the expense and loss of time and damage to valuable cargo involved, is witnessed of vessels with merchandise consigned to the premier port in Nigeria having to steam 120 miles south of it and there discharge their freight into branch steamers for conveyance to destination. An elusive and sinister obstruction is Lagos bar, strewn with wrecks and hitherto refractory to dredging, which shifts its depths three feet in a single week, while the position of the channels is continually altering. As one surveys the coast-line and notes the two, comparatively speaking, deep and roomy anchorages of Forcados and Old Calabar, one cannot refrain from marvelling somewhat at the curious chain of events which has conspired to concentrate effort and expense upon a place so difficult of access. However, the past cannot be undone, and no doubt there is much to be said in favour of Lagos, or rather of the happenings which have ministered to its selection. Be that as it may, the destinies of Southern Nigeria have for the last five years been in the hands of a Governor of large ideas and enormous

73

energy. Sir Walter Egerton, who, despite numerous dis-
appointments and maddening delays, has pursued with
dogged persistence and infinite resource the object dearest
to his heart—that of opening the harbour. A comprehensive scheme of works, entailing the construction of
two stone moles, one on either side of the entrance, combined with harbour and channel dredging, is proceeding
under the direction of Messrs. Coode, Son, and Matthews,
and the constant personal supervision of the Governor,
in the confident belief that its completion will ensure
(combined with dredging) a depth of twenty-seven feet
at high water, corresponding to twenty-four feet at low
tide. When I was in Lagos a month ago * the work on the
eastern mole had advanced 4,500 feet seawards, but the
western mole is not yet started, and will not be, it is
feared, for some time, a further delay having been caused
by the foundering of the *Axim*, with much indispensable
material on board.

One must have stood at the extremity of the eastern
mole and watched the greedy, muddy-coloured sea absorbing like some insatiable monster the masses of grey rock
hurled, at all times of the day and every day in the week,
into its depths, to appreciate the colossal difficulties of a
task which, brought to a successful issue, will always
remain an impressive testimony to human perseverance
under climatic and other conditions of perennial difficulty.
West Africa has certainly never seen anything comparable
to it. Nature disputes with man for every inch of vantage.
As the work progresses the sand twists and writhes into
ever-changing formations ; banks arise and disappear
only to again re-form ; the foreshore on the outer side
of the mole grows and swells and rises weekly, threatening
to become level with the wall itself and even to overwhelm
it ; the scour of the sea scoops into the ocean's floor, thus
forcing the advancing mole into deep water, which

* February, 1911.

demands a proportionately larger meal of stone. From out the greyness of the horizon the remains of the *Kano, Kittiwake, Egga,* and other vessels that once were, lift lamentable spars above the angry breakers. From Abeokuta, thirty miles away, these innumerable tons of granitic boulders must be brought, despatched in "boxes" from the newly-opened quarries to Ebute-Metta by rail. There the "boxes" are lifted from the waggons and hoisted by cranes into lighters, the lighters are towed to the wharf, the "boxes" lifted out of them, run along the mole, and their contents hurled into the sea. Every foot's advance requires sixty tons of stone. At the accelerated rate of progress now ensured the eastern mole will be finished in four years. The labour and organization required to bring this great work to its present stage—initial steps in West Africa being invariably characterized by endless impediments— have been prodigious. Despite the sombre prognostications one hears in certain quarters, there seems no reasonable doubt that the bar will yield in time, as the forest has yielded, to British genius and pertinacity aided by African muscles, but at a cost which, when the time comes to add up the bill, will prove, I think, much heavier than generally supposed.

Lagos is joined to the mainland by two substantial bridges, one connecting the island with another small island called Iddo, which stands between Lagos Island and the continent, and one connecting Iddo with the continent itself at Ebute-Metta. From thence the railway starts on its way northward, traversing the whole of Yorubaland and tapping the Niger at Jebba.

CHAPTER VI

THE YORUBAS AND THEIR COUNTRY

THE administrative problems which confront the Government of Southern Nigeria in the western, or Yoruba, province are very much more complicated than any to be met with in the central and eastern provinces. They arise partly from the character, at once progressive and unstable, of the Yorubas themselves, partly from the curious divergence in the political relations subsisting between his Majesty's Government. and the various sections of the old Yoruba confederation, partly from the influences working in favour of direct British rule which find favour in the Lagos Legislative Council, but mainly through neglect, disinclination to look a situation not without delicacy in the face, and the absence of any serious effort to map out a definite, consistent policy.

In one respect at least, that of the rapid assimilation of every feature, good, bad, and indifferent, which comes to them from the West with the influx of European religious and social ideas, law, and commercial and industrial activity, the Yorubas (who considerably outnumber them) may be termed the Baganda of West Africa. If this capacity spells true progress for a tropical African people, then the Yorubas are infinitely more progressive than any of the peoples, not of Nigeria merely, but of Western Africa. It is, nevertheless, worthy of remark that, without exception, all the native papers published in Lagos which, if not in every case edited by

Yorubas, profess in every case to be the mouthpieces of the " Yoruba nation," ceaselessly lament the Europeanizing of the country, the decay of the national spirit, the decadence of family authority, and the deterioration of the rising generation without, however—so far as many years' perusal of their columns can enable one to judge —ever making an attempt to grapple with the problem in a constructive sense, and, in some cases, perhaps unwittingly, contributing not a little to further the processes which they denounce and deplore. In this, their notable characteristic, the Yorubas may have been influenced by environment, for although a considerable portion of the area they inhabit is forest land, much of it is open park-like country, and the whole of it lies outside the deltaic region altogether. It is among the Yorubas that Christian missionary propaganda has obtained most of its converts in West Africa, although none of the ruling chiefs have accepted the Christian faith, and although Islam is now making much more headway than Christianity. Moreover, official Christianity, already represented in Yoruba by as many sects as we have at home, has been riven by the defection of a body, some 3000 strong, I believe, which has constituted itself an independent Church, the real, though not explicity avowed, motive being a refusal to abide by the monogamous sexual relationship which the Church enforces. With Christian missionary teaching Western education, or, more accurately, and, generally, semi-education (and indifferent at that) has, of course, gone hand in hand, and it is among the Yorubas almost exclusively, so far as Southern Nigeria is concerned, that the problem of the " educated native " and what his part is to be in the future of the country arises and threatens already to become acute.

Nowhere in Africa, it may be confidently asserted, are so many radically different influences, policies and tendencies at work among one and the same people as are observable to-day in this Yorubaland of 28,000 square miles. The situation is really quite extraordinary, and offers an unlimited field of speculation to the student. The natural aptitudes of the Yorubas—of both sexes—are husbandry and trade, not soldiering. But the necessities of tribal defence drove them to concentrate in large centres. These centres have remained and become the capitals of separate provinces, allegiance to the original head having mostly fallen into virtual, in some cases into total, desuetude. Thus we find to-day a series of native towns which for estimated numbers surpass anything to be met with in any part of native Africa—such as Ibadan, 150,000 ; Abeokuta, 100,000 ; Oshogbo, 40,000 ; Ogbomosho, 35,000 ; Ife, 30,000 ; Oyo, 40,000 ; Ijebu-Ode, 35,000 ; Iseyin, 40,000 ; some twelve other towns with a population of between 10,000 and 20,000 ; and twice as many more whose inhabitants number 5000 to 8000. The most surprising contrasts, illustrative of the divergences referred to, are noticeable in these agglomerations of human life—for instance, between Abeokuta, Ibadan, and Oyo. Abeokuta, the capital of the " Egba united Government " (whose authority extends over 1869 square miles), its mass of corrugated iron roofs glaring beneath the rays of the tropical sun, spreading around and beneath the huge outcrop of granitic rock where its founders first settled a hundred years ago, offers the curious picture of a Europeanized African town in the fullest sense of the term, but with this unique feature, that its administration and the administration of the district, of which it is the capital, is conducted by natives—*i.e.* by the Alake (the head chief) in council.

It is, of course, true that the British Commissioner wields very great influence, but he is invested with no legal powers of intervention whatever, because the British treaty with the Egba section of the Yoruba people

78

ONE OF THE SONS OF THE SHEHU OF BORNU. *See p. 163.*

ONE OF THE SACRED STONE IMAGES AT IFE, THE SPIRITUAL CENTRE OF YORUBALAND.

recognizes their independence in all internal affairs ; and all Government notices and pronouncements posted up in the town are signed by the Alake and the Alake's secretary. The Commissioner, Mr. Young, finds himself, indeed, in a position where the utmost tact is required. He has passed through very unpleasant times, and the confidence and respect he has ultimately won constitute a veritable triumph of personality. He has achieved the seemingly impossible task of becoming a real power in a native State over which, save in its external relations and in civil and criminal cases affecting " non-Egbas," the British Government has no legal jurisdiction. The Alake, a burly African, has not—a matter of thankfulness —adopted European dress, as the bulk of his officials have done, but he lives in a two-storeyed European house boasting of a tennis-court which, I am confident, the ample proportions of its owner forbid him from using. The whole machinery of administration is on the European pattern, with its Secretariat, Treasury, Public Works Department, Police, Prison, Printing Offices, Post Office, etc.—all managed by Europeanized Africans. I visited most of the Government departments, the prison, and printing offices, and was impressed with the industry and business-like air which reigned within them. The revenues, thanks to the Commissioner, are in a healthy state. Excellent roads have been and are being constructed. A water supply is being arranged for out of a loan of £30,000 advanced by the Southern Nigeria Government. Labour-saving machinery is being introduced at the Commissioner's suggestion. An imposing college is in course of erection. It is all very remarkable and interesting. Whether it is durable is a matter which I shall have occasion to discuss later on.

Very different is the state of affairs such as I found it early in this year in Ibadan, capital of a district of 4000 square miles with a dense population of 430,000 (107 to the square mile), an enormous, straggling, grass-roofed, rather unkempt town luxuriating in tropical vegetation and whose neighbourhood abounds with rich and delightful scenery. Here, administratively speaking, government is neither fish, fowl, nor good red-herring; neither African, nor European, nor Europeanized-African. All real influence has been taken out of the hands of the Bale (head-chief) and nothing has been substituted for it. Treated at intervals with unwise familiarity and with contemptuous disregard, the present Bale, a man obviously unfitted for his office, has no authority over his chiefs, who in council—as I have myself witnessed—openly deride him. The inevitable consequence is that the chiefs themselves constantly intrigue against one another and have no prestige with the people, while the people themselves have no respect either for their own rulers or for the white man. A visit to the Bale's Court in company with the recently-appointed Acting-Resident was a surprising revelation—quite as painful, I am inclined to believe, to that official as to the writer—of unmannerly conduct, of total absence of respect for his Majesty's representative, of utter lack of decorum and dignity. The "Ibadan Government," as I saw it, is a caricature, and a dangerous caricature, of government, unlike anything, I am glad to say, which I observed in either of the two Protectorates. The town and the inhabitants are obviously out of hand, and in my opinion—an opinion which, having felt bound to communicate it to the responsible authorities in Nigeria, I am the freer to state here—is that if the whole place be not thoroughly overhauled, events must arise at no distant day leading to considerable trouble. I am inclined to think that some people would rather welcome trouble.

Oyo, again, is a singular contrast both to Abeokuta and to Ibadan. The seat of the Alafin, titular head of all the Yoruba-speaking peoples, Oyo is a clean, peaceful, sleepy town charmingly situate in open country and reverentially regarded by many Yorubas. Here the native form of government has been happily preserved against many assaults from both within and without. The Alafin's abode—the Afin—consists of a collection of spacious compounds beautifully thatched with *bere* grass and surrounded by a wall. Here the Court is held, distinguished by all the ceremonial inherent to what was once (and might again become) a wonderfully efficient national Government. In its courtliness, its simple if barbaric dignity, the decorum of chiefs and councillors, and the manifest honour in which the ruling head was held, this Pagan Court recalled the best type of native government I had previously observed in the Mohammedan Hausa provinces of Northern Nigeria, although differing radically from the latter in construction and formulæ. The Alafin himself, a man of great strength and stature, his head surmounted by the national casque or crown of heavy native coral, with a curious face which reminded one of the lineaments of the Egyptian Sphinx (the Yorubas profess to trace their descent from Egypt), is one of the most striking native personalities I observed in Nigeria. A notable incident in the State reception I witnessed was the presence among the prostrated chiefs of several whose dress showed that they had embraced Islam, doing obeisance to their pagan lord.

This brief description of the three most important centres of Yoruba life will serve to show how varied and haphazard are the forms which British policy takes in the Western Province. I fear that much trouble lies ahead if steps are not adopted to evolve something more closely approximating to statecraft in handling the problems of the country. An attempt to show what might be done and the reasons for doing it will be made in the next chapter.

CHAPTER VII

THE political situation in Yorubaland, some aspects of which were briefly sketched in the preceding chapter, is one that, obviously, cannot last. Its inconveniences are too numerous and too palpable and it bears within it the seeds of dissolution. The whole relationship of the different Yoruba States (or, rather, dismembered sections) between themselves and between them and the British *raj* as established by Treaty or by Agreement (which should have equally binding force) abounds in contradictions, irregularities, and potency for mischief. In the Abeokuta district we have theoretically no authority, since, as already mentioned, there is a Treaty guaranteeing the independence of the Egbas in their internal affairs. But every one knows that, given an untactful Commissioner or the development of some more than usually menacing intrigue against the Alake, circumstances might arise at any time which would compel British intervention. With Oyo we have a treaty of friendship and commerce and we have a separate treaty of the same kind with Ibadan, although Ibadan recognizes the paramountcy of, and pays tribute to, Oyo. In Oyo we have not materially interfered with native government. In the Ibadan district native government is, in practice, a myth. Such a state of things leads to singular inconsistencies, and the Southern Nigeria Administration would find it difficult to reconcile its actions in certain directions with its actions in others.

ENTRANCE TO THE "AFIN" OR RESIDENCE OF THE ALAFIN OF OYO,
SHOWING TYPICAL YORUBA THATCHING.

Take, for example, the land question. If there is
one thing upon which all the most experienced Nigerian
administrators are agreed it is the absolute essentiality,
for the future of the people of the country, that their
use and enjoyment of the land should be secured, not
only against a certain type of European capitalist who
covets this rich soil for his own schemes, and, under the
pretence of industrial expansion, would cheerfully turn the
native agriculturist, farmer, and trader into a "labourer,"
but against the class of native who, for his own ends,
for speculative purposes mainly, seeks to undermine
native law and to change the right of user upon which
native land tenure is based, into that of owner at the
expense of the community at large. More especially
does this become a question of vital importance to native
communities where, as in Yorubaland, you have a comparatively dense population which under the *pax Britannica* is bound to increase at a very rapid rate, and thus
requires every inch of land for its own future uses. But
as matters stand at present, we cannot, in the Egba
district, which, being nearer to Lagos, is more accessible
to certain undesirable influences, both European and
native, and to the infiltration of European laws and
customs regulating the tenure of land, take effective
measures to counteract these influences. We could, of
course, if we chose, not in the Egba district only, but
throughout Yorubaland. But there has been a lamentable
reluctance both at home and in the Protectorate to foresee
and cope with a predicament which all realize, which some
from a natural bent of mind inclining them to favour the
substitution everywhere of direct for indirect rule, and
others who are of the same way of thinking but from
motives of self-interest may secretly rejoice at, but which
the officials whose hearts are really in the country and
who have sufficient experience to understand the endless
and disastrous embarrassments that the disintegration

of native law relating to land would produce, deeply deplore. What has been the result ? The Egbas are beginning to buy and to sell land among themselves in absolute violation of their own customs and laws, thereby laying up for their ccuntry a heritage of trouble and inserting the thin edge of the wedge of their own undoing by letting in the land monopolist and speculator. This, according to all its professions and to its actions in some specific circumstances, for which it is to be warmly commended, is, in the view of the Administration, inimical to the public interest of the Protectorate. What is springing up in Abeokuta to-day will spread to the other districts to-morrow—nay, is doing so.

Take another example. The welfare of an agricultural community demands, for many reasons scientifically substantiated, that a stop should be put to the reckless destruction of timbered areas such as has been proceeding all over Yorubaland. This is inherently a public interest, and the Forestry Officer in the discharge of his duties is merely a servant of the public. But in the Western Province, for the same reasons, we cannot or are unwilling to put our case to the native authorities for the protection of the people against themselves with the same moral force as in the case of the other two provinces. We are confined, or think we are confined, to simple persuasion. Now, persuasion by the Forestry Officer alone is one thing, and persuasion by the Forestry Officer supported by direct representations from the Executive at Lagos is a very different thing. It is the latter form of persuasion that has been absent, and very great credit is due alike to the Forestry Officers and to a Commissioner trusted by the native rulers, Mr. W. A. Ross, as well as to the intelligence of those native rulers themselves, that in the Oyo district both State and communal reserves have been created, the latter of great extent including the entire valley of the Ogun.

But in the Abeokuta and Ibadan districts persuasion has failed hitherto to secure any really tangible results. It is almost unnecessary to point out that the interests of the population do not suffer merely indirectly and potentially, but directly thereby. Not only does Southern Nigeria import quantities of timber from Europe when the country should itself provide for all requirements, but even so primitive a necessity as firewood is beginning to make itself felt round such towns as Ede, Abeokuta, and Ibadan.

In these problems the policy of the Southern Nigeria Administration has been to leave the matter to the native authorities, in other words, to let the land question slide down a perilous declivity, and to allow the question of forestry preservation to be left to the unsupported efforts of the Forestry Department. If this policy of non-interference had been consistently applied in other directions an intelligible case, at least, might be made out for it. But the facts are notoriously otherwise. To mention but one instance. Two years ago pressure was put upon the Ibadan authorities to vote unpopular licensing regulations in the interests of temperance, and one of the incidents subsequently arising out of it was the stoppage of the Bale's stipend by the Acting Resident with the concurrence of the Executive at Lagos! Only last February a Bill called the "Foreign Jurisdiction Ordinance, 1911," was passed through the Lagos Legislative Council, which provides for the extension of the laws of the colony to the Protectorate of Yorubaland (except Abeokuta) without the native authorities being even consulted, the Attorney-General adopting, in effect, the extraordinary position that the Government could take no account of "agreements, understandings, or letters" (concluded or written by previous Governors) with the native chiefs! If the native chiefs realized what the logical outcome of the Ordinance might mean for them, by an Executive in Lagos, which adopted the legal argument quoted, there would be ferment from one end of Yoruba to the other.

It must be clear from what precedes that the time has come when the whole position of the Yoruba States in relation to the paramount Power should be reconsidered. The railway and other agencies are causing the country to move forward very fast, and conditions are being evolved through the attempt to drive in two directions at once, which can only lead, if not to the ultimate annexation of Yorubaland, then to what would, if possible, be even worse—viz. the strangulation by successive stages of every effective agency in native government, leaving the chiefs and their councils mere puppets in the hands of the Lagos Legislative Council. Now neither of these courses is, I am convinced, desired by the Imperial Government. The drift is, nevertheless, apparent to all that have eyes to see and ears to hear. There is a strong party in Lagos favouring direct rule. There is a combination of distinct influences—in many respects working unconsciously—making for the breakup of native land tenure and the undermining of native authority. There is the increasing danger of leaving the land question unregulated and the difficulty attending the adoption of adequate measures for forest preservation.

Only one course would appear open to the authorities if they desire to stop the dry rot. The first step would consist in getting the Native Councils—*i.e.* the Chiefs in Council—of all the districts in the Western Province to pass an identical measure of national land preservation which would become known as the Yoruba Land Act. Inalienability of land is the cardinal principle of Yoruba land tenure. The preamble of the measure would define Yoruba law and custom in regard to land. The body of the measure would declare to be illegal all buying and selling of land, either between natives and natives or between natives and non-natives, and would establish limitations of area and time for the holding of leased lands by private individuals or associations, with provision for revision of rentals at specified periods. The need of such a measure should be recognized and the action proposed sanctioned by the Secretary of State, and the matter should be represented to the native authorities with all the additional weight which in their eyes it would under those circumstances possess. It cannot be doubted that were the measure fully and thoroughly explained to the Native Councils and its urgency in the interests of their people emphasized, little or no trouble would be experienced in ensuring its adoption. In the improbable event of difficulties arising it would be the plain duty of the Administration to overcome them. The Administration should be able to count in a matter of this kind upon the support of every patriotic educated Yoruban. The second step would be more far-reaching—viz. the general reconstruction of the machinery of national government over the whole province, and the welding together under the headship of the Alafin of Oyo—the " King and Lord of Yorubaland," as he is described in the British Treaty—working with a Council representative of all Yorubaland, of the separate districts which internal anarchy and external aggression between them have caused to fall away from the central authority. The existing Councils of the various districts would, of course, remain, but we should have what we have not at present, a true " Yoruba Council," a strong central native Government through which the development, the progress, and the common welfare of the country could proceed on definite, ordered, national lines.

This would be Empire-building of the real kind. It would not be unattended with difficulty. It would

require time, much tact, and, above all, full and frank
exposition and explanation.   But it is feasible of accomplishment, and by a policy of this kind alone can one of
the most interesting and promising races of Western
Africa hope to reach, under our supreme direction, its
full development.   The elements necessary to the success
of such policy exist.   They do not need to be created,
but only to have their vitality revived and their course
adjusted and guided.

PART III
NORTHERN NIGERIA

CHAPTER I

THE NATURAL HIGHWAY TO THE UPLANDS OF THE NORTH

A CASUAL visitor provided by private kindness with the hospitality of a stern-wheeler and not, therefore, exposed to the discomforts (soon, it is to be hoped, to be a thing of the past, with the completion of railway communications between Lagos and Zungeru) with which an inexcusably inefficient service of river-boats afflicts the unhappy official on his way to Northern Nigeria, packed like a sardine, and feeding as best he can, may be pardoned for finding much of captivating interest in 400 miles of leisurely steaming, with many a halt *en route*, from Forcados to Baro, the starting-point of the Northern Nigerian Railway to Kano. The heat of the afternoons, the myriad insect visitors which are heralded by the lighting of the lamps, blacken the cloth and invade every part of the person accessible to their attentions, the stifling nights, spent, may be, at anchor under the lee of perpendicular banks ; these are trifles not worthy of mention by comparison with the rewards they bring. Kaleidoscopic varieties of scenic effects enchant the eye as hour follows hour and day follows day on the bosom of this wonderful Niger, passing from serpentine curves so narrow that the revolving paddles seem in imminent danger of sinking into the bank itself or snapping against some one of the many floating snags, to ever broadening and majestic proportions with vistas of eternal forest, of villages nestling amid banana groves, of busy fishermen flinging their nets, of occasional dark massive heads lifted a brief second from the deeps to disappear silently as they arose, of brilliant blue kingfishers darting hither and thither. Now the river flows through some natural greenhouse of palms and ferns, whose nodding fronds are reflected in the still green waters, now past a fringe of matted creepers gay with purple convolvulus pierced at intervals with the grey upstanding bole of the silk cotton tree. Here its course is broken by long stretches of fine hummocky sand across whose shining surface stalk the egret and the crane, the adjoining rushes noisy with the cackle of the spur-winged geese. Here it glides expanding between open plains bordered with reeds, only to narrow once more as the plain heaves upward and the tall vegetable growth gives way to arid granite outcrops, ascending towards the far horizon into high tablelands. If at dawn the Niger veils its secrets in billowy mists of white, at sunset the sense of mystery deepens. For that, I think, is the principal charm of this great highway into the heart of Negro Africa, the sense of mystery it inspires. Cradled in mystery, for two thousand years it defied the inquisitiveness of the outer world, guarded from the north by dangerous shoals and rapids; hiding its outlet in a fan-shaped maze of creeks. To-day when its sanctuaries are violated, its waters churned and smitten by strange and ugly craft, it is still mysterious, vast and unconquered. Mysterious that sombre forest the gathering shades encompass. Mysterious that tall half-naked figure on yonder ledge, crimson framed in the dying sun, motionless and statuesque. Mysterious that piercing melancholy note which thrills from the profundities beyond, fading away in whispers upon the violet and green wavelets lapping against the side of the boat. Mysterious those rapid staccato drumbeats as unknown humanity on one shore signals to unseen humanity on the other.

Mysterious the raucous cry of the crown-birds passing in long lines to their resting-place in the marshes. Mysterious those tiny lights from some unsuspected haunt of natural man that spring into life as the sun sinks to slumber, and darkness, deep unfathomable darkness, rushes over the land there to rest until a blood-red moon, defining once again the line of forest, mounts the sky.

From the point of view of navigation and of commerce the Niger is a most unsatisfactory and uncertain river to work. It can be described, perhaps, as a river full of holes with shallows between them. Its channels are constantly changing. It is full of sandbanks which take on new shapes and sizes every year. The direction of the water-flow below Samabri, where the bifurcation begins, is so unreliable that within a few years the Nun has become virtually useless, the Forcados gaining what the Nun has lost, while there are recent indications that the process may again be altered in favour once more of the Nun to the detriment of the Forcados. In the course of the year the water level varies twenty-seven feet, the period of rise being from June in an ascending scale until the end of September, the fall then commencing, the river being at its lowest from December to May. In the rainy season the banks are flooded in the lower regions for miles around. In the dry season the banks tower up in places fifteen feet above water level. Roughly speaking, the Niger is navigable for steamers drawing five feet in June, six feet in July, and so on up to twelve feet in the end of September; from November to April for vessels drawing between four and five feet. But the conditions of two consecutive years are seldom alike.

Government has done little or nothing to cope with these natural difficulties. The Admiralty charts available to the captains of steamers are ludicrously obsolete, and all wrong. No continuous series of observations have been taken of the river, and no effort made to tackle the problem of improving navigation. Four years ago, by Sir Percy Girouard's directions, soundings were, indeed, taken over a distance of 350 miles from Burutu (Forcados) to Lokoja at the junction with the Benue ; with the result that only seven miles of sand-bars were reported to require dredging in order to secure a six-foot channel all the year round. The experienced merchant smiled. He is a slightly cynical person, is the West African merchant who knows his Niger. Anyhow he is still whistling for his six-foot channel. One dredger, the best which money could buy, was purchased by the Northern Nigerian Administration. It did a little dredging round about Lokoja (and the merchants in the south declare that the performance has made matters worse for them), has been used as a passenger boat up the Benue, and is now, I believe, filling up the swamps at Baro ; but the six-foot channel still exists as an attractive theory in the Government Blue Book. There is so much to praise, administratively speaking, in Nigeria that one feels the freer to speak bluntly of the failure of Government to handle this matter of Niger navigation. It is one of the inevitable, one of the many deplorable, results of dual control over a common territory ; one of the consequences of the long competition between the two rival Administrations, each quite honestly playing for its own hand and each quite satisfied that it alone can think imperially. The upshot has been pernicious to the public interest. The river-service is shocking from the point of view of efficiency, and enormously costly. The steamers themselves are falling to pieces. There is no system of public pilotage, or of lighting. Trading steamers must anchor at night, which involves, in the aggregate, a great waste of time and money. The two Administrations are so busy squabbling over their competing railways and manœuvring to frame rates which will cut one another out, that the great natural highway into the interior is utterly neglected.

It is impossible that feelings of respect should not go out, not only towards the official who labours under these conditions in the Niger waterways but also towards the merchant building up in quiet, unostentatious fashion the edifice of commercial enterprise upon which, in the ultimate resort, the whole fabric of Administrative activity reposes. I do not now speak of the heads of these powerful trading firms in Europe, many of whom, by the way, have themselves gone through the mill in their time. To them England is indebted for the Imperial position she holds in Nigeria to-day, a fact which is too apt to be forgotten. I refer to the men, mostly young, in charge of trading stations on the banks of the Niger and its creeks, living a life of terrible loneliness amid primitive surroundings in a deadly climate, separated in many cases several days' journey from another white face, not nearly so well housed as the officials (I am describing Southern Nigeria, be it remembered), and not, like them, helped by the consciousness of power or stimulated by the wider horizon the latter enjoy. Thrown entirely on their own resources, usually unfitted by their previous life to face the privations and isolation of an existence such as this, very hard-worked—their lot is not an enviable one. No doubt the hardships they have to endure are incidental to a career they freely choose, although often enough with little or no previous comprehension of its character. No doubt the fibres of a minority will be toughened by their experiences. No doubt these hardships are infinitely less severe than those which the early pioneers were compelled to undergo, many succumbing under the process; but in that connection it should not be forgotten that the latter had the incentive of carving out their fortunes with their own hands, whereas the present generation out in Nigeria are not their own masters. One cannot help reflecting upon the irony of the contrast between the commiseration so freely lavished at home upon the spiritual drawbacks of the Nigerian native, and the total lack of interest displayed by the Church in the welfare of these young fellows, many of them mere lads, exposed to all the moral temptations of their savage environment in which only exceptional natures will detect the broadening spiritual influences. What an untold blessing would be a periodical visit to their African homes, fronted by the silent river, invested by the tropical forest, from an experienced, genial, sympathetic minister of God, who for a day or two would share their lives and win their confidence.

There is another matter which should be raised. These young men who come out from England—I refer to the English trading firms only, not having inquired into the system prevailing among the Continental firms—do so under a three years' contract. This is an altogether excessive period for the Niger. It should be cut down one half. Even then it would be half as long again as the officials' term of service. Professors of tropical medicine and magnates at home may say what they like about the improvement of health in the large European settlements. The towns are one thing. The " bush " is quite another. Speaking generally, the climate of Nigeria, and the conditions under which four-fifths of white humanity have to live are such as combine, even in favourable circumstances, to impose the severest strain, both physical and mental, upon all but a select few. At the end of a year's continuous residence, the strain begins to make itself felt in a multiplicity of ways. Not to acknowledge it, and not to make provision for it, is, on the part of an employer, penny wise and pound foolish—to put the matter on the lowest ground.

At Idah we leave Southern Nigeria. That bold bluff

VIEW OF LOKOJA AND NATIVE TOWN FROM MOUNT PATTEY, LOOKING S.E.—THE BENUE IN THE DISTANCE.

of red sandstone crowned with grey-trunked baobabs and nodding palms—black with roosting and repulsive vultures—which overhangs the river at this point, stands out at the dying of the day, a sentinel pointing to the north. Henceforth the appearance of the country undergoes a remarkable transformation, more and more accentuated with every hour's steaming. High valleys, slopes and tablelands; a sparser vegetation; masses of granite or red sandstone vomited promiscuously from broken, arid plains and taking on fantastic shapes; in the distance, mountain ranges and solitary rounded eminences—on our right, King William's range rising to 1200 feet, on our left, Mounts Jervis, Erskine, Soraxte, and many others, varying from 400 to 1000 feet. The river curves, winds and narrows, obstructed here and there by dangerous boulders, which the falling waters bring into view. More substantial, better-thatched huts appear upon the banks, and around them an increasing number of robed Africans. Plantations of yams, and guinea corn set out on parallel, raised ridges, attest a higher skill in cultivation. Cattle are seen cropping the green stuffs near the water's edge, and canoes pass bearing cattle, sheep and goats to some neighbouring market. We enter the spreading domain of Mohammedan civilization, and before long we shall find ourselves in a new world, as our gallant little vessel, none the worse for a narrowly averted collision and grounding on a sandbank or two, casts anchor at Lokoja. Here beneath the wooded heights of Mount Patte the wonderful prospect afforded by the junction of the Niger and Benue unfolds itself, and presently we shall mingle with robed and turbaned African humanity, come from immense distances to this great market of the middle Niger. The mangroves of the Delta, the awesome grandeur of the forests, these are left far behind. We have entered the uplands of the North.

CHAPTER II

THE political events of which Northern Nigeria was the scene last century are well known, but a brief recapitulation of them is necessary by way of introduction to the study of its present conditions, the life of its people, and the accomplishments and problems of the British Administration.

In the opening years of the nineteenth century, what is now Northern Nigeria consisted of the shattered remnants of the once famous Bornu Empire ; of seven independent states more or less (generally less) controlled by chieftains of the remarkable so-called " Hausa " race, invaders of a thousand years before " out of the East," and of the aboriginal inhabitants whose origin is lost in the mists of antiquity. Scattered throughout the region and constantly shifting their habitat in response to the necessities of their calling, were tribes of light-coloured straight-haired people, Fulani, nomadic herdsmen and shepherds. From the ranks of these people, spread over West Africa from the Senegal to the Chad, had sprung from time to time political leaders, divines and men of letters who had played a conspicuous part in the history of the old Niger civilizations. The Hausa Chieftains had established a nominal authority over a wide expanse of territory and were constantly at war with the aborigines on their borders. It was not, however, for warlike feats, but for their commerce, farming, cotton and leather industry ; for the spread of their language ; for the great centres of human activity they had formed and for the fertility and prosperity of the land which they had made their home, that the Hausas were justly renowned all over Western and Northern Africa. They had evolved no great imperial dominion whose various parts acknowledged a central Head, such, alternately, as Melle, Ghanata, Kanem and Bornu ; but they had leavened with their intelligence and fertilised with their industrial achievements some of the naturally richest areas of tropical West Africa, and they had earned for themselves in these respects a widespread fame.

It was at this period that a learned Fulani, Othman Fodio, fell foul of the chieftain ruling over the most ancient and aristocratic of the Hausa States, Gober. The latter, fearing for his authority, ordered all the Fulani in his country to be slaughtered, with the result that Othman found himself at the head of a numerous following. Emerging successfully from the struggle, Othman preached a *jihad*, confided sacred standards to his worthiest captains and despatched them far and wide. The Hausa Chieftains were successively overthrown and replaced by Fulani, and regions unassimilated previously by the Hausas were occupied. Othman's warriors even crossed the Niger and invaded Yorubaland, a large part of which they conquered and retained (Ilorin), the forest belt, Yoruba resistance within it, and, probably, the tsetse fly proving an insurmountable barrier to further progress southwards. Down the Niger they advanced no further than the neighbourhood of Lokoja. Othman adopted the title of *Sarikin mussulmi*, and during his life and that of his son Bello, Hausaland experienced for the first time the grip of a central, directing power. It is doubtful, however, if this change in their rulers had much effect upon the mass of the population, to whom dynastic convulsions mean very little, and it is noteworthy that the Fulani conquerors possessed sufficient statecraft to interfere but slightly with the complicated and efficient system of administration and of taxation which the Hausas had introduced. They took over the government of the towns from the Hausas, the people in many instances assisting and welcoming them. The general condition of the country remained pretty much what it had been. Moreover— and this fact is significant in connection with the arguments I shall presently adduce as regards the inspiring motive of the Fulani uprising—such of the old Hausa families who by their learning and piety had become invested with a special public sanctity were not generally molested by the conquering Fulani. Thus the Kauru, Kajura and Fatika families of Zaria, which had given birth to a long line of Mallams, were preserved in all their authority and dignity by Othman and his successors.

A period of comparative political quiet ensued. Othman issued regulations, and caused them to be strictly enforced, inflicting the severest punishments upon robbers and evil-doers generally. A recrudescence of spiritual influence and of letters everywhere manifested itself. Learned men flocked to Sokoto, where Othman had built his capital, from West and North Africa. The trans-desert trade revived. Security was so well established that Clapperton, who visited the country during Bello's reign, records the common saying of the time that a woman could pass unmolested through the land, even if she carried a casket of gold upon her head. With the death of Bello the influence of the central power, enormously difficult to maintain in any case owing to the greatness of the area and the absence of ways of communication, declined. Administrative decay gradually set in and extended with the years. Little by little the authority of the Emir of Sokoto was openly questioned, in all save spiritual matters. Allegiance slackened. Emirs quarrelled amongst themselves. This or that chief acted on his own responsibility in political affairs affecting the general weal, or entirely broke away from control. The roads became infested with bands of highwaymen whose proceedings differed in no way from the banditti of feudal Europe. Rebellious chieftains formed robber strongholds. Military operations degenerated into mere raiding for the capture and sale of prisoners of war to replenish revenues from ordinary taxation which the disturbed state of the country was causing to decrease.

There has probably been a natural tendency in recent years to exaggerate the aggregate effect for evil upon the country which accompanied the weakening of the Fulani dynasty. There is no proof that the state of affairs was worse than what had obtained previous to Othman's *jihad*. It could hardly have been worse than the condition of Western Europe at sundry stages in its history, when the weakness of the paramount authority and the foraging and strife of rival Barons combined to desolate the homesteads of the people and lay waste the country side. Some notion of parallels in approaching the events of West African history is very desirable, but not often conspicuous. But there can be no doubt —the evidence of one's own eyes in ruined villages and once cultivated areas " gone to bush " is conclusive— that when the alien Britisher arrived upon the scene as a reforming political force, Northern Nigeria was once more urgently in need of a power sufficiently strong to restore order. Such was the condition of the Hausa States. In Bornu matters had gone from disorder to chaos, culminating in the final tragedy of Rabeh's incursion, the slaughter of the *Shehu* and the sack of Kuka, the capital.

There is no need here to describe the events which

led to the British occupation, or to narrate the circumstances attending it. We have replaced the Fulani in supreme control of the destinies of Northern Nigeria. We are there to stay. How are we carrying out our self-imposed mission ? What are the problems with which we have to grapple ? These are the questions to examine. But before doing so, let us first see what manner of people they are over whom we rule henceforth as over-lords. What is their mode of life, their principal occupation, their character, and the material and spiritual influences which direct their outlook and mould their existence ?

CHAPTER III

THE INDIGENOUS CIVILIZATION OF THE NORTH

An attempted reconstruction of the prehistoric period —considered locally—of that portion of Western Central Africa, now known as Northern Nigeria, would take up many chapters, and would be largely founded upon conjecture. It suffices to say that in the course of ages, through the influences of Moorish, Semitic, and probably pre-Semitic Egyptian culture, fused in later times with Mohammedan law, learning and religion, there has been evolved in this region a civilization combining a curious mixture of Africa and the East, to which no other part of the tropical or sub-tropical continent offers even a remote parallel. And this is the more remarkable since these territories have been separated from the east by inhospitable, mainly waterless stretches, and from the north by vast and desolate sandy wastes; while southwards the forest and the swamp cut them off from all communication with the outer world by sea. The peoples responsible for the creation of this civilization did not acquire the art of building in stone, but, at a cost of labour and of time which must have been gigantic (slave-labour, of course, such as built the pyramids) they raised great cities of sun-dried clay, encompassing them and a considerable area around, for purposes of cultivation and food-supply, with mighty walls. These walls, from twenty to fifty feet high and from twenty to forty feet thick at the base, in the case of the larger cities, they furnished with ponderous and deep towered entrances, protecting the gates with crenellated loopholes and digging deep moats outside. They learned to smelt iron and tin ; to tan and fabricate many leather articles durable and tasteful in design ; to grow cotton and fashion it into cloth unrivalled for excellence and beauty in all Africa ; to work in silver and in brass ; to dye in indigo and the colouring juice of other plants ; to develop a system of agriculture including (in certain provinces) irrigated farming, which, in its highest forms, has surprised even experts from Europe ; to build up a great trade whose ramifications extend throughout the whole western portion of the continent ; to accumulate libraries of Arabic literature, to compile local histories and poems, and, in a measure, to become centres for the propagation of intellectual thought.

That is the condition in which Leo Africanus found them in the sixteenth century, when he first revealed their existence to an incredulous and largely unlettered Western world ; in which the pioneer explorers of the nineteenth century found them ; in which the political agents of Great Britain found them ten years ago when destiny drove her to establish her supremacy in the country. That is the condition in which they are to-day in this difficult transition stage when the mechanical engines of modern progress, the feverish economic activity of the Western world, the invading rattle of another civilization made up of widely differing ideals, modes of thought, and aims, assailed them.

Will the irresistible might wielded by the new forces be wisely exercised in the future ? Will those who, in the ultimate resort, direct it, abide by the experience and the advice of the small but splendid band of men whose herculean and whole-hearted labours have inscribed on the roll of British history an achievement, not of conquest, but of constructive statesmanship of just and sober guidance nowhere exceeded in our management of tropical dependencies? Will they be brought to understand all that is excellent and of good repute in this indigenous civilization; to realize the necessity of preserving its structural foundations, of honouring its organic institutions, of protecting and strengthening its spiritual agencies? Will they have the patience to move slowly; the sympathy to appreciate the period of strain and stress which these revolutionary influences must bring with them; the perception to recognize what elements of greatness and of far-reaching promise this indigenous civilization contains? Or will they, pushed by other counsellors, incline to go too fast both politically and economically, impatiently brushing aside immemorial ceremonies and customs, or permitting them to be assaulted by selfish interests on the one hand and short-sighted zeal on the other? Will they forget, amid the clamorous calls of " progress " and " enlightenment " that their own proclaimed high purpose (nobly accomplished by their representatives) of staying the ravages of internal warfare and healing open wounds will be shamed in the result if, through their instrumentality, the seeds of deeper, deadlier ills are sown which would eat away this fine material, destroy the lofty courtesies, the culture and the healthy industrial life of this land, converting its peoples into a troubled, shiftless mass, hirelings, bereft of economic independence and having lost all sense of national vitality? Thoughts such as these must needs crowd upon the traveller through these vast spaces and populous centres as he watches the iron horse pursue its irrevocable advance towards the great Hausa cities of the plains, as he hears the increasing calls from the newly opened tin mines for labour, from the Lancashire cotton-spinner for cotton and markets; as he takes cognisance of the suggestions already being made to break the spirit of the new and admirable land-law, and of the efforts to introduce a militant Christian propaganda ; as he listens in certain quarters to the loose talk about the " shibboleths " and " absurdities " of indigenous forms and ceremonies, the cumbrousness of native laws and etiquette.

CHAPTER IV

A BROAD, sandy road, piercing a belt of shea trees, gnarled and twisted, their bark figured like the markings of a crocodile's back, from which peculiarity you can distinguish the true shea from the so-called "false" shea, or African oak. From the burnt grasses, golden flowers destitute of leaf companionship peep timidly forth as though fearful of such uncongenial surroundings. The heat rays quiver over the thirsty soil, for it is Christmas time and no rain has fallen for nigh upon four months. On the summit of a blackened sapling, exquisite in its panoply of azure blue and pinkey-buff, a bird of the size of our English jay but afflicted with a name so commonplace that to mention it in connection with so glorious a visitant would be cruel, perches motionless, its long graceful tail feathers waving ever so slightly in the still air. The sun beats downward shrewdly, and combined with the gentle amble of the patient beast beneath you, induces drowsiness. You find yourself nodding in the saddle until the loosening grip of thighs jerks the rider once more into sentiency. It is hot, dreamily, lethargically hot. All the world seems comatose, the unfolding panorama unreal as if seen through a fog of visionary reverie. But there is nothing fanciful about the rapidly approaching cloud of dust ahead, which emits a swelling murmur of confused sound. It takes shape and substance, and for the next half-hour or so, drowsiness and heat are alike forgotten in the contemplation of a strange medley of men and animals. Droves of cattle, among them the monstrous horned oxen from the borders of Lake Chad, magnificent beasts, white or black for the most part. Flocks of Roman-nosed, short-haired, vacant-eyed sheep—white with black patches. Tiny, active, bright brown goats skipping along in joyful ignorance of impending fate. Pack-bullocks, loaded with potash, cloth, hides and dried tobacco leaves, culinary utensils, and all manner of articles wrapped in skins or in octagon-shaped baskets made of parchment, tight drawn in a wicker framework, which later—on the return journey—will be packed with kolas carefully covered with leaves. A few camels, skinny and patchy, and much out at elbows so to speak, similarly burdened. The drivers move among their beasts. Keeping in the rear, with lengthy staves outstretched over the animal's back, they control any tendency to straggle across the road. Tall spare men, for the most part, these drivers, small-boned, tough and sinewy. Hausas mainly, good-featured, not un-frequently bearded men, often possessed of strikingly handsome profiles, with clean-shaven heads and keen cheerful looks. But many Tuaregs are here also from the far-distant north, even beyond the Nigerian border ; their fierce eyes gleaming above the black veil drawn across the face, covering the head and falling upon the robe beneath, once white, now stained and rent by many weeks of travel. From the shoulders of these hang formidable, cross-handled swords in red-leather tasselled scabbards. Nor are the Hausas always innocent of arms, generally a sword. But here is a professional hunter who has joined the party. You can tell him from his bow held in the right hand and the quiver of reed-arrows barbed—and, maybe, poisoned—slung across his back. The legs of the men are bare to the knees, and much-worn sandals cover their feet. Some carry loads

A NIGERIAN HUNTER STALKING GAME WITH THE HEAD OF THE GROUND HORNBILL AFFIXED TO HIS FOREHEAD.
(Photo by Mr. E. Firmin.)

(Copyright.)

of merchandise, food and water-gourds ; others have their belongings securely fastened on bullock or donkey. Women, too, numbers of them, splendid of form and carriage, one or both arms uplifted, balancing upon the carrying pad (*gammo*) a towering load of multitudinous contents neatly held together in a string bag. Their raiment is the raiment of antiquity, save that it has fewer folds, the outer gown, commonly blue in colour, reaching to just below the knees, the bosom not generally exposed, at least in youth, and where not so intended, gravely covered as the alien rides by ; neck, wrists and ankles frequently garnished with silver ornaments. Many women bear in addition to the load upon the head, a baby on the back, its body hidden in the outer robe, its shiny shaven head emerging above, sometimes resting against the soft and ample maternal shoulders, sometimes wobbling from side to side in slumber, at the imminent risk, but for inherited robustness in that region, of spinal dislocation. Children of all ages, the elders doing their share in porterage, younger ones held by the hand (nothing can be more charming than the sight of a youthful Nigerian mother gladsome of face and form teaching the young idea the mysteries of head-carriage !). Two tired mites are mounted upon a patient ox, the father walking behind. A sturdy middle-aged Hausa carries one child on his shoulders, grasps another by the wrist, supporting his load with his free hand. A gay, dusty crowd, weary and footsore, no doubt, tramping twenty miles in a day carrying anything from forty to one hundred pounds ; but, with such consciousness of freedom, such independence of gait and bearing ! The mind flies back to those staggering lines of broken humanity, flotsam and jetsam of our great cities, products of our " superior " civilization, dragging themselves along the Herefordshire lanes in the hop-picking season ! What a contrast ! And so the trading caravan, bound for the markets of the south, for Lokoja or Bida—it may well be, for some of its units, Ibadan or Lagos—passes onwards, wrapped in its own dust, which, presently, closes in and hides it from sight.

Throughout the dry season the trade routes are covered with such caravans and with countless pedestrians in small groups or in twos or threes—I am told by men who have lived here for years and by the natives themselves, that while highway robbery is not unknown, a woman, even unattended (and I saw many such) is invariably safe from molestation—petty traders and itinerant merchants, some coming north loaded with kolas, salt and cloth, others going south with butchers' provender, potash, cloth, grass, and leather-ware, etc., witness to the intensive internal commerce which for centuries upon centuries has rolled up and down the highways of Nigeria.

A TRADING CARAVAN.

CHAPTER V

THE LIFE OF THE PEOPLE—THE AGRICULTURIST

Allahu Akbar! Allahu Akbar! The sonorous tones perforate the mists of sleep, heralding the coming of the dawn. *Ashadu Allah, ila-allahu, ila-allahu!* Insistent, reverberating through the still, cold air—the night and first hours of the day in these latitudes are often very cold. A pause. Then the unseen voice is again raised, seeming to gather unto itself a passionate appeal as the words of the prayer flow more rapidly. *Ashadu an Muhammad rasul ilahi! Haya-al essalatu! Haya al el falahi! Kad Kamet essalatu!* Another pause. The myriad stars still shine in the deep purple panoply of the heavens, but their brilliancy grows dimmer. The atmosphere seems infused with a tense expectancy. *Allahu Akbar! Allahu Akbar! La illaha, ila-Allahu, ila-Allahu. Muhammad Rasul ilahi. Salallah aleiheiu, . . . Wassalama.* The tones rise triumphant and die away in grave cadence. It thrills inexpressibly does this salute to the omnipotent Creator ringing out over every town and village in the Moslem Hausa States. "God the Greatest! There is no God but *the* God!" And that closing, "Peace!" It has in it reality. Surely it is a good thing and not a bad thing that African man should be reminded as he quits his couch, and as he returns to it, of an all-presiding, all-pervading, all-comprehending Deity? His fashion may not be our fashion. What of that? How far are we here from the narrow cry of the " Moslem peril " ! Whom does this call to God imperil ? The people who respond to it and prostrate themselves in the dust at its appeal ? Let us be quite sure that our own salvation is secured by our own methods, that the masses of our own people are as vividly conscious of the Omnipotent, as free and happy in their lives, as these Nigerian folk, ere we venture to disturb the solemn acknowledgment and petition that peal forth into the dusk of the Nigerian morn.

And now a faint amber flush appears in the eastern sky. It is the signal for many sounds. A hum of many human bees, the crowing of countless roosters, the barking of lean and yellow " pye " dogs, the braying of the donkey and the neigh of his nobler relative, the bleating of sheep and the lowing of cattle. The scent of burning wood assails the nostrils with redolent perfume. The white tick-birds, which have passed the night close-packed on the fronds of the tall fan-palms, rustle their feathers and prepare, in company with their scraggy-necked scavenging colleagues the vultures, for the useful if unedifying business of the day. Nigerian life begins, and what a busy intensive life it is ! From sunrise to sunset, save for a couple of hours in the heat of the day, every one appears to have his hands full. Soon all will be at work. The men driving the animals to pasture, or hoeing in the fields, or busy at the forge, or dye-pit or loom ; or making ready to sally forth to the nearest market with the products of the local industry. The women cooking the breakfast, or picking or spinning cotton, or attending to the younger children, or pounding corn in large and solid wooden mortars, pulping the grain with pestles—long staves, clubbed at either end—grasped now in one hand, now in the other, the whole body swinging with the stroke as it descends, and, perhaps, a baby at the back, swinging with it ; or separating on flat slabs of stone the seed from the cotton

WATER-CARRIERS.

FRUIT-SELLERS.

lint picked the previous day. This is a people of agriculturists, for among them agriculture is at once life's
necessity and its most important occupation. The sowing
and reaping, and the intermediate seasons bring with
them their several tasks. The ground must be cleared
and hoed, and the sowing of the staple crops concluded
before the early rains in May, which will cover the land
with a sheet of tender green shoots of guinea-corn, maize,
and millet, and, more rarely, wheat. When these crops
have ripened, the heads of the grain will be cut off, the
bulk of them either marketed or stored—spread out
upon the thatch-roofed houses to dry, sometimes piled
up in a huge circle upon a cleared, dry space—in granaries
of clay or thatch, according to the local idea ; others
set aside for next year's seeds. The stalks, ten to fifteen
feet in height, will be carefully gathered and stacked for
fencing purposes. Nothing that nature provides or man
produces is wasted in this country. Nature is, in general,
kind. It has blessed man with a generally fertile and
rapidly recuperative soil, provided also that in the more
barren, mountainous regions, where ordinary processes
would be insufficient, millions of earth-worms shall
annually fling their casts of virgin sub-soil upon the sun-
baked surface. And man himself, in perennial contact
with Nature, has learned to read and retain many of her
secrets which his civilized brother has forgotten. One
tree grows gourds with neck and all complete, which
need but to be plucked, emptied and dried to make
first-rate water-bottles. A vigorous ground creeper yields
enormous pumpkin-shaped fruit whose contents afford a
succulent potage, while its thick shell scraped and dried
furnishes plates, bowls, pots, and dishes of every size,
and put to a hundred uses : ornaments, too, when man
has grafted his art upon its surface with dyes and carved
patterns. A bush yields a substantial pod which when
ready to burst and scatter its seeds is found to contain

a fibrous substance which resembles—and may be identical
with, I am not botanist enough to tell—the loofah of
commerce, and is put to the same uses. From the seeds
of the beautiful locust-bean tree (*dorowa*), whose gorgeous
crimson blooms form so notable a feature of the scenery
in the flowering season, soup is made, while the casing
of the bean affords a singularly enduring varnish. The
fruit of the invaluable *Kadenia* or shea tree is used for
food, for oil, and medicinally. The bees receive particular attention for their honey and their wax, the latter
utilized in sundry ways from ornamenting Korans down
to the manufacture of candles. As many as a dozen
oblong, mud-lined, wicker hives closed at one end, the
other having a small aperture, may sometimes be seen
in a single tree. Before harvest time has dawned and
with the harvesting, the secondary crops come in for
attention. Cassava and cotton, indigo and sugar-cane,
sweet potatoes and tobacco, onions and ground-nuts,
beans and pepper, yams and rice, according to the
locality and suitability of the soil. The farmers of a
moist district will concentrate on the sugar-cane—its
silvery, tufted, feathery crowns waving in the breeze
are always a delight : of a dry, on ground-nuts : those
enjoying a rich loam on cotton, and so on. While the
staple crops represent the imperious necessity of life—
food, the profits from the secondary crops are expended
in the purchase of clothing, salt and tools, the payment
of taxes, the entertainment of friends and chance ac-
quaintances (a generous hospitality characterizes this
patriarchal society), and the purchase of luxuries, kolas,
tobacco, ornaments for wives and children. It is a
revelation to see the cotton-fields, the plants in raised
rows three feet apart, the land having in many cases
been precedently enriched by a catch-crop of beans,
whose withering stems (where not removed for fodder,
or hoed in as manure) are observable between the healthy

shrubs, often four or five feet in height, thickly covered with yellow flowers or snowy bolls of white, bursting from the split pod. The fields themselves are protected from incursions of sheep and goats by tall neat fencing of guinea-corn stalks, or reeds, kept in place by native rope of uncommon strength. Many cassava fields, the root of this plant furnishing an invaluable diet, being indeed, one of the staples of the more southerly regions, are similarly fenced. Equally astonishing are the irrigated farms which you meet with on the banks of the water-courses. The plots are marked out with the mathematical precision of squares on a chess-board, divided by ridges with frequent gaps permitting of a free influx of water from the central channel, at the opening of which, fixed in a raised platform, a long pole with a calabash tied on the end of it, is lowered into the water and its contents afterwards poured into the trench. Conditions differ of course according to locality, and the technique and industry displayed by the farmers of one district vary a good deal from the next. In the northern part of Zaria and in Kano the science of agriculture has attained remarkable development. There is little we can teach the Kano farmer. There is much we can learn from him. Rotation of crops and green manuring are thoroughly understood, and I have frequently noticed in the neighbourhood of some village small heaps of ashes and dry animal manure deposited at intervals along the crest of cultivated ridges which the rains will presently wash into the waiting earth. In fact, every scrap of fertilizing substance is husbanded by this expert and industrious agricultural people. Instead of wasting money with the deluded notion of " teaching modern methods " to the Northern Nigerian farmer, we should be better employed in endeavouring to find an answer to the puzzling question of how it is that land which for centuries has been yielding enormous crops of grain, which in the spring is one carpet of green, and in November one huge cornfield "white unto harvest," can continue doing so. What is wanted is an expert agriculturist who will start out not to teach but to learn; who will study for a period of say five years the highly complicated and scientific methods of native agriculture, and base possible improvements and suggestions, maybe, for labour-saving appliances, upon real knowledge.

Kano is, of course, the most fertile province of the Protectorate, but this general description of agricultural Nigeria does not only apply to Kano Province. I saw nothing finer in the way of deep cultivation (for yams and guinea-corn chiefly) than among the Bauchi pagans. The pagan Gwarri of the Niger Province have for ages past grown abundant crops in terraces up their mountainsides whither they sought refuge from Hausa and Fulani raids. The soil around Sokoto, where the advancing Sahara trenches upon the fertile belt, may look arid and incapable of sustaining annual crops, yet every year it blossoms like a rose. But the result means and needs inherited lore and sustained and strenuous labour. From the early rains until harvest time a prolific weed-growth has continuously to be fought. Insect pests, though not conspicuously numerous in most years, nevertheless exist, amongst them the locusts, which sometimes cover the heavens with their flight; the caterpillar, which eats the corn in its early youth; the blight (*daraba*), which attacks the ripening ear. In some districts not so favoured, the soil being of compact clay with a thin coating of humus, intensive cultivation has proved exhausting, and it is a study to note how every ounce of humus is tended with religious care. Very hard work at the right time is the secret of success for the Nigerian agriculturist. It is little short of marvellous that with all he has to do he somehow manages to build our railways and our roads. Indeed, if that phenomenon

A GWARRI GIRL.

A HAUSA TRADING WOMAN.

See p. 152.

has in many respects its satisfactory, it has also its sombre, social side. One can but hope that the former may outweigh the latter as the country gradually settles down after the severe demands placed upon it these last few years.

Truly a wonderful country, and a wonderful people, a people who with fifty years' peace will double its numbers, a people whom it is our paramount duty to secure for ever in the undisturbed occupation and enjoyment of the land, precluding the up-growth of a middleman class of landlord from which the native system is free, and being so free need never be saddled with.

CHAPTER VI

THE LIFE OF THE PEOPLE—THE HERDSMAN AND THE ARTISAN

THE word " peasant " as applied to the Fulani is, no doubt, a misnomer. I employ it merely to distinguish the herdsmen from the caste of statesmen and governors, evolved in Nigeria by the genius of Othman Fodio, but, as their recorded history throughout Western Africa shows, inherent in this mysterious race whose moral characteristics have persisted through all degrees of admixture with the negro. The Fulani peasant is but rarely an agriculturist in Nigeria, but he plays an important, if indirect, part in the agriculture of the Hausa provinces. Over the face of the land he wanders with his great herds—which may number upwards of several thousand head in one herd—of beautiful hump-backed cattle, mostly white, ever seeking " pastures new." Speaking under correction, in Borgu only does his settlement partake of permanency. Elsewhere he is a wanderer. One month a given district may be full of Fulani camps, come from where his fellow-man has but the vaguest of notions. The next, not a single Fulani will be seen within it. But they return, as a rule, the ensuing year to their old haunts. To the Hausa farmer the *M'Bororoji* or " Cow-Fulani " are an invaluable asset, and he enters into regular contracts with them for turning their cattle on to his fields ; and he buys milk from them. I struck several of their encampments, at distances

A FULANI GIRL.

hundreds of miles apart. The first, at the crossing of the Bako, between Badeggi and Bida, was in charge of a patriarch who might have stepped out of the book of Genesis : a Semite every inch of him : spare of form, emaciated in feature, with high cheek-bones, hawk-like nose, flashing, crafty eyes, a long white beard and a bronzed skin without a trace of black blood.

There is no more interesting sight in Nigeria than a Fulani encampment. It is usually pitched well away from the beaten track, albeit within convenient distance of a village. You rub your eyes and wonder if you can really be in the heart of the Dark Continent, as these gracefully built, pale copper-coloured men and women— one may say of some of the young girls with the sun shining on their velvety skins, almost golden coloured— appear tending their herds and flocks, or standing and sitting at the entrance to their temporary shelters. Even the latter differ frequently from the African hut, resembling in shape the wigwam of the North American Indian. As for the people themselves, you are aware of an indefinable sentiment of affinity in dealing with them. They are a white, not a black race.

I have discussed their origin and West African history elsewhere,* and will only say here that delicacy of form, refinement of contour and simple dignity of bearing distinguish this strange people, just as the ruling families possess the delicacy of brain and subtlety of intellect which impress their British over-lords. A fact worth recording, perhaps, is that while the Hausa woman spins and the Hausa man weaves cotton, the Fulani woman does both the spinning and the weaving.

If the agricultural life of the Northern Nigerian peoples is a full one, the industrial life, especially in the northern provinces of the Protectorate, is equally so. It is an extraordinarily self-suffing country at present,

* "Affairs of West Africa." Heinemann, 1902.

and the peasant-cultivator and artisan are inter-dependent, the latter supplying the domestic wants and making the requisite implements for the former. The variety of trades may be estimated from the old Hausa system of taxation. This system the Fulani adopted, modifying it slightly here and there by enforcing closer adherence to the Koranic law, and we are modifying it still further by a gradual process tending to merge multiple imposts under two or three main heads, with the idea of establishing a more equitable re-adjustment of burdens and to ensure greater simplicity in assessment. The Hausa system provided that taxes should be levied upon basket and mat-makers, makers of plant for cotton-spinners, bamboo door-makers, carpenters, dyers, black-smiths and whitesmiths, as well as upon bee-keepers, hunters, trappers and butchers. Exemption from taxes was granted to shoe-makers, tailors, weavers, tanners, potters, and makers of indigo ; but market taxes were imposed upon corn measurers, brokers, sellers of salt, tobacco, kolas, and ironstone.

The chief agricultural implement is the Hausa hoe, the *galma*, a curious but efficient instrument, which simultaneously digs and breaks up the soil and is said to be of great antiquity, but which is easier to draw than to describe. There is also in daily use among the Hausas a smaller, simpler hoe and a grass-cutter, while the pagan favours a much heavier and more formidable-looking tool. This pagan hoe somewhat resembles our English spade, but is wielded in quite different fashion. Iron drills, rough hammers and axes, nails, horseshoes, stirrup-irons and bits are included among the ordinary forms of the blacksmith's art. Iron-stone is common in many parts of the country and is extensively worked, furnaces being met with in every district where the use of the metal is locally in vogue. It is to be hoped that " Civilization " will not seek to stamp out this native industry

DYE-PITS.

PANNING FOR IRON.

as the tin-miners have done their best—and, unless
the promise made to the smelters of Liruei-n-Kano by
Sir H. Hesketh Bell is not speedily carried out, but
too successfully—to crush the interesting tin-smelting
industry. The history of native tin smelting in Nigeria
furnishes a remarkable proof of the capacity of the
Nigerian native, but is too long to set forth here in
detail. Suffice it to say that for a hundred years, a
certain ruling family with numerous branches, has
succeeded in turning out a singularly pure form of the
white metal whose sale as an article of trade brought
prosperity to the countryside. When I left the tin
district, owing to unjust and stupidly selfish interference
with immemorial rights, the native furnaces had been
closed for nine months and poverty was beginning to
replace comparative affluence.

Hoe-handles, mortars, pestles, beds, doors, gins,
spindles, bobbins, looms, shuttles, saddles, riding-boots,
sandals, slippers, bridles, scissors, razors, rope, fishing-
nets, earthenware cooking-pots, lamps, water-bottles
and pipes are among the innumerable articles turned out
by the artisan in Northern Nigeria. Indigo dye-pits are
to be found in many towns, but the great tanning centre
is Kano. Cloth-beating is a recognized branch of the
former industry. After removal from the circular pits
sunk *à fleur de terre*, the clothes are hung up to dry and
then handed over to the beater. In a dark and spacious
hut perspiring men kneel in rows facing one another on
either side of a huge log of wood, stained black and
smooth-polished with constant use, upon which the
cloths are spread and vigorously beaten with rounded
wooden mallets. Very hard work it is, as I can personally
testify, having tried my hand at it, much to the entertainment of the dusky experts. The Kano tanneries
are in appearance disappointing ; in odours surpassing
anything that can be imagined. But the product is

astonishingly excellent. The completed skins, dyed deep red or orange with native dyes, the roots, leaves and bark of sundry shrubs and trees being utilized in the many processes through which the raw hide passes, are as soft to the touch as Russian leather. They are greatly appreciated in the Western world, and the trade is a rapidly increasing one.

CHAPTER VII

THE CITY OF KANO AND ITS MARKET

You are permanently conscious that this country has a history and traditions. Nowhere, perhaps, does the fact impress the new-comer more vividly than at Kano. It is a wonderful place to find in Central Africa, this native city with its great enfolding walls, twelve miles in circumference, pierced by thirteen deep gateways (*kofas*), with platform and guardhouses and massive doors heavily clamped with iron; with its written records dating back nearly eight hundred years. And although incomparably the most important it is not the oldest of these Hausa cities—Katsina, now in the same "province," is probably older. When the West-Saxon realm fell before the onslaught of the Danes and the first Danish King reigned over England, Hausaland was conquered by an unknown people from the East, and when the prosperity of the English towns was beginning to revive under Henry I., Gijimasu, the third King of the invading dynasty, was building Kano. When Henry VIII. was laying the foundations of personal government, the "rich merchants and most civil people" of Kano were entertaining Leo Africanus. Three hundred years later (1824) Clapperton entered this "great emporium of the kingdom of Hausa," which Barth forty years afterwards termed the "far-famed entrepôt of Central Africa;" which Lugard was subsequently to describe as exceeding anything he had ever seen " or even imagined " in Africa.

Tributary now to this, now to the other, evanescent African kingdom, frequently at war with its neighbours, repeatedly besieged, it has survived every vicissitude. Neither the disastrous struggles with Katsina in the seventeenth, and with Gober in the eighteenth centuries, nor the deposition and defeat of the forty-third (and last) King of the original dynasty by the Fulani early in the nineteenth century, nor yet the occupation of the country by the British seven years ago, have destroyed its influence or impaired its commercial prestige—a tribute to the staying power and to the sterling qualities of the truly remarkable African people whom, in the providence of God, it has now fallen upon us to rule. Its market-place, still the scene of clamorous activity, continues to attract merchants and merchandise from all parts of western Central Africa. It still remains the nerve-centre of a district whose natural fertility, aided by the labour and skill of a hard-working, industrious population, not only supports, as it has done for many centuries, a population of equal density to the square mile as England boasts, but exports large quantities of grain to less-favoured regions ; and its looms continue to supply the requirements of an immense area ranging from the Chad to Timbuktu and the borders of Tripoli, and (in part, at least) southwards to the Niger.

Picturesque by day, with numerous and gaily dressed pedestrians and horsemen perambulating its tortuous streets, busy crowds around its markets, dye-pits, tanneries, and looms, Kano is still more so when the moon floods its broad open spaces with light and flings strange shadows across the sandy thoroughfares where they abut upon the dwelling-places of its inhabitants. Then, but for the occasional howl of a dog, this city which has endured so long and withstood so much lies wrapped in impenetrable silence. The ugly sores of Africa—not, assuredly, as ugly or as numerous as those of Europe, but more conspicuous

A VIEW OF A PART OF KANO CITY (INSIDE THE WALL).

—are mercifully hidden. No one walks abroad. Yet you know as you wander with noiseless footsteps through its curves and labyrinths, escaping for once from your inevitable native attendants (delightful people, but sadly hampering at times), that behind these thick clay walls and closed doors, the mysterious world of Africa is awake and stirring, that social world with its primitive impulses, but also with its many courtesies and refinements, that world of habit and of thought, guarded with jealous reticence from the alien, unfathomed and unfathomable even by the most experienced of Residents. And, again, at sunrise, when from the summit of the minaret outside the Emir's residence, the pink flush of dawn steals down the sides of the city's guardian hills, Dala and Goronduchi, flickers upon the fronds of the palm trees, and reveals the seemingly interminable vista of houses, mostly flat-roofed, but varied here and there by others of humbler thatch and conical in shape ; when the blue wreaths of smoke from many fires mount perpendicularly into the crisp, still air, mingled with the aromatic scent of burning wood and a confused murmur of awakening life—then, too, the city holds you in the grip of a fascinated interest. It is difficult to explain this fascination, for the architecture of Kano, though imposing in its way, is rude. There are no flashing domes and sumptuous buildings as in the East ; yet the few who have visited it, and the handful of officers—all travelled men—who by turn have had responsibility for the good order of the Emirate would be prepared, I fancy, one and all to confess that not even the blunting effects of familiarity can do away with the curious influences it exercises.

A visit to the famous market-place—the *Kasua Kurumi* —which covers a wide expanse, and where anything from 4000 to 7000 persons may be congregated together, according to the day, is a bewildering experience. In this tumultuous sea of humanity, shot with brilliant colours, details are swamped at first in general impressions. You are aware of a vast concourse of men and women, cheery-faced, closely packed together, clad in robes of many hues —white and various shades of blue predominating; of tossing arms and turbaned heads; of long lines of clay-built booths where piled-up merchandise awaits the customer; of incessant movement, the strife of many tongues, the waft of many scents, mostly the reverse of fragrant—over all, blue sky and fierce hot sun. As you move along with frequent pauses necessitated by the crush, and the eye gets more accustomed to the scene, some at least of its component parts stand out more clearly from the ever-shifting view, and the extraordinary variety of human types and the multiplicity of articles on sale is realized.

The home of the Kanawa (people of Kano), whose industry is famed from the Atlantic to the Mediterranean, one would naturally expect to find their numbers in the ascendant. Keen-featured men of business, women with elaborate coiffures resembling pictures of old Assyrian helmets, their cheeks often disfigured by exaggerated " beauty spots " daubed on with lead or antimony. Other Hausas, visitors from Katsina, Gober, or Daura, each with the distinguishing facial mark of his clan, six strokes with a dot for Katsina, two for Daura, and so on. Pale-complexioned Fulani from the country, the women wearing their straight hair in ringlets, with silver earrings and gentle eyes. The Nupe, with his characteristic headgear of red, black, and yellow straw. Thick-lipped Kanuris from Bornu. Tall, lithe Tuareg from distant Sokoto, or Asben. The Arab merchant, arrogant and intriguer, making his way through the market to the " Arab quarter," a quarter of the city remarkable for its Moorish architecture and unpleasantly notorious for its smells.

Each trade has its quarter. Beneath the shelter of

the booths vendors sit cross-legged, their wares spread out before them. Cloths of every hue and texture under the sun, it would seem, absorb one whole quarter, and form, perhaps, the most important article of sale, although the more valuable clothes are seldom seen, for the Kano market is essentially a retail one, transactions in objects of more costly worth taking place within the shelter of private houses. You will see enough in the cloth quarter, however, to appreciate the diversity of quality and design, from the beautifully embroidered Kano *riga* (a sort of hoodless cloak universally worn by the better classes, covering the body from neck to knee) to the common shirting of Manchester, the white *bullan* or gown from Bornu, the *arigiddi*, or woman's cloth from Zaria, the *faringodo*, or plain white cloth from Ilorin, the *majai*, or webbing made by the pagan tribes of Bauchi, and used by the Fulani for girths. The products of native looms from towns hundreds of miles distant, enjoying special renown for some attractive peculiarity, are purchasable here, together with the manufactures of Europe. The former are almost infinite in diversity, and each has its particular uses. Black, white, and blue gowns, brocade, striped brocade, striped shirting, white shirting, shirting with a red border, white and black checks, drill, red baft, cloths for turbans, caps, fezzes, expensively embroidered trousers, sleeveless under-vests, velvet—all in endless variety.

In the leather quarter you will find great quantities of saddlery from Tripoli, and also of local manufacture, highly ornamented bridles, stirrup-leathers, despatch-bags, *Korans* in leather cases, purses, red slippers, sandals, quilted horsecloths, undyed goatskins and cowhides, swords in scabbards, many of them admirable in workmanship. An examination of the latter will disclose the interesting fact that the blades of the most expensive specimens bear the Sölingen mark, a curious example of the conservatism of this interior African trade, for as far back as the middle of the last century Sölingen sword blades were imported into Kano across the desert. Passing out of the leather quarter you will find silver, brass, and tin ware ; among the former necklaces and earrings which would not disgrace a London jeweller's shop-window, ruder bangles and anklets, partly tin, partly silver ; brass urns and bowls, and glass bracelets from Bida. Necklaces of beads, Venetian and local, of agates imported from Tripoli and polished and cut at Bida, of cheap European coral, of different kinds of bright-coloured local seeds. Rough pottery, but often of elegant design, such, for example, as the small lamps used for burning ground-nut oil, in the manufacture of which mica enters.

Sheds and stalls, in addition to the booths, are devoted to the sale of numerous merchandise. The store of an elderly white-turbaned Hausa contains a mass of rough silk mixed up with the cocoons ; these are produced by the silkworm, which feeds on the tamarind tree. The *rigas* made from it are very dear, and also very pleasant to the touch, resembling in that respect and in colour tussore. Here is a stall containing the products of the local smithy, stirrup-irons, locks for doors, every kind of agricultural implement used by the native farmer, axes, knives, and skin-scrapers used in preparing goat and sheep skins for export. There a stall filled with native herbs used as medicines, from the *tafarnua* for rheumatism to the *karijiji* for colds, the *kula* and *passakori* much used by women after child-birth. Much space is taken up by the sellers of foodstuffs, mostly vegetable, such as guinea-corn and millet in variety, beans, yams, sugar-cane, sweet potatoes (in variety), pepper, onions, the fruit of the tamarind, the red flowers of the tobacco plant, cassava, and ginger.

In another direction you will observe on sale European salt and native potash in cakes and cones, zana-mats, firewood, native rope, roofing, sticks with branches, guinea-corn and millet stalks for fencing, native beds,

ONE OF THE GATEWAYS TO KANO CITY, SHOWING OUTER WALL.

ANOTHER OF THE ENTRANCES TO THE CITY.

doors made of palm sticks, baskets, mats in great diversity of size and colouring. Round about the booths and sheds on every side sit men and women (mostly the latter) selling articles of local or European origin ; by their side, and, apparently, no more carefully watched than the articles themselves, small piles of cowries and sometimes the new nickel coinage we have introduced, and threepenny bits represent the takings of the day. Among such articles are to be observed indigo, antimony, ground-nuts, the inevitable kola-nut, shea-butter, spices, cow-dung in small packets (very precious), raw cotton, henna (*lelli*) for staining hands or feet, fresh honey, cakes and sweetmeats (of a fearful and wonderful composition), native soap from Nupe (*sabouni*), bobbins, shuttles, and other necessities of the national industry, cigarettes, red wool, green wool, crochet-thread, water-pots, and sundry cheap trinkets from Europe. The butchers' quarter it is best to pass by swiftly ; unsavoury in Europe, the flies and tropical sun do not improve it in Africa. Long files of cattle, donkeys, sheep, and goats can be seen winding their way to the cattle market, where many thousands are daily on sale.

CHAPTER VIII

A VISIT TO THE EMIR OF KANO

KANO PROVINCE under the British Administration includes a number of independent Emirates which we found existing and which we have maintained, viz. : Kano, Katsina, Katagum, Daura, Kazaure and Gummel. The total area of the Province is 28,600 square miles, *i.e.* almost the size of Scotland, and its population 2,600,000, or what that of Scotland was in the middle of last century.

The present Emir, Abbas, a reserved and very dark Fulani, with refined regular features and long aristocratic hands, is a fine figure of a man. The description of a visit to him may serve to convey some idea of the ceremonious etiquette observed at the courts of the Mohammedan Emirs (Kano being typical of all the great Emirates, with the exception of Sokoto where formalities are even more elaborate), besides throwing light upon several questions of interest and moment connected with the problems of British administration. To depict the Emir's residence as a compound built of clay is, while accurate, to give but an inadequate idea of the imposing character of these solid structures, the best of which are, with supervision, capable of resisting for centuries the action of the weather. I am probably understating the case when I say that the tall and bulky wall—some fifteen feet in thickness—surrounding the residence encloses five acres. Dismounting at the principal entrance, we are escorted through the gateway by several functionaries and emerge into a vast enclosure open to the sky. At its extremity, facing us, is an inner wall and another deep embrasured gateway leading to the state apartments. On our right stands the Emir's private mosque, a building of considerable proportions but smaller, of course, than the public mosque outside the walls. Here and there a few picturesque figures are noticeable. For, perhaps, a minute we wait. Then a blare of trumpets resounds, and through the inner gateway emerges a brilliant gathering which advances slowly towards us, the Emir in the midst. Within a dozen yards or so it halts, and the Emir, separating himself from the throng, greets us with hand outstretched—the only African in the Emirate to whom etiquette allows this particular form of salutation with the White man. Towering above most of the councillors, officers of state and heads of leading families by whom he is accompanied, and bearing himself with great dignity, the Emir murmurs some words of welcome. He is dressed entirely in costly white robes and turban ; his feet are encased in ostrich-feather sandals, a footgear introduced in the sixteenth century by Mohamma Rimfa, the twentieth Emir of Kano, justly revered for a reign full of years and usefulness, and he carries the silver-mounted staff of office presented to all the ruling Emirs by Sir Frederick Lugard after the British occupation. He invites us to follow him and leads the way in silence to his apartments, his courtiers closing round us as we proceed. In the same impressive silence we pass through the inner gateway and find ourselves in a broad passage flanked on either side by lofty audience chambers whose dimensions it is difficult to gauge in the semi-obscurity which reigns within them. At the end of the passage is yet another gateway. Thenceforth we proceed alone with the Emir and the *Waziri* or Vizier— the present holder of that office being a man of great independence and strength of character, whose fearless candour and ripe judgment have been of inestimable service in assisting successive Residents to understand the many complex problems of native administration. Crossing a courtyard we enter the outer room of the Emir's private apartments. And here for an hour we discuss many things, chairs being provided for us while the Emir and Waziri, in accordance with the etiquette of the country, sit cross-legged before us. A word as to the architecture and appearance of the room, which, as we were subsequently to ascertain, is roughly similar to the audience chambers we have left behind. It is some twenty to twenty-five feet in height, with an arched roof supported by wooden beams on the cantilever principle ; both beams and roof are, like the floor, stained a deep black with the varnish obtained from the shell of the locust bean ; a few plates of European manufacture are let into the supporting rafters ; the walls, constructed of the usual sun-baked clay mingled with other substances, have a glittering appearance due to the admixture of mica ; two doors, an outward and an inward one, of massive timber bound with iron bars affixed by native nails ornamented with large circular brass heads, and a divan of rugs and shawls complete a picture which suggests a certain austere simplicity.

After the usual interchange of compliments, I said it was desirable the Emir should understand clearly in respect to any subjects which might be touched upon, that I had no connection direct or indirect with the British Government, or with any British commercial or other interest; that I was merely visiting his country as an independent traveller, and would report what I had seen and heard, and that I hoped he would feel free to tell me frankly what was in his heart, for the people of England only wished to know the truth. Conversation then ranged over the part of the province of Kano I had, up to that time, visited; the industry of the inhabitants, their methods of agriculture, the care they bestowed upon secondary crops, such as cotton, cassava and onions, the great city

INSIDE KANO CITY.

market and the variety of goods sold therein. I expressed
a wish to see the irrigated farms, and the Emir named
certain localities near the city where such farms were to
be seen. The increasing prosperity of the country through
the preservation of peace was touched upon *de part et
d'autre.* The antiquity of the city and its interesting
records was the next subject approached. It would, I
remarked, be a very great pity if its essential characteristics were not maintained amid the innovations which the
railway would bring in its train. From that point of view
I ventured to express regret that the ancient walls of the
city were, in parts, falling into disrepair. In time to come
future generations of Kanawa would, I thought, lament
the fact. Would it not be possible to start repairs on one
section at first, performing the needed work gradually,
doing a certain amount every year and finishing section
by section ? The Emir fully concurred, saying that his
people themselves wished the walls restored. He hoped
to deal with the matter, but thought that it might be
easier to commence preliminary repairs on a general scale
rather than start one part and finish that first as I had
suggested. From the question of the wall we turned to
the more difficult one of European traders and educated
Native traders from the coast whom the railway would
bring, settling in the city. The Emir remarked that,
while foreign merchants were welcome, it would be better
for them and for the city and its inhabitants if those who
wished to trade with the Kanawa founded places of business at convenient spots outside.

Missionary propaganda in the Muslimised Hausa States
of the north was next touched upon. The subject has
already given rise to discussions at home, which are being
followed in Northern Nigeria with anxious concern, and
such momentous consequences are bound up in it
that I felt it incumbent to ascertain through personal
contact, the views of one of the most important,

in a certain measure the most important, of the Mohammedan chiefs through whom we exercise supreme control.
I told the Emir I would be quite frank with him, and
hoped that he would be equally frank with me. The
English people and the Kanawa people, I said, worshipped
the same Almighty Creator of the universe. The English
people followed the teachings of Christ, the Kanawa people
the teachings of Mohammed, and both peoples thought their
religion the best. But although the people of England
held firmly to their beliefs, they had no desire to interfere
with that of the Kanawa. Their representative, Sir
Frederick Lugard, had pledged himself in their name to
that effect, and the English people always kept their word.
But, I went on, some of my countrymen who wished well
to the Kanawa, thought Christianity could be preached
in Kano without breaking this pledge, because there would
be no interference and no moral pressure would be put
upon the people of Kano to change their religion even
though Christian teachers sat down in the city and taught.
The Kanawa could come and hear them, or not, as they
pleased. That was the view held by some of the people in
my country. What I wished to know were the Emir's
opinions in the matter. Did he, or did he not, see
objections to the presence of Christian preachers in the
city ?

For some time the Emir kept silent, his fingers
twitching nervously. One could see the struggle passing
in his mind and realize some of the difficulties of his own
position. Presently he spoke thus—I reproduce the words
as literally as possible :—

"Mohammedanism is a matter of the heart. Our fathers and
our grandfathers were Muslims. For many generations we have been
Muslims. What is the use of preaching if there are no converts?
Even if the Christian missionary tried to meet the native on equal
terms he could not do so because all white men are Sarikis (chiefs),
and the people cannot help so regarding them. The missionaries
might not wish to use force. But they would exercise pressure

THE EMIR OF KANO ON THE MARCH.

amounting to force, because of the prestige all white men have, and the people would be disturbed and troubled in their minds.

" There would be unrest."

I asked the Emir whether he would have any objection to confirming in writing the views he had expressed. After a further period of silent consideration, he said he had none. Here is the letter subsequently received from him, rendered from the Arabic text :—

" Praise to God who only is to be praised.

" Salutations.

" This letter is directed to the stranger, Mr. Morel, who has come.

" Know that as regards the preaching (of Christianity) which we discussed here, my opinion is that it were better to stop it altogether, from the first—because, if our people are disturbed about their religion they will become suspicious and afraid. Hence the country will become unsettled. Neither you nor we desire the country to become unsettled, for that would be harmful. On the other hand, as regards secular matters and the affairs of this world, we can do anything— however great a change it might be—since our people are accustomed to law and to obey the orders of their rulers as their fathers and grand-fathers were before them. Also, as regards white men living in the city of Kano, if they do so many of our people will leave it, since the white men are too strong, and every one of them is in our eyes, a great man and powerful. The lion and the lamb cannot lie down together. My opinion is that the white man who may wish to settle should have a separate town outside the city of Kano—then we shall have our town and they will have theirs. This is the wisest course, and far more advantageous for our subjects than a mixed city of natives and non-natives.

" Peace."

At the close of the interview we were reconducted with the same ceremonious politeness and in the same silence as before to the centre of the outer enclosure, where we took our leave.

CHAPTER IX

GOVERNING ON NATIVE LINES

THE fundamental principle aimed at by the Government in Northern Nigeria is indirect administration, *i.e.* administration through the native rulers of the communities, the Chiefs and their executives, under the supervision and with the assistance of the Residents. That was the policy laid down by Sir Frederick Lugard in a series of comprehensive Memoranda which form not the least notable feature of the great work he carried out during his tenure of office, a work entirely creative, be it remembered, a work of which the value can but grow in public estimation as the sense of perspective deepens with the years, and as additional information supplies what in the early days of the occupation was largely lacking. That was the policy Sir Frederick Lugard's successor, Sir Percy Girouard, found in being, not, indeed, unthreatened, but enthusiastically upheld by the most experienced members of the Political Staff. He not only gave it his full official support and checked certain leanings of an opposite kind, but he brought to bear upon the situation a personal sympathy, an illuminating and penetrative genius which popularized the policy in quarters previously hostile or indifferent. Sir Henry Hesketh Bell has loyally followed in the footsteps of his predecessors. That nothing should be allowed to divert us from keeping on the same road is the writer's conviction, for what it may be worth, after several years' study at a distance and recent investigations on the spot.

GOVERNING ON NATIVE LINES

A genuine and honest endeavour is being made not only to rule through the native Chiefs, but to rule through them on native lines. Too much importance can hardly be ascribed to the distinction. The success already attained would be thrown away if policy were deflected in the direction of substituting European for native ideas. If the native machine is expected to perform functions for which it is unqualified, the works get out of gear. If the Chiefs are called upon to exercise their authority in enforcing measures essentially alien to the native constitution, their prestige over the individual lapses. They become mere puppets, and indirect rule breaks down. I hope to make clear what the native constitution is, and what is meant by ruling on " native lines." The difficulties of improving and purifying when required a native administration, without impairing its general efficiency, are always considerable. In Northern Nigeria they are, for several reasons, peculiarly so. If the result, so far, has shown the wisdom of the original conception, it has been due to the determination and tact of the senior Political Residents, and to the excellence of the native material. Our task has been furthered by the administrative capacities of the Fulani Emirs. Some were, indeed, found unfit and had to be removed, but the majority are increasingly showing themselves not only capable but quite indispensable to the work of government.

It would, however, be mischievous to conceal the fact that indirect rule in the proper sense of the term, *i.e.* involving the preservation of native law and custom, has to bear, in West Africa, the brunt of constant and insidious assaults on the part of interested, or prejudiced, or ill-informed opinion. This opposition is often quite honest and quite easy to understand if the conditions are grasped. It is important they should be grasped. Indirect rule is an obstacle to employment and promotion in some branches of the service. It restricts the scope of secretarial, judicial, police and military activities. It robs the educated native barrister trained in English law, and the educated native clerk, of a field for the exercise of their professions. It checks the European capitalist in a hurry to push on " development." The missionary is apt to regard it as a stumbling-block to Christian propaganda. Finally, there is the type of European who is racially biased against the retention of any sort of control by the native in his own country. Indirect rule, therefore, has very many enemies, and it cannot have too many friends among the thinking public at home. So far as Northern Nigeria is concerned, strenuous efforts will have to be put forward by all who are convinced of the necessity of upholding indirect rule therein, when the amalgamation of the two Protectorates is taken in hand. That time cannot be far distant and the wind which blows from the south is charged with many hostile particles. There would seem, then, to be solid reasons for the public to appreciate the conditions, at once severely practical, and of the moral order, which make the continuation of the existing policy necessary to the welfare of the Northern Protectorate.

Let us first consider geographical verities and ways and means. Northern Nigeria is 255,000 square miles in extent and the territory is divided into thirteen provinces. Of these provinces, Sokoto, the most considerable in point of area, is nearly as large as Scotland and Wales ; Bornu is the size of Ireland ; Kano is almost as large as Scotland ; Kontagora-Borgu is slightly larger than, and Bauchi and Muri the size of, Greece ; the Niger Province is as extensive as Servia ; Yola is as large as Denmark, and Nassarawa exceeds the area of Switzerland. It is only by realizing space, by realizing that months of travel still separate some provinces from others, that the expense, to say nothing of other considerations, which would be entailed in gathering up all the administrative threads of such a territory into the hands of a staff of British officials can be understood. I have never heard it suggested that the Lords of the Treasury parted enthusiastically with the meagre sum allotted to Northern Nigeria. One cannot imagine that their Lordships' satisfaction would increase if they were presented not with a bill of a quarter of a million but of two millions. The single Province of Kano, which under the present system is supervised by seventeen political officers, and more than pays its own way, would require at least three hundred officials if direct rule were established, or the prestige of the Emirs so weakened as to deprive them of all real authority over the people, and this, exclusive of a swarm of native officials who could not be done without in any case. That brings me to my next point. Direct rule would, of necessity, involve an erormous, directly paid, native staff. For its every action the Government would be compelled to accept responsibility, and its members would, perforce, be largely composed of the class of native—the most undesirable type, it may be added—from which the policemen and soldiers are now recruited. Putting aside the question of expenditure altogether, can any sane man, disposed to look the facts squarely in the face and knowing anything of the country, contemplate with equanimity the consequences of such a *régime* ? Then, assuming for purposes of argument the non-existence of these impediments, where would lie the moral justification, let alone the purely political expediency, of sweeping away the rule of the natural rulers of the country ?

CHAPTER X

THE FOUNDATIONS OF NATIVE SOCIETY—THE TENURE OF LAND

HAVING indicated some of the quagmires into which direct rule would lead us, one may now pass to an examination of the foundations upon which native law and custom repose in the organized society of the north, as revealed by systematic inquiry extending over the past five years. Essentially the same groundwork is found in the more rudimentary pagan communities which have remained without the area of Mohammedan organization. Incidentally, it may be well to mark that Northern Nigeria has not evolved powerful pagan organisms comparable with those of Yoruba and Benin in the south. The basis of the social system is the village community. A number of village communities form the tribal community. The partly hereditary, partly elective rule of the tribal community constitutes, with the Executive, the Government of the entire community. The ruler himself is the " Governor," against whose actions the people can appeal to native law and custom. For the welfare of that community the ruler is guardian. Land is the common heritage of the community. The ruler is trustee for the land. Upon him devolves the granting of rights of occupancy. The structural law of tenure is the right of occupier and user, not of owner. Private ownership of land is unknown. The cultivator is, in reality, a licensee. Alienation of land is unknown. The unit of taxation is the village community. Each individual is supposedly assessed according to his earning capacity. If he is an agriculturist he furnishes a proportion of his crop, which, in effect, is a rent paid to the community for the use of land. If an artisan, he pays a tax upon his trade. If a herdsman, upon his cattle. The community as a whole is subject to specific imposts which assist in maintaining the civil list of the ruler. The character of the taxes and imposts follows the requirements of the Koranic law modified, when considered expedient, by pre-Koranic customary law. Justice is administered by judges conversant with the sacred books, appointed by the ruler and exercised on the principles of Koranic law. If a balance could be struck, it would probably be found that a system of this kind ensures a greater amount of human happiness than many of the forms of government even now existing in Europe. Indeed, the closer one's knowledge of African life and the more insight one obtains into the immense sea of human misery heaving beneath the crust of Western civilization, the more one is led to marvel at the shallow commonplaces which picture the African wallowing in degraded barbarism. Like all institutions, the African system lends itself to abuse. Those abuses the British Administration has set itself to correct, while maintaining the system itself. Upon the Colonial Office continuing to support that policy, and upon the men who are applying it on the spot being enabled to go on with their work free from interference, depends the future happiness and prosperity of the Nigerian peoples, which, in effect, is at once the Imperial interest and the justification of Imperial rule.

The British, having replaced the Fulani, are in native law and custom the conquering tribe. The urgency of devoting as much time as it was possible to spare from the pressing problems of the hour demanding daily solution, to an investigation of the exact conditions prevailing in each province was, therefore, imperative. In so extensive a territory, differing local circumstances affecting soil, population, occupation, distribution of power, and so on, had obviously created different methods or rather heads of taxation and variation in the formulæ of Government, assessment and levying of revenue, etc. One question above all others had to be elucidated, that of the ownership of land—basis of the whole social edifice. Sir Frederick Lugard initiated these inquiries. They were vigorously prosecuted by Sir Percy Girouard and the Residents, and when it became apparent beyond all possibility of doubt that the land, whether actually occupied or not, was national ; that freehold property was foreign to all native ideas; and that, under native law and custom, the new rulers of the country were recognized as holders of the land in trust for the people and, thereby, the grantors of occupants' rights, Sir Percy Girouard pressed for these cardinal principles being given force of law. Legislation which should embody them was, moreover, of additional moment for two reasons. First, because the opening up of the country was bound to give rise to the danger of alienation of occupancy rights creeping in and being incorporated into native custom, out of which would automatically evolve a customary sanction for the mortgaging of land, the creation of a class of landlords, a wide field for the European speculator in land, and a general break-up of the native system. Secondly, because the approach of the railways, the development of roads, the increasing demand for foodstuffs and the all-round intensifying economic pressure were bound, once more automatically, to originate, independently of the industry of the cultivator, an incremental value in the land. Before that state of affairs was brought home to the native and had, perhaps, been made under native law and custom, the subject of private property, which would have meant the creation of vested interests difficult to displace, it was the obvious duty of a Government trustee for the community to step in and secure these expanding values for the future benefit of that community. But things move slowly in West Africa, and legislation of the kind referred to was novel : unique, indeed. West Africa's problems had never been thought out ahead before. Just as matters were ripening, Sir Percy Girouard was suddenly transferred to East Africa. But the Colonial Office was sympathetic, and there were men in Nigeria who, comprehending well the perils of leaving the land question unregulated, were determined to do their utmost to push the matter through.

On January 1st of this year the most far-seeing measure of constructive statesmanship West Africa has ever known was put upon the statute-book. " The Land and Native Rights Proclamation " consecrates the three main principles of native law and custom. First, that the whole of the land whether occupied or unoccupied is " native land." Secondly, that the land is under the control and subject to the disposition of the Governor, to be " held and administered by him for the use, need and common benefit of the natives of Northern Nigeria." Thirdly, that the Governor's power shall be exercised in accordance with " native laws and customs." For the rest, and without going into detail, the measure can be described as expressing the native system, and the natural developments of the native system, in English. It is not, in Nigeria, an innovating measure, but a conservative measure ; not an experiment, but a preservation of the *status quo*. It is not a measure of land nationalization, because land nationalization means State control of the land and all that is done upon it. What this measure does is to provide for the communalizing of the communal value of the land, leaving the occupier full control over the use of land and full benefit for his private enterprise upon it, with payment of rent to the community to which the land belongs, instead of to a landlord. The individual's right to all that is due to individual work and expenditure, but not to the communal value, is secured. No freehold can creep in and no monopoly profit can be made out of the land. The holding up of land for speculative purposes is, in effect, penalized, while the man who is industrious is not made to pay more as the outcome of his enterprise. At the same time the basis is laid for a land revenue which, with the years, will be the chief source of income of the Government—the healthiest form of income, perhaps, for any Government. For the first time in the history of West Africa, the art of governing the native on native lines has become consecrated in British legislation and the pernicious tradition of applying the law of England to African land questions has been set aside. It is impossible to exaggerate the potentialities for good of such a departture from crude, ignorant and unscientific precedent. It will be the duty of the Colonial Office, to whom everlasting credit is due for having sanctioned this proclamation, to watch strictly that the principles laid down therein are not departed from in practice, and to apply them, with the modifications of method which differing and pre-existing conditions render advisable, to Southern Nigeria also. That attempts to undermine the provisions and the spirit of the Northern Nigerian law will arise, may be unhesitatingly assumed.

CHAPTER XI

THE FOUNDATIONS OF NATIVE SOCIETY—THE ADMINISTRATIVE MACHINERY

THE policy of governing Northern Nigeria on native lines—in other words, of training the natives to govern themselves instead of trying to govern them ourselves—has the approval of the entire native community except the criminal classes, who would be the only ones to benefit by a weakening in the position of the native authorities and in the decay of the etiquette attaching to their position. It is being pursued in every branch of the Administration concurrently, with a steadily marked improvement in the efficiency and purity of the public service.

The native administrative machinery varies slightly in the different Emirates, and is better organized in some than in others, but a description of the system as it obtains in the Kano Emirate, which is a little larger than Belgium and Luxemburg, will serve as a general indication applicable in its essentials to the others. The executive consists of the Emir—advised and assisted by the Resident—and his judicial and executive Council, composed of the Waziri (Vizier, or Chief of Staff), the Maji (Treasurer), the Alkali (Chief Justice), and five Mallamai (" teachers," men versed in the law and in the customs of the country) of repute. This is the Supreme Court of Appeal. The Emirate is divided into districts under a district Chief or Headman (Hakima) responsible to the Executive. Each district is divided into sub-districts under a sub-district

Chief or Headman (Maijimilla) responsible to the District Headman. Each sub-district is composed of townships or villages with village-heads (Masugari) responsible to the sub-district Headman.

Kano city itself is under the supervision of the *Maajen-Wuterl*, who corresponds roughly with our English mayor with twenty town police (dogarai), picturesque individuals in red and green, and twenty night watchmen (masugefia) under him. Ninety more police are spread over the various districts and attached to the District Courts. There are no British native police whatever. That experiment was tried for a time, being attended with such conspicuous ill-success and being accompanied by such an increase in crime that it was wisely abandoned. Nothing could surely convey a more striking proof of the order reigning throughout the Emirate and of the law-abiding character of the people, than the fact of its being policed with ninety men armed with nothing more formidable than a sword. Think of ninety constables sufficing for Belgium and Luxemburg or any other area of 13,000 square miles in Western Europe ; or take the population of the Emirate—one and a half millions—and point to a single comparable proportion of police to population in Europe. Crimes of violence are extraordinarily scarce, and the Native Administration, backed by the British " raj," has now such a hold upon the country that for a case to be unreported would be hardly possible. The roads are safe for the solitary traveller—I frequently passed women alone, or accompanied by a child, sometimes husband, wife and child, many miles from the capital. I have walked alone save for one white companion through the deserted streets of Kano city at night. Kano city is not, however, free from thieves, and seeing that so many strangers are constantly coming and going it is hardly to be wondered at. Some two years back night burglaries became unpleasantly frequent. Native ingenuity hit upon a plan to cope with

them.   The services of the professional rat-catchers were
enlisted.   They were enrolled as night-watchmen, paid
£1 a man, and told they would be fined 2s. 6d. every time
a robbery was committed.   Very few fines were inflicted,
and Kano was cleared of its nocturnal undesirables " one
time."

The general standard of probity among the inhabitants
of Kano themselves is, however, shown by the free and
easy manner in which merchandise is left unguarded in
the great market, and it appears that lost property is
constantly being handed over to the Alkali, who has the
articles called out by a public crier in the market-place.

The absence of a fixed scale of emoluments for public
servants is always the weak point of native government.
Northern Nigeria was no exception to the rule.   The
proportion of the taxes actually collected which eventually
found its way into the so-called Public Treasury, was used
by the Emir with small regard to the public interest and
with a great deal for his own.   The Alkalis and their
assessors, though by no means universally corrupt, were
dependent for their living upon such sources as the fees
(usheri) upon judgment debts and upon the estates of
deceased persons (ujera).   To Mr. Charles Temple, now
Acting Governor, whose knowledge of Northern Nigeria
and its peoples is unequalled, belongs the credit of having
instituted in the Kano Emirate the Beit-el-Mal or Public
Treasury in the proper sense of the word, which has since
been extended, or is being extended, into all of them.   The
system follows traditional lines but vastly improves them.
In practice it works out as follows.   Half the total revenue
collected goes direct to the Northern Nigeria Government.
Of the remaining half, fifty per cent. is paid into the Beit-
el-Mal to provide salaries for the native officials and to pay
for necessary public works.   The balance is divided into
fifths on the basis of two-fifths of each district's yield to
the District Headman ; two-fifths of the sub-district's

yield to the Sub-district Headman ; one-fifth of his own village's yield to the Village Headman. It will doubtless be possible, as the system becomes perfected, for each district to have its own Beit-el-Mal with limited powers, receiving its instructions from the central Beit-el-Mal, just as the local British Treasuries receive instructions from the Treasury at Zungeru. This would enable the District Heads, Sub-district Heads and Village Heads to have fixed salaries like the Native Executive, a very desirable ideal to aim at.

The Emir draws a fixed sum monthly from the Beit-el-mal for his private expenses, which are numerous, and the public expenditure is accounted for and overlooked by the Resident. The *Waziri* draws £1000 a year, the *Maji* £360, the *Alkali* £600, the *Limam* (High Priest) £72. There are thirteen districts in charge of thirteen local *Alkalis* drawing £60 a year each. The public works completed out of the Beit-el-mal funds during the last year or two include the rebuilding of the Kano market at a cost of £600, a new jail at a cost of £1000, a new Court House, £250, besides keeping the thirteen gates of the city in repair, additions to the mosque, etc. In regard to the latter, it is interesting to note that the work of adding to the mosque and repairing the minaret, was entirely carried out by contract labour. The contract was given out by the Emir and the contractor paid the workmen to the number of over a thousand, a previously unheard-of event in native annals and an example of one of the many improvements which the Native Administration is carrying out under British influence. The Emir has also directed that £1000 shall be contributed to the National School at Nassarawa, which I shall have occasion to speak about in a subsequent letter. Legislation for the purpose of legally constituting the native Beit-el-Mals would seem to be called for.

The administration of justice has been vastly purified

CORNER OF A NATIVE MARKET.

ANOTHER CORNER.

by the inauguration of fixed emoluments. The District Courts and the Supreme Court administer Koranic law, or customary law, *i.e.* traditional law based on custom, or Government proclamations. Speaking generally, the Alkalis are a fine body of men, and they appear to be realizing more and more the dignity and responsibilities of their position. The chief Alkali in particular is a man of very high character. The legal code in criminal and civil matters is, of course, mainly inspired by the sacred books, and the Alkali is generally a Doctor of Mohammedan common law. His influence and power appear to be more extensive than that of the Egyptian *kadi*, since he has jurisdiction in criminal cases and in land suits, which the latter has not. Of the cases tried in the courts of the Kano Emirate, about 30 per cent. are matrimonial, such as divorce, restitution of conjugal rights, alimony, etc. The courts are very hard worked, dealing with about 7000 to 8000 cases *per annum*, and the Alkalis fully earn their salaries. I attended the chief Alkali's court in Kano city, and was greatly impressed by the general decorum, the respect shown to the Alkali, the activity of the assessors, the marshalling of the witnesses, the order, rapidity, and business-like manner in which the whole proceedings were conducted. It was an example of *native* self-government in Western Africa which would have astonished a good many people in Europe. No British court, no alien magistrate, could possibly deal with these " affairs of the people," which require a complete mastery of Koranic law and customary law, such a mastery as only a trained native can ever acquire, and it is to be hoped that any attempts which may arise to curtail the jurisdiction of the native courts—accepted by all classes of natives—will be promptly discouraged, together with similar attempts to interfere with the present Beit-el-mal system. From a practical point of view the maintenance of the Native Administration, guided and supervised by the Resident, *i.e.* indirect rule, is inseparable from the financial question. If the Native Administration were not financially provided for it would cease to exist. If the Emirs and their executives were converted into mere civil pensioners of the Government, they would become figure-heads deprived of all power and prestige. Under the system I have described the Emirs have power, and only hyper-sensitiveness and short-sightedness can see in their power our weakness. It is, on the contrary, our strength and defence against the reactionary elements which exist, and which are bound to exist in a country but newly occupied, and which are certainly not less hostile to the native authorities, who pursue their labours under the ægis of the British " raj," than they are to the British " raj " itself. Anything that impairs the influence of the native authorities, not only impairs the efficiency of the Administration of the country, but is an invitation to lawlessness and disorder.

It is only fair to state in this connection that the initiative of perpetuating, under British rule and with the modifications required, the system of land taxation indigenous to the community, was due to the suggestion of Sir William Wallace, for many years Acting High Commissioner of Northern Nigeria.

CHAPTER XII

THE PRESERVATION OF THE NATIONAL LIFE

AMONG those to whom the government of the coloured races of mankind appears in the light of a sacred trust committed to an Imperial white people, as to the servants of that people possessing the widest experience in the practice of such government, the preservation of the national life of these races must be a matter of paramount importance. Increased knowledge born of familiarity in the art of tropical government and of anthropological knowledge, a clearer realization of human needs which an expanding mental horizon brings with it, are teaching us many things. They are teaching us that there can be no common definition of progress or common standard for all mankind; that the highest human attainments are not necessarily reached on parallel lines; that man's place and part in the universe around him must vary with the dissimilarities of race and environment; that what may spell advance for some races at a particular stage in their evolution may involve retrogression, if not destruction, for other races in another stage; that humanity cannot be legislated for as though every section of it were modelled on the same pattern; that to disregard profound divergence in culture and racial necessities is to court disaster, and that to encourage national growth to develop on natural lines and the unfolding of the mental processes to proceed by gradual steps, is the only method by which the exercise of the Imperial prerogative can be morally justified. Our one and only conspicuous Imperial failure was due to a misguided belief that we could, and that it was desirable in our own interests that we should, crush out nationality by violence. It inflicted upon the victims immense misery and upon the performers embarrassments which have endured for centuries. Elsewhere we are experiencing the discomforting reflex of a policy based upon the supposition that East is capable of assimilation with West under alien guidance. British India is rent with confusion and mentally unsettled by a jumble of conflicting ideals, to which the Protected Native States offer a contrast that cannot but carry with it its own very significant lessons.

All the good work accomplished in Northern Nigeria during the last seven years can be flung away by a refusal to benefit from experience in other parts of the world. In pleading for the slow but sure policy everywhere in Nigeria, and in pleading that where in Nigeria national life has already expanded through the exercise of its own internal forces into organized communities, possessing their own laws and customs, their own machinery of government and their own well-defined characteristics, that national life shall be protected, preserved and strengthened to enable it to bear the strain of new conditions, one is pleading, it seems to me, for the true welfare of the people and for the highest concept of Imperialism.

These considerations hold good as regards every branch of European activity. Effective British political control does not require constant encroachments of departmental activity. British industrial interests can be allowed to find a natural outlet in the ordinary play of economic forces without calling upon Government assistance, for example, to undermine a national weaving industry in which, as Barth remarked of it many years ago, there is something that is " truly grand," giving employment and support as it does to innumerable families without compelling them to sacrifice their domestic habits or to pass their lives in immense establishments detrimental to health. British commercial necessities do not demand that the big native cities should be thrown open to the White trader, who can pursue his useful avocations just as well, and certainly with much greater regard to health conditions, outside than inside them. In the same way the advent of the missionary into the organized Mohammedan provinces of the north before the country is ripe to receive them, would be a positive danger, besides being an act perilously akin to a breach of faith. Surely we have become sufficiently intelligent to take a broadly human view of these things ? There is a field in pagan Northern and pagan Southern Nigeria sufficiently extensive to occupy all the energies of all the missions put together, without invading the heart of Moslem Nigeria. The advent of Christian missions into Kano or Katsina or Sokoto, for example, would be regarded as an act of aggression. Their presence in Zaria is a great mistake, and I make bold to assert that it is only comparable to a man smoking a pipe on a barrel of gunpowder. We hold this newly occupied country by the force of our prestige, far more than by the very small number of native troops in our service. That it is the duty of Government to prevent the introduction of elements, whatever their character and however lofty their motives, whose presence is calculated to cause unrest, is sufficiently self-evident as not to need emphasizing. No Government can afford to disregard so clear a view as that formulated, for example, in the Emir of Kano's letter given in Chapter VIII. But one would desire, if possible, that the leaders of the Christian Churches themselves should be brought to appreciate the justice of the contention. The establishment of Christian missions in the Mohammedan Emirates would not succeed in damming up the self-propelling currents of Islamic propaganda which are permeating Nigerian paganism. That is the true problem which the Churches have to face.

The question of economic development is on the same plane. That peace, the advent of railways and the growth of population will eventually result in the creation of a large commercial movement of affairs with Northern Nigeria—apart from the mineral output—is not to be doubted. But exaggeration as regards immediate prospects is to be deprecated, and the claims of economic development, important as they are, should not be allowed to play too great a part in administrative solicitude. The main concern of the Administration for the next few years should be that of placing the political, financial and educational organization of the country upon secure foundations. Political unrest and social confusion are stumbling-blocks to commercial progress, and everything should be done to avoid them. Those in a position to realize the marvels already accomplished in this region of Africa by the handful of British officials administering the country, and the many problems requiring on the part of those who are called upon to deal with them the utmost delicacy and tact in adjustment, cannot but enter a *caveat* against all tendencies, from whatever source they may emanate, be they of self-interest or of unselfish devotion, to " rush " Northern Nigeria. Rapid expansion does not necessarily mean progress. Sometimes it means exactly the reverse. Let us, rendered wise by experience elsewhere, set our faces like flint against the " Europeanizing " of Northern Nigeria. In Sierra Leone, in the Gold Coast, in the Western Provinces of Southern Nigeria we have daily object-lessons of the deplorable results of this denationalizing process. That Northern Nigeria should be preserved from it must be the earnest wish of all who are acquainted with its peoples and alive to their possibilities.

CHAPTER XIII

A PAGE OF HISTORY AND ITS MORAL

IF we have the imagination to grasp the true significance of the events which led, a century ago, to the break-up of the Hausa dynasty by the Fulani, we shall find the key to the moral side of permanently successful government in Northern Nigeria. The motive of the Fulani *jihad* has usually been attributed either to mere religious fanaticism or to personal and racial ambition; or, again, as an incident in the prolonged struggle for power on the part of this or that ruler or dynasty which has destroyed the fertile uplands of Western Africa south of the Sahara since the shattering of the ancient Niger civilizations by the Moorish invasion at the end of the sixteenth century. It appears to me that this appreciation is superficial, and that we must look deeper than the surface results. I am not sure that these surface results themselves do not suggest the need of doing so. A man of letters galvanizing a whole countryside to revolt against oppression. Shepherds and cowherds flinging away their sticks and staves and rallying to his standard. Initial defeat turned into victory. A number of independent States converted into a homogeneous entity acknowledging a temporal and spiritual over-lord. An immense region ill-provided with means of internal communication brought to recognize one common authority—and all within a year or two. These are remarkable occurrences. They insinuate the existence of some driving force below the surface. Is it possible to trace that force in the chequered annals of this part of Africa?

The Moorish invasion dealt the great Negroid Empire of the middle Niger—the Empire of the Songhay—a blow from which it never recovered. The invasion did not actually swamp the Hausa States, but its indirect consequences must have been felt throughout them in everywhere shaking established order, and in the decay of spiritual influence following upon the heels of anarchy. In the absence of any continuous written records, the history of the period following the advance of Morocco's musketeers into the Western Sudan, appears to Western minds as a confused medley of internecine strife without defined objects of any kind. One can imagine, let us say, a Chinese historian picturing the history of England from the tenth to the fifteenth century much in the same light, if his materials for composing it were almost wholly confined to oral traditions. But a close study of the few documents at our disposal must, I think, induce the belief that, dating from the introduction of a higher spiritual influence into the country—Mohammedanism had begun to acquire a footing by the eleventh century—the land was never free from an agency which sought the uplifting of society. Before the Moorish generals carried fire and sword into the Niger Valley, holy voices were raised in protest against the " decay of faith with the increase of infidelity." " Not one of the acts forbidden by God " —lament learned Arabic historians—" but was openly practised ; wine was drunk, and adultery had become so frequent that its practice seemed to have acquired legality." The terrible punishment which ensued was ascribed to these lapses : " It was on account of these abominations that God avenged Himself by calling in the victorious Moroccan army." We seem to be listening to another Moses denouncing the wickedness of the people of Israel. In the midst of all these disordered turmoils, when the worship of the true God was being swept aside by a wave of recrudescent paganism, when mosques were being destroyed and desecrated and social lawlessness reigned supreme, little knots of true believers gathered, forming as it were islands in the sea of turbulence and moral abasement, to which Christian Europe added a renewed element of subversion by her demand for slaves, thus intensifying internal warfare by furnishing it with a new and deadly incentive.

There is evidence that in the middle and towards the close of the eighteenth century the Hausa Kings were relapsing into paganism (in Zaria, for instance, the old Hausa " Tsafi," customs—rock worship—had been revived). It was at this period that the spark of a spiritual renascence arose in the most northerly of the Hausa States, Gober. Othman Fodio, a Fulani, ultimately the leader of the uprising, was above all a moral and spiritual reformer, as was his teacher the Mallam Jibrila. He sought to raise the whole tone of society. He used his influence at the Court of the Hausa King to secure the building of schools and the spread of letters. He himself and his brother and his son—into whose hands he placed affairs of state after the conquest—wrote a number of books whose titles are sufficient to indicate their character. Here are some of them : " The Book manifesting the Path of Righteousness and Unrighteousness," " The Book for the saving of the People of the Time and the Teaching of the Ignorant to understand the Knowledge of the Word," " Explanation to the Rulers as regards their Duties and what is due from them in the execution of their Duties," " The Book expressing the Difference between Right and Wrong," " The Book the Window for Students in the holding of the Doors of the Faith in God the Giver," " The Book to prevent others from following the promptings of the Devil," " The Book plainly showing

that the love of the World is the cause of every Fault."
A reflection by the way. When the Fulani reformers
were composing these works, and for many years afterwards, European and American slavers were periodically
visiting the lower Niger, six hundred miles south, and, by
presents of guns and powder, hounding on the natives
to raid one another for the benefit of the Western
plantations!

Othman's converts were by no means limited to men
of his own race, as was subsequently shown in the adherents he obtained. But it was not unnatural that such
a man should have been an offence to many ; that his
converts should have been molested ; and that finally, by
his personal action in releasing a number of them from
bondage, a collision with the authorities should have been
precipitated, which eventually led to the proclamation of
a holy war. Othman engaged in the struggle with
the words : " If I fight this battle that I may become
greater than my fellows, may the unbelievers wipe us
from the land." Upon its successful termination, the
statesman and the warrior became once more the social
reformer. Othman returned to his preaching and to the
compilation of his books.

A consideration of these facts irresistibly suggests
that the root causes of the Fulani outburst were
spiritual in their nature. Othman led a moral and
spiritual revival, among a people who, like all negroes
and negroids, are naturally more accessible to spiritual
influences than are the white peoples of the earth.
He gave a renewed inspiration to letters. That the
country, after half a century, fell back once more into
political chaos does not in the least weaken the moral
to be gleaned from these events. The religious revival
has not gone back. From that political chaos the country
has been rescued by the British power. One of the
obvious duties of the Administration is to continue the

work of the great Fulani reformer in everywhere extending and broadening the intellectual horizon, and doing nothing to weaken the national spiritual influences, of the people of the land. The creation of a system of education which shall be truly national is imperative at this moment when the whole fabric of native society is being shaken by disturbing elements. The field is clear : the slate clean. We are here unfettered by those bitter experiences of the West Coast of Africa and of India which are perpetual reminders of past blunders and daily handicaps to true progress.

CHAPTER XIV

A SCHEME OF NATIONAL EDUCATION

THE predominant characteristic of our educational methods—official and unofficial—in Western Africa hitherto may be summed up in one word—denationalization. The result is so notoriously unsatisfactory as to need no specific illustration. If readers of Mr. Valentine Chirol's book on India will turn to his chapters on the failure of our educational methods there, and substitute West Africa for India, they will be furnished with a replica of the situation on the West Coast of Africa. It is not an exact replica—for the reason that while the ties of caste in India are a deterrent to denationalization, such deterrent is non-existent in West Africa. But there is not one charge which Mr. Chirol brings against the Indian system that could not be equally brought against the West African system, and identical consequences are ensuing. We are barely beginning to realize that the policy, or rather impolicy, of the last half-century has been a hideous example of misdirected effort, and there is hardly an administrator who does not contemplate the development of the " educated native problem " with the gravest foreboding.

The object of the Northern Nigeria Administration is to set on foot an educational system throughout the country which shall save the Protectorate from these follies, while at the same time affording the rising generation the intellectual pabulum we are bound to provide, and ultimately laying the basis for a native civil service. At the present moment the scheme is only in its infancy, but the infant is robust and full of promise. It is at Nassarawa, a beautifully situated and healthy spot a few miles outside Kano, close by the Emir's country residence, that the first Government schools have been started. They consist at present of the *Mallamai* school, or school for teachers, a school for the sons of Chiefs, an elementary vernacular school and a technical school with carpenters', blacksmiths', leather-workers', and agricultural classes. The creation of a primary and secondary school will follow as soon as the work is sufficiently advanced. Special importance attaches to the elementary schools, as through them the mass of the population will be influenced. As soon as the teachers now being trained are ready they will be supplied to the Provinces, where the Residents are eagerly awaiting them, and it is the intention in every case that they shall be accompanied by a technical instructor. The training of Government clerks and of artisans for the Public Works Department is recognized as a necessity, but it takes quite a secondary place in the general educational plan which has been so successfully initiated, and these men will be trained so as to retain both their national instincts and their national dress.

A ride out to Nassarawa and some hours spent in investigating the work already accomplished (there are some 350 pupils) I shall always remember as one of the most pleasurable experiences of my visit to Northern Nigeria. Here at last, one saw, was a common-sense, well-thought-out, scientific scheme to enlarge the mental outlook of the West African on African lines, to preserve his racial constitution, to keep him in touch with his parents, in sympathy with his national life. Here, one felt, was the nucleus of a future Hausa university to be raised some day by the people themselves on their own initiative, a university which should far outshine the ancient glories of Timbuktu and Jenne, which should herald the dawn of a real African renascence, which instead of divorcing the people from their land should bind them to it in intensified bonds of pride and love. For one thing, the preservation of the national tongue is aimed at, the general teaching being given in the vernacular, for the present in Hausa—the *lingua franca* of the country—although in course of time, as the system extends, classes in Fulfulde (*Fulani*), Kanuri (the language of Bornu), and, perhaps, Nupe, will doubtless suggest themselves; not, however, to the exclusion of Hausa, but in combination with it. For another thing, the fatal mistake of taking in pupils free, or even paying them to come, is not being repeated here ; the principle of every pupil paying a fee, paying for his books and paying for his medical attendance having been laid down from the start.

The *Mallamai* school was full of special interest, being composed of grown men from eighteen to thirty ; for these are the teachers of to-morrow. I was told, and I can well believe it from their intellectual faces, that the rapidity with which they acquire and the ease with which they retain knowledge, is amazing. Land surveying and farm measuring is included in their *curriculum*, and some of them, although their course of instruction is not completed, have already rendered very considerable assistance, their work (which I was able to examine at a later date), calculated in acres and roods and covering many assessment sheets, being neat and generally accurate. I attended the geography lesson which was then going forward, and found these future teachers studying, not the configuration of the Alps or the names of the English counties, but the map of Africa, the rivers, mountain ranges and political divisions of their own continent : not the distances between Berlin and St. Petersburg,

A SCHEME OF NATIONAL EDUCATION

Rome and Paris, but between Kano and Lokoja, Zaria and Yola, and the routes to follow to reach those places from a given spot. The various classes, I observed, were not puzzling over, to them, incomprehensible stories about St. Bernard dogs rescuing snow-bound travellers, or busy bees improving shining hours, but becoming acquainted with the proverbs and folk-lore of their own land ; not being edified with the properties of the mangel-wurzel or the potentialities of the strawberry, but instructed in the culture requirements of yams, sweet potatoes, and sugar-cane. I did not see rows of lads in European costume, unsuited to the climate, hideous (out here) and vehicles for the propagation of tuberculosis, but decently clothed in their own graceful, healthy African garb.

The school for the sons of chiefs—which, I venture to hope, will not, as rumoured, be abandoned without very careful consideration—struck me as a triumphant proof of what a sympathetic Administration can accomplish in a very short time out here by way of winning confidence and removing suspicions. Here were perhaps threescore youngsters, the older and more advanced boys forming a separate class, and a more intelligent, keener crowd it would be difficult to select in any country. Their presence—among them were sons of the Emirs of Sokoto, Kano, Bauchi, Bornu, Katsina, Katagum, Bida, Gombe, Gando, Daura, and Muri—together, was evidence of the revolution which a few years have brought, for their respective fathers were until our advent more or less in a state of chronic friction and sometimes of open warfare. These *Yan Sarikis* (sons of chiefs) are not only allowed, but encouraged, to correspond with their parents, and constant are the mounted messengers passing to and fro.

In the technical school, the leather-workers were particularly interesting. The encouragement of this branch of native art should prove a great incentive to what is a national industry. There is no reason why in time the Hausa leather-workers should not only cut out the trade in Tripoli saddlery and boots, imported across the desert and sold at fabulous profits in the local markets, but supply, as the Hausa cotton manufacturer supplies, the needs of French and German territory. Indeed, there is no limit to the vistas which this national system of education opens up. A people of considerable intellect, of notable industrial aptitudes, having the sense of history, possessed of singular national vitality, guided on national lines of thought expansion, the old-time barriers of internecine strife wiped out—what a magnificent experiment, and how great the privilege of the initiators! I referred to the opportunity for true Empire-building which lies before us in Yorubaland, if we will but seize it. Here at Nassarawa is Empire-building of another kind in actual progress. One other fact needs chronicling in connection with these national schools. It is the intention of the Administration to insist that all pupils receive careful religious instruction from teachers of their own creed. When I visited the schools, lessons in reading and writing the Koran were being given by a Kano Mallam specially selected by the Emir of Kano, somewhat on the model of the Egyptian schools. It is earnestly to be hoped that the Colonial Office will resist any attempt at interference with this policy. Interference would be disastrous. It has been a prodigious labour of tact and careful steering, for which Mr. Hanns Vischer, the director of education and the founder of these schools, deserve the greatest credit, to secure the support of the Emirs for a truly national system of education. Many prejudices have had to be overcome. The older school of Mallams do not look with a favourable eye upon an innovation which must gradually displace their influence in favour of a younger generation,

IRON-SMELTERS.

FULANI CATTLE.

See p. 29.

broader-minded and more tolerant because better educated than they. Attempts both internal and external have not been, and are not, wanting to warn the chiefs of the danger of permitting their sons to become contaminated by foreign doctrines inimical to Islam. Justification for the confidence which the chiefs repose in our good faith can alone enable us to defeat these influences. Were that confidence to be shaken, the effort to train the future rulers (under the British suzerainty) of the country with a view to making them mentally and physically better fitted to assist the Administration, and to bring them into closer contact with one another and with the Government official, would receive a fatal blow, and the prestige of the Government would be deeply shaken. Let us once more turn to the pages of Mr. Chirol's weighty volume and note the consequences which have followed the elimination of religious instruction from the Government schools. To allow a weakening of the spiritual forces at work among the peoples of the Northern Hausa States would be to perpetuate a cruel wrong upon those who have come under our protection and from thenceforth are our wards.

A rapid multiplication of national schools in Northern Nigeria, so eminently desirable, entirely depends upon the financial support which the Administration, hampered in every direction for lack of funds, is able to contribute. The Imperial Government would be displaying wisdom in making a special grant for the purpose, the present sum available being altogether inadequate for the importance and urgency of the object in view, and in seriously broaching the problem of control over all unofficial educationary agencies in the Protectorate.

CHAPTER XV

COMMERCIAL DEVELOPMENT

THE external, by which I mean non-indigenous, trade of Northern Nigeria plays as yet but an insignificant part in the commercial and industrial activities of the country. It is largely in the hands of one company, the Niger Company, Limited, to the enterprise of whose founder, Sir George Taubman Goldie, is due our possession of the Northern Protectorate. Three or four other commercial houses have extended their operations to the territory, and more will certainly follow. At present the only other European firm, outside the Niger Company, which is doing a large general business is that of Messrs. John Holt & Co., Limited. Another alien commercial element is the Arab trader. His seat of interest is Kano city, where he has been established for several centuries, and where, as already stated, there is a recognized Arab quarter. The trans-desert trade from Tripoli has always been in his hands, but he is now beginning to use the parcel post and the western route largely. Ten thousand parcels, weighing eleven pounds each, were despatched or received by Arab traders during the first half of last year. The Arabs appear to deal in lines of trade with which European firms are not in touch. Several of them have been in England, and the business headquarters of one of them is in Manchester. They are intelligent men, but form an uncertain and not particularly safe element in the affairs of Kano. A representative of these traders who visited me at the house kindly placed at my disposal near the Residency, two miles from the city, gave it as his opinion that the railway would double the trade of the country in five years.

The two principal articles of import at present are cotton goods and salt. The articles of export are shea-nuts or butter, dressed and dyed goat and sheep skins, ostrich feathers, rubber, ground-nuts, gum arabic, hides, gum copal, beeswax, various kinds of oil-beans, cotton, and a fibre resembling, and equal in value to, jute. Tin and other minerals stand, of course, in a different category, and cannot be regarded as " trade." Of these I formed the opinion that a very large future expansion in the shea-nut trade and ground-nut trade may be legitimately expected. I rode for days through woods of shea, and I found these trees growing abundantly all over the parts of the Niger Province and Zaria Province I visited, and in many parts of the Kano Province. The ground-nut is already cultivated, its cultivation is easy, and the soil in many districts along the Baro-Kano railway is suitable. I see no reason why that railway should not, in parts, and in time, attract to itself a population of ground-nut cultivators, as the Dakar-St. Louis railway has done, and the new Thiès-Kayes railway is doing in Senegal. The industry is at present handicapped because the merchants will not buy the undecorticated nut, and the price offered to the native is not sufficiently attractive to induce him to go to the great labour involved in decortica-tion. Seeing that the Niger ground-nut fetches much higher prices than the Senegal and Gambia nut, it is astonishing that the merchant is not prepared to deal with the nut himself, and to purchase the undecorticated article from the native. The present policy strikes one as short-sighted.

A great many hopes have been engendered touching an immediate and large export of raw cotton consequent upon the termination of the railway. I should be

extremely loath to say anything here which would tend
to throw cold water upon the commendable enterprise
of the British Cotton Growing Association, to which
Imperially we owe much, and the problem is one which
is affected by so many varying local influences that to
dogmatize upon it would be unwise. Enormous quantities of cotton are undoubtedly grown, some districts in
the Zaria and Kano Provinces being almost entirely
devoted to its production, and many more off the beaten
track could be, if transport were available. But at
present there are two difficulties, apart from the general
difficulties affecting all economic development in Northern
Nigeria, to which I shall refer in a moment. One is the
question of price. The other is the local demand. In
one sense they are inseparable. The local demand for
the raw material by local weavers exceeds the supply,
and the result is that the price the Association finds
itself, either directly or through its agents, the Niger
Company, able to pay is insufficient to tempt the growers.
To overcome these obstacles the Association relies upon
the attraction offered by a permanent market at a fixed
price irrespective of local fluctuation ; an increased
yield *per* acre through an improvement in the varieties
produced, and improvement in methods of cultivation ;
and the inroads upon the local weaving industry through
the increasing import of Manchester cotton-goods. These
views may be quite sound, but, granted their soundness,
some time must elapse before they become appreciably
operative, and I have difficulty myself in believing that
any really substantial export of raw cotton is to be
looked for in the *immediate* future. But that the Association's general line of policy in seeking to develop and
expand the existing native-growing industry, as such, is
right, and that its labours are calculated to achieve these
ends, I am persuaded ; while I see no reason to doubt
that a considerable export of raw cotton will eventually

be the outcome of those labours.* Among agricultural products, corn should also figure largely in course of time. The export of dressed goat and sheep skins is steadily increasing. The trade now amounts to over one million skins *per annum*, of a total home value of £50,000 to £60,000. Until a few years ago it was an entirely trans-desert trade, and the skins were purchased at Tripoli for the American market. Latterly the *London and Kano Trading Company* have diverted more than half of this trade by the western route, and London is to-day the principal purchaser.

There would seem to be a good future for a trade in hides, especially if Kano becomes a slaughter-centre for cattle for the southern markets. The possible obstacle to this is partly political and partly ethnological, and the first, at least, is worthy of special attention on the part of the Administration. Virtually all the herds in the Hausa States are the property of the Fulani. Now the Fulani M'Bororo, as already pointed out, is a nomad, and it is very doubtful if he will ever be anything else. Indeed, his very calling necessitates that he should be continually on the move to seek out pasture-land, according to the seasons, and the localities he knows. But the more the Protectorate is organized the more ill at ease will the nomad Fulani become, especially as he dislikes most intensely the *jangali* or cattle-tax, at the best of times an unsatisfactory tax to enforce, and one which, moreover, operates unfairly towards the small herdsman. Here the ethnological peculiarity comes in. The Fulani is very fond of his cattle. He does not breed them for slaughter, but because he literally loves them. He knows every one of them by name, and lavishes as much attention upon them as he does upon his children. This is peculiar to him not in Nigeria only but all over Western Africa. Often have our officers in

* The subject is discussed at greater length in Part IV.

Northern Nigeria found it impossible to resist the pitiful appeal of some old Fulani herdsman or his wife, begging with eyes full of tears for the restitution of a favourite ox or heifer taken with others under the " jangali " assessment. The dual problem must be thought out or the M'Bororo will silently disappear into the vastness of Africa, as the Shuwa—his nomadic colleague of Bornou —has already partly disappeared from Nigeria. Fulani migration eastwards towards the Nile valley is a marked phenomenon of the last ten years, both as regards French and British territory in West Africa. Khartoum now numbers some 5000 Sokoto Fulani alone. The disappearance of the Fulani M'Bororoji from the Hausa States would not only arrest any development of the cattle and hides trades, but would be an incalculable loss to Hausa agriculture for the reasons given in a previous chapter.

The forest resources of the country are as yet practically untapped, for lack of adequate transport. They are not as rich in Northern as in Southern Nigeria, because the forests are much fewer, but there are very extensive gum-copal forests in Bornu ; there is a good deal of rubber in Bauchi and in some other provinces, the Benue region especially abounding in rubber, copal, and fibres of great value. The Muri province is particularly rich. A forestry department organized on the lines of Southern Nigeria is urgently needed. But in this, as in almost everything else, the Administration is hampered for lack of funds.

There can be no doubt whatever, that Northern Nigeria has immense potentialities but they are not going to be developed in a day, or in a decade, and no useful purpose can be served by pretending otherwise. The very vastness of the country and the natural difficulties of communication preclude rapidity in development. In West Africa the game is generally to the tortoise, not to the hare. And several factors must ever be borne in mind. Northern Nigeria, as already stated, is a remarkably self-sufficing country, one part of it supplying the wants of another; peopled with born traders busily occupied in furthering the needs of a comprehensive internal traffic. For instance, the river-borne traffic of the Benue, both up and down, is entirely in the hands now of Nupe and Kakandas trading on behalf of native merchants, mostly Yorubas, at Lokoja. There is an active overland trade between the Benue region, north towards Kano and Bauchi, south with Southern Nigeria right down to Calabar on the ocean. Native merchants from the north import cloth, sheep and cattle, and corn, taking away cash, galena and silver from the Arifu native mines. Between district and district, province and province, all over the country there is a ceaseless interchange of commercial commodities. That is one factor to take into account. Another is that we must revolutionize our ideas as to general conditions and capabilities for labour, proportionately to the needs and extent of population. The belief that the majority of the inhabitants of Northern Nigeria pass their time in idleness, or what approximates to idleness, is a pure delusion. Even from the European standpoint, which is not and cannot be the African's from climatic causes alone, the Northern Nigerian, speaking generally, is the reverse of idle. Moreover, if on the one hand our political administration tends to root the people in the soil and increase the area under cultivation; on the other hand, our roads and railways and the opening of the tin mines tend to take the people off the land and to create an increasing class of casual, floating labour which cannot itself provide for its own sustenance, and has to purchase its food requirements. The economic consequence is a steadily ascending price of foodstuffs in the neighbourhood of all the great centres. From this the farmer benefits, but at the expense of an increase in the production of raw material for the export trade with Europe. The Northern Nigerian farmer will grow the crop which it pays him best to grow, and if he sees a larger profit in corn for local consumption than in ground-nuts or cotton for export, he will grow corn. These economic questions do not appear to me to be given their due proportion in the estimates which are made. The whole country is in a state of transition, and it must be given breathing space in which to adjust itself. Patience and statesmanship are the main necessities of the moment. Sir Henry Hesketh-Bell, who takes a keen interest in all questions of economic development, may be trusted to do all that is humanly possible to encourage the commercial progress of the territory.

The outsider who attempts any detailed investigation of trade conditions in Northern Nigeria must be pre-pared to walk as delicately as any Agag, and even then he is pretty sure to ruffle somebody's feelings. The fact of the matter is, that the paramount position held by the Niger Company—the " monopoly " as some call it, although it hardly amounts to that and must decreasingly do so—is a very sore point with many of the officials. The aims of the latter and the aims of the company necessarily diverge, but there is, I think, a tendency on the part of some of the officials to forget the fact that the Niger Company's enterprise is the explanation of our presence in the country. One very sore point is the question of " cash " for produce," and this affects not the Niger Company only, but the other merchants. The official case is, that the natives desire cash for their produce, but that the merchants will not pay cash, or pay as little cash as possible, because they make a very much larger profit on the barter business ; that this strangles trade development by discouraging the native producer, who is automatically forced to accept goods he often does not require, and must afterwards sell at a loss in order to get the cash he wants. Indeed, the official case goes further. It is contended not only that the merchants will not buy produce against cash when asked for cash, but on occasion actually refuse to sell goods against cash offered by the native, demanding produce in lieu thereof. For example, if a native has sold his produce against cloth and then, possessing some loose cash, desires to purchase, shall we say, earthenware or salt, he is told that his cash will not be accepted, but that he must bring shea-nuts or ground-nuts, or whatever may be the product out of which the merchant can make the biggest margin of profit. Instances are given of merchants having refused to sell salt to natives for cash ; of natives being able to buy cloth in the open market for actually less than the merchants reckon in paying the native producers, and so on. Why, it is urged, should the political officer encourage the native to bring produce for sale to the merchant when all he will get is cloth that he must sell at a loss in the market in order to get silver to pay his taxes ? Hence we arrive at a point when, as in the last published Government Report, the " pernicious barter system " is denounced, lock, stock, and barrel. The views of the merchants are various. In certain quarters the official allegations are altogether denied. In others it is contended that the barter trade is the best means of getting into touch with the actual native trader ; that it would not pay to import cash to buy rough produce like shea-nuts or ground-nuts, which in many cases are all the natives have to offer ; that the out-stations are in charge of native clerks from the coast, who cannot be trusted with cash ; that the native gets as good value in goods as he does in cash, and so on. Proceeding from the defensive to the aggressive, many of the merchants contend that competition, and competition alone, can be expected to put large quantities of cash into commercial circulation, and that the Government, instead of fostering competition by encouraging new-comers, and especially the small man, to go into the country, handicaps the merchant by disproportionately heavy taxes. The £20 trading licence for every trading station, even far away in the bush, is particularly resented. It is pointed out that if the Administration of Southern Nigeria, whose economic resources are so much richer, makes no such charge, it is preposterous that the Administration of Northern Nigeria, whose economic fortune, in the European sense, depends so largely upon the growth of trade, should do so. One firm of merchants showed me their books, which disclosed in rent, assessment, and licences a total annual charge of £150 for a single station. No doubt there is much to be said on both sides, and each side has a case. It was, for instance, proved to my satisfaction that in certain instances cash had undoubtedly been refused to native traders bringing produce to the merchant stores for sale, and that, in other instances, when cash had been given, the prices paid, as compared with the local price governing mer-chandise, was so much less as practically to drive the native to accept merchandise. On the other hand, to dub as " pernicious " the barter system, which is respon-sible for the vast bulk of the trade that provides the Government all over West Africa with such large revenue, must appear a straining of the use of language; nor does the Administration, I think, allow sufficiently for the innumerable difficulties which the merchant has to face in Northern Nigeria. For example, in many of the out-stations produce has often to be stored for six months or more, depreciating all the time, before the state of the river permits of its shipment. But, after all, cash is spreading rapidly, and the key to the situation undoubtedly lies in competition. The more the Administration can do to attract new blood the better will be the all-round results.

CHAPTER XVI

THERE appears to be no doubt that Nigeria is a highly mineralized country. Iron exists in considerable quantities and in many districts, in Southern but more particularly in Northern Nigeria. In the Southern Protectorate large deposits of lignite have been discovered 40 miles inland from Onitsha, and require more than a passing mention.

Lignite, as is well known, stands about halfway between wood and coal. It forms an excellent combustible, and if it can be produced in the proper form for the purpose, it would be invaluable for the Nigerian railways and for the steamers and steamboats plying up and down the river, besides saving the Administration, which is a large importer of coal, much expense. The first experiments made with the raw material, as extracted, by the Marine Department, the Northern Nigerian Railway, and the Niger Company were not altogether satisfactory, which is, perhaps, not surprising. The Imperial Institute in London is giving close attention to the matter. That the deposits are of commercial value is undoubted. An analysis of the Nigerian lignite and a personal investigation of lignite deposits in Bohemia and elsewhere, conducted by Professor Wyndham Dunstan, the Director of the Institute, have shown that the Nigerian article is virtually identical with the German and Austrian. Lignite is extensively used in Germany, where it is manufactured into briquettes, and excellent briquettes have been made by a German

175

firm from specimens of the Nigerian lignite supplied by the Institute. It is probable that the difficulties experienced locally in utilizing the material in its raw state would vanish if the necessary machinery for the manufacture of briquettes could be erected at or near Asaba. Meantime the Administration has had a road constructed from Asaba to the lignite-fields.

Great importance is attached locally to the Udi deposits, specimens of which I was able to examine. To the non-expert eye they have every appearance of rather dirty-looking coal. Credit for this discovery is wholly due to the mineral survey party sent out by the Imperial Institute under Mr. Kitson. I am told that the deposits cover an area of no less than five square miles. To work them commercially a railway between Onitsha and Udi will, of course, be necessary. The Udi district can hardly be described as " open " at the moment, but a metalled road to connect it with Onitsha is in a fair way of being completed.

There can be little doubt that in these deposits the Administration has a valuable source of potential revenue, and that the Colonial Office will be called upon before long to come to a decision as to the best means of reaping advantage therefrom. It is an open secret that demands for prospecting licences and even for concessions are already being made. In some quarters the opinion is entertained that the home and local authorities would be well advised to refuse to part with control over the fields, but, for some years to come at any rate, to let the Southern Nigeria Administration itself develop them. There seems to be no reason why these deposits of fuel should not be made to play as important a part in the future economy of West Africa as the Nile Sudd appears likely to do in the economy of Egypt and the Sudan.

Mineral oil has also been discovered in the Southern Protectorate, but the extravagant hopes held out of being able to work the latter at a profit seem in a fair way of being abandoned, and the financial assistance lent by the Administration has not so far justified itself. West Africa is a peculiar country and is apt to turn the tables upon the company promoter with a disconcerting completeness. In the Northern Protectorate salt exists in Bornu, Sokoto, Muri, and Borgu. Monazite has been found, although not in large deposits, in Nassarawa and Ilorin. Mica and kaolin occur in Kano. Tourmaline has been found in Bassa. Kabba contains limestone deposits favourably reported upon by the officers of the Imperial Institute as suitable for agricultural purposes and the preparation of mortar. Certain parts of Muri are rich in galena, containing lead and silver. I am told that quite recently extensive supplies of silver have been discovered in the same district, the natives of which have, of course, been trading in both silver and in lead for many years. Rumours of the existence of gold and copper have not so far, to my knowledge, been justified. Of precious stones, I have only heard of small garnets being won, although I was shown a handful of inferior diamonds supposedly discovered in Southern Nigeria, and the blue clay formation certainly exists in some parts of Bauchi. A number of mineral surveys have been carried out by the Imperial Institute, but the potentialities of the vast bulk of the country are still unknown.

The chief discoveries have been concerned with tin. The industry was originally, and in restricted form, a native one, and has a somewhat romantic history. Its brief outlines, obtained from conversation with the native authorities of Liruei-n-Kano and Liruei-n-Delma, are as follows. Some eighty years ago the people of the former place, a small town in the south-east of Kano Province, whose inhabitants carried on an iron smelting industry under the direction of an able woman, *Sariki*, found the white metal. They ascertained that it possessed a trading value. They invented an ingenious but simple method of treating and producing it in an exceedingly pure form, which remained a secret among the members of the ruling family and their adherents, but which was explained to me by them in detail, by the side of one of their furnaces at Liruei-n-Kano. After honeycombing the neighbourhood of Liruei-n-Kano with vertical pits, they wandered in course of time over the whole stanniferous area, washing and digging in the beds, as far south as the tenth parallel. Further than that they could not move owing to the hostility of the pagan tribes. Tin, in thin, rounded rods, became a regular article of sale in the markets.

The first sample of tin ore was sent home by Sir William Wallace, then Acting High Commissioner, in 1902. It was examined by the Imperial Institute and was found to contain over 80 per cent. of tin di-oxide, equal to about 64 per cent. of metallic tin. From that time onwards the Niger Company which, under the arrangement contracted with the Imperial Government at the time of the abrogation of the Charter, stands to gain very largely through the development of the mineral resources of the Protectorate, has spent considerable sums—at first without return—in proving and in encouraging the industry. To the company is due the fact that the field has been opened out at all. It is but fair to state this because the company is the butt of much criticism in Northern Nigeria, and in some respects, I think, criticism inspired by jealousy of its own remarkable enterprise. In the last three or four years no fewer than eighty-two companies have been floated to exploit Northern Nigeria tin with a total capital of £3,792,132.* Hardly a week passes but that some fresh company is not floated, or the attempt made to do so. It has, therefore, become a very big thing

---

* In the case of some of these companies, such as the West African Mines, Ltd., the Anglo-Continental Mines Company, Ltd., etc., only a part of their capital is invested in the tin mines.

indeed, and an outside non-expert opinion may be of some use from the point of view of the " man in the street " at home. The country is flooded with prospectors, on the whole of a much better type than is usually attracted to a new mining region, and the Government, under guarantee from the Niger Company, are now building a light railway in the direction of the principal deposits.

Needless to say, there has been the usual amount of swindling, and, perhaps, more than the usual amount of lying. Tin has been located in districts where there never was and never will be the slightest vestige of tin; imaginary " bore-holes " have been sunk and companies have been formed in London on the strength of utterly fraudulent reports. Statements have been issued proclaiming that the country is self-supporting for the white prospector in the matter of supplies, which is totally untrue; and that it is a health resort, which is equally false. Young fellows have been sent out on agreements which are a disgrace to those who drew them up, and in some cases, their bones are rotting in the ground. An unpleasant feature of the affair has been the indecent precipitancy with which in certain instances ex-Government officials have identified themselves with syndicates formed in London, a practice which appears to be growing and which is to be deprecated in the interest of the high standard and general purity of our public service.* No doubt these incidents are common in the initial stages of every such enterprise. They are none the less to be deplored.

The western portion of the Bauchi province is the true

* Perhaps the above remarks are a little too sweeping. It has been brought to my knowledge that in one such case where permission was sought by an experienced ex-Government official and granted by the authorities, the former's action was, as a matter of fact, twice instrumental in preventing a fraudulent concern from being unloaded upon the public ; and no doubt there is something to be said in favour of the practice from that point of view, arguing from an isolated case. But I must adhere to the opinion that, speaking generally, the practice is objectionable, and lends itself to incidents which are calculated to impair the very high standard of public service of which Great Britain rightly makes a boast.

centre of the nascent industry. The country about here is wild and beautiful, broken by mountain ranges which cannot always be negotiated on horseback, and rising to a considerable height, up to 5000 feet round about Bukuru and Pankshin. Anything more at variance with the forest regions of the south it would be impossible to imagine. The whole province is well watered, and the mineral section lies in the watershed of three fluvial systems, one feeding the Chad of which the Delimi (or Bunga) is the most important ; another the Benue, of which the Gongola, Kaddera and Sango are the principal contributory offshoots ; another the Niger, through its tributary the Kaduna which branches out into a fan of numerous lesser streams. Naraguta, on the Delimi— where most of the mining is actually concentrated—is situate almost at the heart of these three systems. There appears to be no bed of tin-bearing wash over the whole country, but for centuries upon centuries hundreds of feet of rock—chiefly granite of sorts, with gneiss and basalt— have been denuded by the action of the weather, and the tin discovered is the concentration of the tin disseminated throughout those rocks which has been washed into the beds of the rivers. Practically (there is one known exception, perhaps two) all the tin as yet discovered is alluvial, and there is virtually no alluvial tin except in the river-beds themselves. It occurs in patches, which explains, although it does not excuse, the flamboyant statements issued on the strength of specific returns, over a given area, from washings. A company may have secured a licence, or a lease, over a wide area in one particular corner of which one or more of these patches has been met with. The returns from washings in these patches, some of which are very rich, are made to apply in prospectus-framing to the whole area, when the bulk of it may be virgin not only of tin in payable quantities, but of any trace of tin at all.

It is unwise to dogmatize about a new country where further discoveries may give a different complexion to the situation. But in the present state of our knowledge, the statements describing Northern Nigeria as the " richest tin field in the world," are, to put it mildly, a manifest exaggeration, and the happiest thing which could happen to the country and to the industry would be a cessation of the " boom." It may be fairly urged that the Government's business is not the protection of the home investor. All the same, it is not in the public interest that Northern Nigeria should get a bad name, through wild-cat schemes and dishonest finance. Five years hence a boom may be justified by results. At present it is not. Disinterested expert opinion on the spot estimates the eventual output of the discovered field at 5000 tons per annum. It is always possible that further and valuable deposits may be struck. On the other hand, the life of an alluvial tin mine is, by general consent, a short one, and ten years will probably cover the life of the existing mines. Under the circumstances it is very evident that a great number of the companies which have been floated are over-capitalized and will never pay an honest dividend. Companies with a small capital, whose property is a good one and favourably situated, have every chance of doing so. For the small man, working with a modest capital, who is fortunate enough to select a good site and who is prepared to come in and do the actual mining, the prospects, I should say, are distinctly good ; and prospectors of that sort could count upon receiving every assistance from the Administration, which is anxious to encourage them. For two energetic men—it is always better to be *à deux* out here— a capital of £3000 would be ample, and the conditions made to licence and lease-holders are not onerous, although the staff for dealing with applications is too small, entailing vexatious delays. There is no serious labour trouble, and there is not likely to be any, provided the natives are properly treated. The representative of the Niger Company, who has considerable knowledge of the country and whom I saw at Joss—a beautiful station reflecting the greatest possible credit upon the company and its local staff—was very emphatic on this point, and his views were borne out by the most experienced people I consulted. In this connection I feel impelled to remark that both from the political point of view, as from the standpoint of the interests and progress of the industry itself—not to mention other considerations—it is absolutely essential that abusive acts, such as the incident which occurred at the close of last year at Maiwa, should be punished with exemplary severity. On that occasion the guilty party escaped with a substantial fine. Should anything of the sort recur, expulsion from the country ought to accompany the fine. The Bauchi province is not yet entirely "held," and much of it is peopled by very shy and timid pagan tribes. These are amenable under just treatment to regular labour on short terms and prompt pay, as has been proved in the final stages of the completion of the Riga-Chikum-Naraguta road, although such labour is quite foreign to them. Harsh and unjust handling would send them flying to the inaccessible hills. While on this subject I am also bound to say that the political staff of the Bauchi province is hopelessly and dangerously undermanned, or was when I left the country last January. It is tempting Providence to allow three hundred white prospectors to go wandering over the face of a vast country like this (27,000 square miles) with a political staff amounting to no more than thirteen all told ; and that number, a purely nominal one, be it stated. Twenty political officers at least should be permanently on duty in the province.

The question of transport has been a difficult one and still remains so. The situation has been somewhat alleviated by the construction of a road connecting Naraguta with the Baro-Kano railway at Riga-Chikum,

although, following that road for its whole (then) completed length, I fail to see for my part that it will be of
much use in the rains without a series of pontoons over
the rivers which cut it at frequent intervals, and no measure
of the kind was in contemplation last January. Possibly
the situation has changed since. The scarcity and the
distance of the villages and, consequently, of food supplies
for men and beasts, from the road is also a drawback. But
doubtless the road will fall into disuse and turn out to have
been more or less a waste of money with the completion
of the railway which, mercifully, be it said, has been started
from Zaria instead of following the deserted country from
Riga-Chikum as was originally proposed. This railway is
being constructed in the direction of Naraguta. But not
to Naraguta itself, which is wise, for the development of
the industry in that immediate neighbourhood is still a
sufficiently doubtful quantity to permit at least of the
supposition that the centre of gravity may shift to Bukuru
or some other spot. The railway traverses the region
where the Kano tin deposits are situate—virtually the only
ones not entirely alluvial in character. At the present
time the road chiefly used for the transport of the tin is
that opened and maintained by the Niger Company
between the mines and Loko on the Benue, a distance of
180 miles. The Niger Company have established ferries
across the rivers and organised a system of carriers and
donkeys. But at best the route is not an ideal one, costs
a great deal to keep open, and is hardly capable of dealing
with more than 500 tons *per annum*. I found complaints
rife as to the alleged favouritism shown by the company
in its management of the transport, but I failed to dis-
cover any specific facts justifying them. Of course the
company enjoys a complete monopoly of that road, even
the Government, it seems, having to apply to the company for carriers ; and a monopoly is always undesirable in theory and sometimes very irritating in practice.

(Apparently the same situation has come about in regard to the Riga-Chikum road.) But it is difficult to see how any tin at all could have been got down, or machinery and stores got up, to and from the river if it had not been for the company's enterprise and far-seeing methods. Certainly the loudest of its local critics would have been quite unable to have coped with the problem.

Something remains to be said of the Bauchi province. The province consists of the Bauchi and Gombe Emirates, the Ningi Division, an independent community half Muslim, half pagan, of erstwhile noted freebooters and fighters, and the purely pagan section, of which the Hill Division is the most important. The total population is about half a million. In no part of Africa probably is there such a conglomeration of different tribes—Angass, Sura, Tangali, Chip, Waja, Kanna, Bukurus, etc., etc.—as is to be found in the pagan division of Bauchi which, for centuries, has been the refuge of communities fleeing from Hausa, Fulani and Beri-Beri (Kanuri) pressure. No fewer than sixty-four distinct languages—not dialects—are said to have been noted within it. The men are an upstanding race, lithe rather than muscular, great archers and in many cases daring horsemen, riding bare-backed, covering immense distances in a phenomenally short space of time and shooting accurately (with the bow) while mounted. Most of them go about absolutely naked but for a sanitary adornment of special character. For a picture of primitive man commend me to the spectacle of a naked Bauchi pagan carrying a bow in his hand, on his back a quiver of arrows ; on his head, its horns sticking out on either side, the gory and newly severed head of an ox—the " Boar of the Ardennes " in variation and in an African setting of rugged mountains and dying sun ! I observed this sight one evening riding into Naraguta from a distant mining camp, passing, ten minutes later, a gorgeously attired Mohammedan *Sariki* in his many coloured robes on a richly

SCENE IN THE BAUCHI HIGHLANDS.

caparisoned horse. Northern Nigeria is a land of extraordinary contrasts, which to some extent no doubt is the secret of its fascination. The women's clothing is also of the scantiest, consisting of a bunch of broad green leaves fixed round the waist and falling over the hips and lower abdomen. Their chastity is proverbial even among the dissolute camp-followers.

Among these people many customs of great anthropological interest must linger, many religious practices and philological secrets that might give us the key to much of which we are still ignorant in the history of the country, and assist us in the art of government. It seems a pity that their gradual Hausa-ising, which must be the outcome of the *pax britannica*, should become accomplished before these facts have been methodically studied and recorded. The pagan division of Bauchi is a unique corner of Africa, and it would be well worth the while of Government and of some scientific body at home to prosecute research within it. The Administration has no money to spare. But it is really a misfortune that public opinion in England is so lax in these matters. We wait in order to understand the ethnological lore of our African dependencies, until German scientists have gone through them and told us what they contain of anthropological value, incidentally sweeping the country bare of its ethnological treasures. In these things we appear to have no national pride whatever. If any British scientific body should be stung by these mild remarks into some sort of action, I would advise its communicating with Captain Foulkes, the Political Officer until recently in charge of the Hill Division, who is keenly interested in the people and their customs which he has more knowledge of than any one else.

The soil of the province is supposedly poor, but I observed it to be covered in many places with millions of casts of virgin soil flung up by earthworms, and these must, when the rains come, enrich its recuperative properties. The province would probably grow wheat. The pagan cultivation is very deep and remarkably regular, and these communities, for all their primitiveness, weave grass mats of tasteful finish, colouring and design ; grow cotton which they manufacture and sell, and tobacco which they smoke, and snuff, and smelt iron. They are also readily taking to the rubber trade and learning how to tap the rubber trees which, in some parts, are to be met with in every village, without destroying the tree. In the plains there are large herds of cattle, which form the principal wealth of the inhabitants, and an abundance of good grazing land. The Fulani herdsman, ubiquitous as ever, may be seen tending his beasts.

On all hands the Barchi plateau is looked upon as an eventual sanatorium whe re officials can recoup, and thanks to which the term of service may be ultimately prolonged, which, with the keenness which distinguishes this service, they all seem to want—the Politicals, I mean. Even now they play hide-and-seek with the doctors, and keep uncommonly quiet when the time comes round for furlough, lying low like Brer Rabbit. I hesitate to strike a discord where so much unanimity prevails. No doubt it is a generally accepted maxim that the bracing air of a mountainous region, its cool nights and mornings, have recuperative effects upon the system undermined with malaria and other ills, and it may well be—I devoutly hope so—that in course of time the plateau will become the Nigerian Simla and may also contain a population of white settlers engaged in stock-raising and, perhaps, agriculture. But the period within which these things can come about strikes me as still remote. If they are to be, it will mean the expenditure of much money, and, under existing circumstances of transport and housing, the climate of Bauchi has been over-praised. You have always the tropical African sun to reckon with, and there appears to be some subtly dangerous quality about it which even men who have lived in other tropical lands find very trying.

CHAPTER XVII

THE NECESSITY OF AMALGAMATING THE TWO PROTECTORATES

No interested student of Nigerian affairs can fail, I think, especially after an examination of the problem on the spot, to arrive at the conclusion that the present dual system of administration, with its artificial territorial boundaries, its differing methods, and its inevitable rivalries, has served its turn and should be brought to an end as speedily as possible. The situation, as it obtains to-day, is incongruous—in some respects almost absurd; and the absence of a sense of proportion in estimating responsibilities and acknowledging public services is conspicuous. No comprehensive scheme of development and, what is more important, no unity of principle in public policy is possible while it lasts. Moreover, just as each Administration settles itself more firmly in the saddle and pursues its own aims with increasing determination, so will differences in the handling of great public issues accentuate themselves and eventual adjustment on a common basis of principle be attended with additional perplexity. It is not only quite natural, but under the existing circumstances it is right that the Administration of Southern Nigeria should work for the interests of Southern Nigeria and the Administration of Northern Nigeria for the interests of the latter. But Nigeria is geographically a single unit, and Imperial policy suffers from a treatment which regards the interests of one section as not only distinct from, but in certain

187

cases antagonistic to the interests of the other. It is not suggested that administration should everywhere be carried out on the same pattern. No one would contend that the problems of government in the Northern Hausa provinces can, for instance, be assimilated to the problems of government in the Eastern Province of the Southern Protectorate. But that the main principles of government should be identical, and that the governing outlook should be directed to a consideration of the interests of Nigeria as a whole, can hardly be disputed. Take, for example, the question of direct and of indirect rule. The tendency in Southern Nigeria, as the Secretariat gets stronger and the initiative of the Commissioners decreases, is towards direct rule, especially in the Western Province. Northern Nigeria has resolutely set the helm in the contrary direction. Take the question of taxation. North of the imaginary line which separates the two Protectorates the native pays a direct tax to the Administration, and tribute from the people to their natural Chiefs and to the Government is assured on specific principles. South of that line the native pays no direct tax to Government, and in the Western Province the Central Administration doles out stipends, apparently suspendable, to the Chiefs, while the paying of native tribute to the Chiefs, where it has not altogether ceased, exists only by the internal conservatism of native custom. Take the question of education. The Southern Nigerian system is turning out every year hundreds of Europeanized Africans. The Northern Nigeria system aims at the establishment of an educational system based upon a totally different ideal. In Northern Nigeria the land question has been settled, so far as the Northern Protectorate is concerned, on a broad but sure foundation ; but the Southern Nigerian native is an alien in Northern Nigerian law. In Southern Nigeria there is no real land legislation, and the absence of such, especially in the Western Province, is raising a host of future complications.

Every year the gulf widens between the two ideals, and its ultimate bridging becomes a matter of greater difficulty. While on the one hand the Northern Nigeria Administration has had the priceless advantage of " starting fresh " and has been compelled to concentrate upon political and administrative problems, British rule in Southern Nigeria has been the slow growth of years, advancing here by conquest, there by pacific penetration, here by one kind of arrangement with native Chiefs, there by another kind of arrangement. Politically and of necessity British rule in Southern Nigeria is a thing of shreds and patches. The last two Governors, both very able men in their respective ways, have had, moreover, strong leanings in particular directions ; sanitation was the loadstar of the first ; road construction, clearing of creeks and channels, harbour improvements and commercial development the chief purpose of the latter. It is no reflection upon either (the material advance of the Protectorate under Sir Walter Egerton's administration has been amazing) to say that, between them, questions vitally affecting the national existence of the people, the study and organization of their laws and courts and administrative authority, have been left somewhat in the background. In criticizing a West African Administration it must always be borne in mind that no broad lines of public policy are laid down from home. None of the Secretary of State's advisers have ever visited Nigeria, and however able they may be that is a disadvantage. There is no West African Council composed of men with experience of the country, as there ought to be, which would assist the Permanent Officials in advising the Secretary of State. The result is that each Governor and each Acting-Governor " runs his own show " as the saying is. One set of problems is jerked forwards by this Governor, another by another. The Governor's position is rather like that of a Roman Emperor's, and the officials responsible for large districts, never knowing what a new Governor's policy is going to be, look upon every fresh change with nervous apprehension, which has a very unsettling effect. A vast wastage of time as well as many errors would be avoided if we had clear ideas at home as to the goal we are pursuing, and laid down specific principles by which that goal could be attained. This could be done without hampering the Governors. Indeed, the very indefiniteness of the home view on all these problems is often a serious handicap to a Governor who, for that very reason, may hesitate to take action where action is required, fearing, rightly or wrongly, the influence which Parliamentary questions may exercise upon the Secretary of State, and who may also find himself committed by an Acting-Governor, in his absence, to actions of which he personally disapproves. In other instances the existence of definite plans in London would act as a salutary check upon sudden innovations by a new and inexperienced Governor. Frequent changes of Governors there must be until the conditions of life in Nigeria are very much improved ; but the inconveniences arising therefrom would be largely mitigated if there were continuity of a well-thought-out policy at home.

This digression is not, perhaps, altogether irrelevant to the subject under discussion.

The position of Northern Nigeria is very anomalous. A vast Protectorate shut off from the seaboard by another less than four times its size ; having no coastline, and the customs dues on whose trade are collected by the latter. Southern Nigeria enjoying a very large revenue ; its officials decently housed and catered for ; able to spend freely upon public works and to develop its natural resources. Northern Nigeria still poor, a pensioner upon the Treasury, in part upon Southern Nigeria ; unable to stir a step in the direction of a methodical exploration of its vegetable riches ; its officials housed in a manner which is generally indifferent and sometimes disgraceful, many of them in receipt of ridiculously inadequate salaries, and now deprived even of their travelling allowance of five shillings a day. The latter measure is so unjust that a word must be said on the subject. The reason for the grant of this allowance [which the Southern Nigerian official enjoys] was frequent travelling, expensive living, and mud-house accommodation. As regards the two first, the arguments to-day are even stronger than they used to be. The safety of the roads and the increased pressure of political work compels the Resident and his assistants to be more or less constantly on the move if they are worth their salt. When travelling about the country, 4s. to 5s. a day and sometimes a little more is an inevitable expenditure ; at present, a clear out-of-pocket one. As to living, it is a commonplace that the price of local food supplies is very much higher than it was seven years ago, while the price of goods imported from abroad have not all appreciably decreased. So far as the mud-houses are concerned, probably more than half the officials, except at places like Zungeru and Kano, live in mud-houses to-day. The Resident at Naraguta, for instance, lives in a leaky mud-house, while the Niger Company's representative at Joss, five miles off, has a beautiful and spacious residence of brick and timber. A good mud-house is not to be despised, but the money to build even good ones is quite inadequate. I could give several examples where officials have spent considerable sums out of their own pockets to build themselves a decent habitation of mud and thatch. Some of the juniors have to be content with grass-houses, draughty, bitterly cold at night and in the early morning, and leaky to boot. Moreover, many of the brick-houses supplied are an uncommonly poor exchange for £90 a year. They are made of rough local brick, which already show symptoms of decay, and the roof is often so flimsy that in the verandah and supper-room one has to keep one's helmet on as protection against the sun. I am not at all sure that the real official objection to all but leading officials bringing out their wives is not to be sought in the assumption that married officials, other than of the first grade, would no longer put up with the crude discomfort they now live in, and would be a little more chary of ruining their health by touring about in the rains—at their own expense. That Northern Nigeria is not under present conditions a fit place for other than an exceptional type of woman I reluctantly admit ; but that the constant aim of Government should be to improve conditions in order to make it so I am fully persuaded. Our women as well as our men have built up the Empire and made it, on the whole, the clean and fine thing it is, and what a good woman, provided she is also a physically strong one, can accomplish in Northern Nigeria is beyond calculation. It is not too much to say of a very extensive region in the eastern part of the Protectorate, that the moral influence of one such woman is powerfully felt throughout its length and breadth. Other aspects of this question will obviously suggest themselves, and they ought to be boldly tackled; but the national prudery makes it difficult to discuss such matters openly. The salaries paid in Northern Nigeria fill one with astonishment. The salary of a first class Resident appears to vary from £700 to £800 ; that of a second class Resident from £550 to £650 ; that of a third class Resident from £450 to £550. Kano Province when I visited it was in charge of a third class Resident, admittedly one of the ablest officials in the country, by the way ; that is to say, an official drawing £470 a year was responsible for a region as large as Scotland and Wales, with a population of 2,571,170 ! The Bauchi Province was in charge of a second class Resident, drawing £570 a year ; it is the size of Greece, has a population of about three-quarters of a million, and additional administrative anxieties through the advent of a white mining industry. These two instances will suffice. The men saddled with these immense responsibilities are really Lieutenant-Governors and should be paid as such. It is perfectly absurd that an official in whom sufficient confidence is reposed to be given the task of governing a huge Province like Kano should be paid the salary of a bank clerk, when, for instance, the Governor of Sierra Leone, with half the population,* is drawing £2500, exclusive of allowances. A comparison of the Northern Nigeria salaries with those paid to the Governors of the West Indian Islands gives furiously to think. The Governorship of the Bahamas, 4404 square miles in extent, with a population of 61,277, is apparently worth £2000; that of the Bermudas, with an area of twenty-nine square miles and a population of 17,535, £2946; that of Barbados, 166 square miles and a population of 196,498, £2500.

* Whose administration offers no problems comparable with the task of governing a Hausa province.

CHAPTER XVIII

RAILWAY POLICY AND AMALGAMATION

To all these incongruities must be added the series of
events which have led to the creation of two competing
railway systems, and, consequently, to open rivalry
between the two Administrations in the effort to secure the
traffic from the interior, a rivalry which is certainly not
lessened by the circumstance that the method of railway
construction followed in one Protectorate differs radically
from that pursued in the other. This rivalry, needless to
say, is perfectly honourable to both sides, but it is deplorable, nevertheless, and not in the public interest, and
were the two systems placed under one management before
the amalgamation of the Protectorates, *i.e.* if Southern
Nigeria took over the Northern line, which it very naturally wishes to do, having lent the money for its construction, and not appreciating the *rôle* of milch cow without
adequate return, friction between the railway management and the Political Staff would be inevitable owing to
the fundamental divergence of method already referred
to. Moreover, the results achieved by Mr. Eaglesome and
his staff in laying the Baro-Kano railway have been of so
revolutionary a character as to suggest the advisability of
reconsidering the whole policy of railway construction in
British West Africa, such as has been pursued hitherto.
I will refer briefly to this method in a moment. Mean-
while the position of the competing lines is roughly this.
Southern Nigeria has built—or rather is building, for the last
section is not quite finished—a railway from Lagos which

194

SCENE ON THE SOUTHERN NIGERIA (EXTENSION) RAILWAY.

PLATE-LAYING ON THE NORTHERN NIGERIA RAILWAY.

crosses the Niger at Jebba, proceeds therefrom to Zungeru, the capital of Northern Nigeria, and onwards to a place called Minna.* Northern Nigeria has built a railway from Baro, a spot 407 miles up the Niger to Minna, where the junction is effected, and thence to Kano. Southern Nigeria, which looks upon the Northern Protectorate as its natural hinterland, wishes to attract the trade of the north over its line to Lagos, and desires that the through rates it has drawn up should be accepted by Northern Nigeria, and claims the right of fixing the rates on the section of its railway from the point where it enters Northern Nigeria territory (Offa) to the point of junction. The Northern Nigeria Administration, which does not in the least regard itself as the natural appanage of Southern Nigeria, desires to feed the Baro-Kano railway in conjunction with the Niger, and declares that the through rates proposed by Southern Nigeria are so manipulated as to ensure the deflection of the northern trade to Lagos and thus to starve the Baro-Kano line, which would tend to reduce a considerable section of it, apart from its very definite strategical importance, to scrap iron. That was the position when I left the country, and I do not gather that it has greatly advanced since. There has been a conference, but it has not resulted, and could not result, in agreement as to the question of what line is to get preferential treatment ; and that, of course, is the main question which should be decided by an impartial authority, having regard to the interests of Nigeria as a whole. Now a word as to the two systems. So far as governing principles are concerned, it would probably be regarded as a fair description to state that the Southern Nigerian method is less concerned with capital expenditure and with rapidity of construction, as with the advisability of securing permanently good construction and putting in permanent work throughout, including stone ballast, fine stations and so

* Now the capital of the Niger province.

on. The Northern Nigerian method, on the other hand, aims at keeping down initial capital expenditure and interest, exercising strict economy in the matter of buildings, both for the public and for the staff, combined with rapidity of construction and improving the line as the traffic grows. These ideas represent two schools of thought, and beyond the general remark that a rich Administration may be able to afford what a poor one certainly cannot, the non-expert had best not venture upon an expression of opinion lest. peradventure he be ground between the upper and the nether millstone. But as regards the respective systems under which these principles are carried out, it is impossible to resist the conclusion that Northern Nigeria has demonstrably proved its superiority so far as actual construction is concerned. The Southern Nigeria line has been, and is being, constructed on the old model. Consulting engineers in London are employed by the Colonial Office, and appoint the staff in Africa. They are unchecked, for the Colonial Office has no independent railway adviser for tropical Africa, no railway board, or department, or anything of that kind. Thus there are two distinct staffs concerned, a staff appointed by and responsible to the Consulting Engineers in London, and the General Manager's Staff in the Dependency. Where the responsibility of one begins and the other ends, both would probably find it difficult to define ; and no one who knows West Africa can fail to appreciate the divided counsels, the friction, the waste of time and money which such a system must inevitably entail, even though every human rivet in the machine were endowed with superlative qualities. It is very difficult to arrive at a clear idea as to what the average expenditure of the Southern Nigerian railway has been per mile, but it does not appear to be disputed that the cost of construction of the first section of 120 miles to Ibadan, plus the capital expenditure incurred on the open line and the working capital for stores, was

LANDING-PLACE AT BARO.

GROUP OF RAILWAY LABOURERS—BARO.

enormous, viz. £11,000 per mile. The expenditure upon the remaining sections will probably be found to work out at an average of between £5000 and £6000 per mile, exclusive of railway stock and maintenance. Contract labour has been employed except in the later stages, when the line entering Northern Nigeria territory has come under the system of political recruiting which will now be described.

The great advantage which the Northern Nigerian system possesses over that of Southern Nigeria is unity of direction. But the vital difference between the two systems is this : Northern Nigeria has shown that it is possible to construct a railway without the services of Consulting Engineers in England at all. Now this is a fact which cannot be too pointedly emphasized ; because Consulting Engineers are most expensive luxuries if they are not necessities. The logical deduction is, either that Consulting Engineers can be, and if they can be should be, dispensed with for any future railways in West Africa ; or that the Baro-Kano railway, without them, is a failure. It appears to me that the Baro-Kano railway has been a marvellous success from the point of view of construction. What are the facts ? The Administration, *i.e.* its Public Works Department, with the help of a few Royal Engineer officers lent by the Home Government, has been its own builder. The absence of any foreign body has reduced friction to a minimum. In fact, there has been no friction whatever, because the Railway Staff has co-operated in every way with the Political Staff, and the exercise of the Political Officers' legitimate duties in protecting the interests of the natives has not been resented or looked upon in the light of vexatious interference by the railway management. I should be the last to wish to minimize the excellence of the individual work performed by the engineers in charge of the Southern Nigeria line, which I was able to admire, and from whom I received the greatest hospitality and kindness at various stages in my journey; but the nature of the system there followed precludes that enthusiastic co-operation of all the elements concerned which is the predominating characteristic of Northern Nigerian methods. And, as already stated, there is a very considerable item of expense to be considered through the employment of Consulting Engineers in London. In the Northern Protectorate every one, from the Governor—the Baro-Kano railway owes, of course, its inception to Sir Percy Girouard—down to the foreman, has been, as it were, a member of a single family. In fact, one might almost say that the line has been built on the communistic principle. In no direction does the system show better results than in the organization of labour. It has proved to demonstration what is the right way of dealing with native labour in West Africa, viz. : that the labourer on public works shall be drawn from the neighbourhood where the public works are situate, that he shall proceed to the scene of his labours accompanied by his own Village or District Headman, the native authority to whom he owes allegiance, and whom he knows and trusts ; that he shall perform his duties in the presence and under the supervision of that Headman, and that for the conduct of the Headman himself, and for the whole proceedings under which recruitment is carried on and labour performed, the Political Officer shall be responsible. In other words, it shows the right procedure to be that of recruiting through and with the co-operation of, and by the orders of, the natural authorities of the people under the supreme control of the Resident, combined with a form of payment which shall ensure the wage being placed in the wage-earner's own hand, not in somebody else's hand. By this system alone can the labour of the country employed in agricultural and industrial pursuits be capable of bearing an additional burden for public purposes, without injustice, without ferment, without dislocating the whole

VILLAGE HEAD-MEN.

VILLAGE HEAD-MEN.

labour system of the region. Persuaded of this truth, the
Political Officers of Northern Nigeria, aided by the ready
willingness of the Railway Staff, have achieved a veritable
triumph of organization which should ever remain a model
to follow. And in that triumph can be read a deep
political lesson. That such organization has been possible
in Northern Nigeria is due, primarily, to the existence of
a native political organization to which we could appeal
and upon which we could rely. The principle adopted on
the works themselves has been to give to each foreman his
own set of Headmen, with their own gangs to look after,
and to so regulate the labour that no individual should
work more than eight hours *per diem*. Built under
conditions such as these, the Northern Nigeria railway,
constructed under great difficulties with wonderful
rapidity and at a cost of well under £4000 per mile,
rolling-stock and stores included, is not only in itself a
striking performance—with, I believe, if free conditions of
development are assured to it, a bright economic future—
but a political and educational work of permanent value.
It has helped to bring the Political Officers into closer
personal touch with the population. It has increased the
confidence of the people in the honesty of their alien
overlords, and has imbued them with a personal interest
and friendly curiosity in the railway. It has taught them
many things which they did not know before, things which
will be useful to themselves in their own social life. It has
brought previously hostile tribes together into the same
trench, effacing tribal barriers and burying old feuds. It
has largely increased the use of silver coinage, and stimulated commercial activity. The same system is being
followed in the construction, now proceeding, of the branch
line towards the tin-fields ; but many more railways will be
required to develop the commercial potentialities of
Northern Nigeria, and the fact constitutes one more
argument to those already given in favour of an

amalgamation of the two Protectorates, and the evolution of one set of governing ideas.

I cannot leave the question of railway construction in the Nigerias without expressing regret that in authorizing the construction of the new line, the Colonial Office should have been led to break the gauge, and to decide upon a 2 feet 6 inch line instead of the 3 feet 6 inch standard. Apart from other objections, which can be urged more fittingly by experts, it is obvious that this departure necessitates a complete equipment of new rolling stock, and the erection of special engineering shops to deal with it. Every freshly constructed line is bound to have a surplus of rolling stock. The Baro-Kano railway is no exception to the rule, and its surplus stock could have been utilized on the new branch line. It is a penny wise and pound foolish policy, and, in all probability, the ultimate result will be that this 2 feet 6 inch line will cost very little, if at all, less than a 3 feet 6 inch would have done.

CHAPTER XIX

AN effort was made in the previous chapter to depict some of the disadvantages and drawbacks arising, and likely to become accentuated with time, from the dual administrative control now obtaining in Nigeria. For the following suggestions as to the character amalgamation could assume, the writer claims no more than that they may, perhaps, constitute an attempt, put forward with much diffidence, to indicate a few constructive ideas which might form the basis for expert discussion.

The objects an amalgamation might be expected to secure, apart from the inconveniences needing removal, would, in the main, be four in number. (*a*) Financial management directed not only to meeting present needs but to making provision for the future. (*b*) The right sort of man to fill the important and onerous post of Governor-General. (*c*) The division of the territory into Provinces corresponding as far as possible with natural geographical boundaries and existing political conditions, involving as few changes as possible. (*d*) A comprehensive scheme of public works.

These various points can, in the limits of a chapter, be best examined collectively.

In the accompanying map Nigeria is divided into four great Provinces. I. The Northern or Sudan Province, comprising the regions where a Mohammedan civilization has existed for many centuries, and where the majority of the people, except in Kontagora, are Muslims. The ruling families in Kontagora are, however, so closely related with those of Sokoto that it would probably be found expedient to incorporate the former into the same Province, which would, therefore, consist of Sokoto, Kano, Bornu, the Zaria Emirate and Kontagora. Its headquarters would be Kano. II. The Central Province, comprising the pagan section of the present Zaria province, *i.e.* Zaria outside the limits of the Emirate proper, and the Nassarawa, Bauchi, Niger, Yola, and Muri (north of the Benue) provinces. It is not quite easy to forecast where the centre of gravity of the Central Province will ultimately fall, but if, as is possible, the Bauchi highlands become in time a second Simla for the Central Executive, the headquarters of the Central Province would presumably be fixed at Zungeru, the present capital of the Northern Protectorate. III. The Western Province, comprising all that is now incorporated in the existing western province of Southern Nigeria, plus—to the north—Kabba, Ilorin and Borgu, while the right bank of the Forcados and Niger would form the eastern boundary, the boundaries of the Province following natural lines. Its headquarters would be Oshogbo, or its immediate neighbourhood. IV. The Eastern Province, comprising what is now the eastern province of South Nigeria, but with its western frontier coterminous with the left bank of the Niger and Forcados and its northern frontiers pushed up to the south bank of the Benue, embracing Bassa and part of Muri, Yola, however, being left, for political reasons, in the Central Province, as noted above. Its headquarters would be Old Calabar, the starting-point of the future eastern railway (see map).

Each of these great provinces would be ruled by a Lieutenant-Governor, with Residents and Assistant Residents under him, and, wherever possible, the present political boundaries of what are now provinces, but would become known as districts and sub-districts, would be retained. Thus in the Northern or Sudan Province nothing would be changed in this respect, save the separation of Mohammedan Zaria from pagan Zaria ; nothing would be changed in the Central Province, so far as the units remaining within it were concerned, except the division of Muri, which would offer no political embarrassments. The enlargement of the Eastern Province as proposed, would in some respects facilitate the work of administration and would not cut across any ethnic divisions. In the Western Province the principal alteration would be the re-grouping of the different Yoruba sections in their old state form (*vide* Part II.) under a Resident who would reside at Oyo ; Ilorin, Kabba, and Borgu would remain under Residents as at present. Warri (the capital of the existing central province of Southern Nigeria) would become the seat of a Residency for the Bini, Sobo, Ijaw and Jekri speaking peoples.

Lagos town would continue to be what the expenditure of much money, and the enterprise of the Yorubas, have made it, the commercial emporium of at least the western portion of the Protectorate, and the headquarters of the small surrounding area known as the " Colony " (*vide* Part II.), administered by a " Lagos Council," which would replace the present " Lagos Legislative Council," and be composed of much the same elements as the latter now consists of, presided over by a Resident. The functions of the Lagos Council would be confined to the Colony.

The headquarters of the Governor-General and the central seat of Government would be the high plateau immediately behind Lokoja, known as Mount Patte, situated in the very centre of the Protectorate, commanding the Niger and the Benue, within easy steam of Baro the starting-point of the central railway, and linked up with the western railway by a branch line to Oshogbo as indicated on the map. The Governor-General would be assisted by an Executive and Legislative Council. Of the former the Lieutenant-Governors and Senior Residents would be *ex officio* members, together with the Chief Justice, the Colonial Secretary, the Financial Secretary, and the officer commanding the troops. The official members of the Legislative Council would include the Directors of rail and river transport, of public works, of agriculture, of forestry and of commercial intelligence ; the Director of mining ; and the Principal Medical Officer. The unofficial members would include selected representatives of the educated native community, and, later on, one or two distinguished Mallams, and selected representatives of the European commercial and mining communities.

Possibly, in course of time, the work of the Council could be carried out in conjunction with periodical Durbars attended by all the important Emirs, but in no case would the functions of the Council be allowed to conflict with the Native Administrations of the Mohammedan Provinces.

The method of handling the finances of the Protectorate would depend to a large extent upon the capacity of the Home Government, in conjunction with the potential Governor-General and other advisers, to map out ahead a considered scheme of railway construction and improvement of fluvial communications, which would proceed from year to year and for which provision would be made. The whole problem of communications, both rail and river, ought to be placed under a special department, subject to periodical inspection by an independent expert sent out from home by the Colonial Office, and the services of consulting engineers in England disposed of if possible. The situation financially lends itself, in a general sense, to a certain boldness of treatment and departure from ordinary British West African precedent. Two distinct classes of budgets might with advantage, perhaps, be

SKETCH MAP OF NIGERIA,

SHOWING SUGGESTED REARRANGEMENT OF PROVINCES.

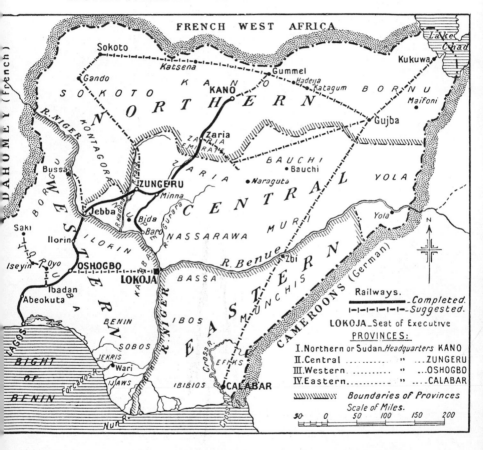

evolved, viz. a Colonial budget and the Provincial budgets. In other words, there would be a central budget and four local budgets, one for each Province. The Colonial budget would be fed by the customs revenue, the whole of which would be credited to it. (It may be estimated that two or three years hence the total customs revenue collected in Nigeria will amount to £2,500,000.) It would be augmented by the profits on the railways, the mining royalties, harbour dues, and pilotage fees (there should be a system of public pilotage on the waterways). The Protectorate could be authorized to raise a loan on its own recognizances of £5,000,000 redeemable in a term of years. This loan would be expended in a succession of public works—some of the necessary lines of rail are indicated in the map—in accordance with the scheme of construction mapped out as previously suggested. The Colonial budget would determine the successive instalments of expenditure out of loans, and would provide the interest on the new loan and on the existing loan of £5,000,000 contracted by Southern Nigeria (for public works in Southern and Northern Nigeria). The revenues of the Colonial budget from whatever source derived, other than from loans, would.be distributed by the Governor-General in council for the administration of the four Provinces in accordance with their respective needs. These needs would show marked variation for some years to come. For instance, the hypothetical Northern and Central Provinces (*i.e.* the territory which now comprises the bulk of Northern Nigeria), relying upon the increasing regularity and juster assessment of internal direct taxation, the nature of which may roughly be termed a graduated property tax, might be expected to advance steadily towards the self-supporting stage. When that stage had been reached, the surplus would be set aside under the Provincial budget for extending the system of fixed salaries to native officials, for expenditure on provincial public works and economic research, improvements in sanitation, and so on, in collaboration with the native authorities of its various sections. A portion of my hypothetical Northern or Sudan Province is already self-supporting, viz. Kano. Indeed, but for the military establishment the whole of that Province would be showing to-day a handsome surplus and, apart from the public works to be met out of loans, would require—even if it continued to be debited with the military establishment—very little assistance from the Colonial budget. The hypothetical Central Province would require more assistance for a time, but, as in the Northern Province, the basis of an expanding land revenue is securely laid and a not inconsiderable mineral development bringing revenue, apart from royalties, is assured to it. On the other hand, most of the hypothetical Western Province and almost the whole of the Eastern Province—*i.e.* in combination, Southern Nigeria of to-day—produces no internal revenue whatever except licences, the amount derived from which will assuredly grow but will not become really large for many years. Therefore, until and unless the delicate problem of introducing direct taxation among peoples—the majority of whom we have been in touch with for years without requiring of them the payment of any form of tribute— were approached, the Colonial budget would have to furnish these Provinces with most of their administrative revenues.

An alternative scheme would be to abandon the idea of a Central Legislative Council for the whole Protectorate and of a new administrative headquarters, the Governor-General spending a certain time at the headquarters of each Province. Lagos would, under such a scheme, become the capital of the extended Western Province (see map), and the action of the Lagos Legislative Council would extend to the whole of that Province. A Legislative Council would be created for the extended Eastern

Province. The administrative machinery of the new Central and Northern Provinces would be left as it is now. On the finance side the alternative scheme to the one I have sketched would be to let each Province contribute to the Colonial budget in accordance with its capacities upon a definite proportionate basis, the sums thus accruing to the Colonial budget, *plus* the loan funds, being utilized in the creation of public works on the lines already sketched. This alternative scheme, amalgamation on federation, would possess some advantages over the first, and compares unfavourably with it in others.

It will be objected that these suggestions do not take into account the present military expenditure of the Protectorates and are dumb with regard to the Imperial grant to Northern Nigeria. I have left a consideration of these two questions until now because they can, I think, be taken together. The military establishment of Southern Nigeria costs £100,000 per annum. That of Northern Nigeria costs £160,000 per annum. Neither is excessive in itself, although in the latter case it amounts to no less than 33 per cent. of the total expenditure of the Protectorate ! It is not one penny too much, and to reduce the number of troops would be folly, having regard to the immensity of the country and the kind of political problem facing us. And yet could anything be more topsyturvey ? Here is a financially struggling Protectorate urgently in need of the most vital necessities ; incapable even of building decent houses for its over-worked and short-handed staff ; forced to deprive the latter of even their travelling allowances, and to sacrifice considerations of reasonable comfort and, therefore, of health for its *personnel ;* in a position to pay so little for posts of enormous responsibility that the entire political expenditure is only some £70,000 per annum ; able to devote but a miserable £1300 a year upon economic forestry, but saddled with this incubus of £160,000 upon a military establishment which has already been called upon (in the case of the last Ashanti war) to provide contingents for service outside the Protectorate, which would infallibly happen again, in the by no means remote contingencies of a further outbreak in Ashanti or disturbances in the Sierra Leone hinterland. This situation needs to be examined in conjunction with the Imperial grant about which so much fuss is made.

The nation imagines that Northern Nigeria is costing the Imperial Treasury something like £250,000 to £300,000 per annum. Nothing of the kind. The grants in aid from 1906 to 1909, inclusive, amounted to £1,220,000, or an average of £305,000. But against this must be set the direct profit to the revenues of the United Kingdom derived from the profit which the Mint makes upon the silver coin exported, in ever increasing quantities (and the process will go on extending), to the two Nigerias. The average yearly cost of silver in the last nine years has, I believe, varied between 2s. 0¾d. and 2s. 6⅞d. The coin at par value is issued at 5s. 6d. an ounce, and I am credibly informed that the profit to the Mint is considerably more than half the net import by Nigeria, seeing that half the face value of the coinage is greater than the cost of minting, plus maintenance of gold reserve and provision for remitting. The net export of coinage, virtually the whole of it silver, to the two Nigerias (*i.e.* the total exported *minus* the coin returned) amounted from 1906 to 1909 to £981,582. If the profit of the Mint is taken at only 50 per cent., it will thus be seen that the nation is making a direct average profit of nearly £125,000 a year out of the two Nigerias, against an average of £305,000 paid to Northern Nigeria by way of a temporary grant in aid. To say, therefore, that Northern Nigeria is costing the British taxpayer a quarter of a million a year or more, is to make a statement which is not in accordance with fact. What the nation advances directly, it recoups itself for directly in part; without counting that these grants are in the nature of a capital investment. Let this grant under amalgamation be cancelled, and let the Imperial Government, on the other hand, foot the bill for the military expenditure (which, as we have seen, amounts to £260,000), looking upon it, say, for the next ten years as Imperial expenditure. Nothing would so alleviate the whole situation, while at the same time simplifying it, and, as has been shown, the actual disbursement of the nation on this item would be considerably less, even now, than what it would appear nominally to be, owing to the profit made by the Mint on the silver coin sent out.

As already explained, the above proposals, illustrated in part by the accompanying map, are put forward merely as a basis for the discussion of a problem of some difficulty but of great urgency. I claim for them nothing more than that, and no conceivable scheme of amalgamation could be set down which would not lend itself to copious criticism. But that the mush of anomalies now obtaining cannot be perpetuated without increasing detriment to Imperial interests in Nigeria, I am fully persuaded. The existence of two public policies side by side in a single territorial area, where internal peace is rapidly fusing the indigenous communities, divided by an imaginary line which does not even correspond to natural boundaries and exhibiting multiple differences of aim and method—in some cases, acutely antagonistic interests—presents many obvious inconveniences and paves the way for future embarrassments of every kind. If these remarks can influence in any way an early and serious examination of the problem by the Colonial Office, they will not, however open to criticism, have been made in vain. Amalgamation must come. All realize that. Unforeseen events might very well, at a given moment, compel decisions of far-reaching moment being precipitately reached without due consideration being given to all the features of the case, such as characterized the amalgamation of the Lagos Colony and Protectorate with old Southern Nigeria in 1899. The advantages of clear thinking out ahead, and of taking the inevitable step before the situation has got tied up into more knots than it already contains, with calm deliberation, after a full and serious study of all the facts, surely needs no emphasizing. As to the man, a last word. The responsibility of selecting the official to be in supreme control over the amalgamated Nigerias is no light one. The task confronting a Governor-General, especially in the first five years, will be replete with difficulties. The post will need heavy calls upon tact, patience, and a peculiarly high type of constructive statesmanship. The only remark I would venture to make on the point is this. Any serious administrative error perpetrated in handling affairs in the north would be attended with consequences of exceeding gravity. That is a proposition I think no one will be inclined to dispute. It suggests either that the Governor-General himself should be personally acquainted with the political conditions of what is now known as Northern Nigeria, or, at least, that the Lieutenant-Governors of the hypothetical Northern and Central Provinces should be chosen from among the most experienced of the existing Senior Residents.

PART IV

ISLAM, COTTON GROWING, AND THE LIQUOR TRAFFIC

CHAPTER I

CHRISTIANITY AND ISLAM IN SOUTHERN NIGERIA

I HAVE referred to Christian missionary propaganda in Mohammedan Northern Nigeria. There has now to be considered the question of Christian missionary propaganda in Southern Nigeria, and the corresponding growth therein of Mohammedanism. The relative failure of the one and the admitted success of the other are at present the subject of much debate and give anxious thought to the heads of the Church. The fundamental cause appears to lie in a disinclination to face the fact, however obvious, that a religion which took centuries upon centuries to take root in Europe, owing, very largely, to its ethical demands upon man, cannot hope to establish itself in the now accessible tropical forest regions of West Africa in a few decades, while a religion embodying a distinct advance upon paganism but not involving the complete structural change in native society which the Christian Church exacts, has every chance of doing so. Then, too, there is another question which the ecclesiastical authorities may never, it is true, find it possible frankly to confront, but which laymen, it seems to me, are bound to do—those, at any rate, who are persuaded that the African race is one of the great races of mankind, not intended by the Almighty Architect to disappear from the scene of human affairs. I refer to the physiological requirements, in the present age, of the Nigerian forest peoples in their struggles with the forces of primeval Nature.

NIGERIA : ITS PEOPLES AND ITS PROBLEMS

All that remains of the Portuguese attempts to Christianize the deltaic region of Nigeria in the fourteenth and fifteenth centuries are a few names and the addition of crucifixion to native punishments of criminals or happy despatch of sacrificial victims. The chief obstacle to the modern efforts of the Anglo-Saxon in Southern Nigeria and the real explanation of the successful modern efforts of the African Muslim, are to be sought in the appeal respectively made by Christianity and Islam to the patriarchal communities to which they are addressed, and in the methods and character of the respective propaganda. Christianity in West Africa either cannot be divorced, or cannot divorce itself, from Europeanism and the twentieth century. It remains for the people of Nigeria, and of all West Africa, an alien religion taught by aliens who cannot assimilate themselves to the life of the people. Islam, on the other hand, has long ceased to be an alien religion. It is imparted by Africans. It is disseminated by Africans. It has its roots in the soil. It has become a religion of the people, losing much of its rigidity and fanaticism as it works down to the coast absorbing the true negro.

Everything is against Christianity as presented to the Nigerian (I venture to emphasize this), and everything is in favour of Islam, although Christianity, in itself, contains more that should appeal to the Negro character than does Mohammedanism. The conditions of Southern Nigeria are the conditions of the Old Testament. The crying need of the country, as of all western tropical Africa, is the need which is proclaimed in, and stamps itself upon, every page of the book of Genesis, the Divinely ordained requirement—population. Vice plays only a microscopic part in the relationship of sex in Nigeria. Race propagation is the motive force which regulates sexual relationship. The Nigerian, incessantly striving with the destructive agencies of Nature, responds to the instinctive and mysterious call of racial necessity. Infant

214

mortality is terrible. With the Nigerian the reproduction of the species is the paramount, if unanalyzed and, no doubt, uncomprehended obsession. It must continue to be so for a period whose limit will be determined by the rate of his progression in coping with these destructive agencies.

This is not the place to discuss what the attitude of the Christian missionary should be to this paramount racial need, but it is obvious that his insistence upon an acceptance of a sex relationship contrary to the promptings of Nature must present a barrier—one of the greatest, if not the greatest—to the acceptance of the Christian faith, or, perhaps, it would be better to say, of orthodox Christianity. One might be permitted, perhaps, to suggest that those who are disposed to regard the condition of the Nigerian forest-dweller in these matters as calling for hard and rigid regulation, are too prone to forget what Lecky describes as the " appalling amount of moral evil, festering uncontrolled, undiscussed and unalleviated under the fair surface of a decorous society," in civilized Europe, monogamistic social laws notwithstanding. Sex relationship, whatever its character and whatever the conditions of society or climate, is never, and can never be, free from abuses. West African polygamy contains many ugly sores, and so does the European system.

Family bonds are equally threatened by Christianity, *as propounded to the Nigerian,* for it trains the child, whether deliberately or otherwise, to look upon his parents as living a life of sin, thus introducing a subversive element into the household. Those who assert the absence of affections and sanctities in Nigerian family life assert that which is untrue. Native authority is likewise menaced, for how can the convert entertain his former respect for rulers whom he has been taught to regard as morally and spiritually his inferiors ? These are some of the reasons why Christianity, *as propounded to the Nigerian,* at the opening of the twentieth century, presents itself to him in the light of a hurtful and disintegrating influence. And this creed is proffered either by aliens between whom and the inner life of the people there yawns an unbridgeable gulf, or by denationalized Africans who have become in the eyes of the people, strangers well-nigh as complete as the alien himself, part and parcel of the alien's machinery. As if these did not constitute sufficient deterrents to the permanency of its footing, the alien race which tenders to the Nigerian this creed—this creed claiming for all men equality before God —is the conquering, controlling, governing race that scorns to admit—because, being an Imperial race, it cannot— equality of racial status with the Nigerian whom it sub- jugates and controls. Between the race of the converter and that of the would-be convert there gapes an abyss of racial and social inequality which does not lessen, but, if anything, widens with conversion—the colour line.

Finally, there is the lamentable intolerance displayed by Christian proselytizers towards one another. Only the other day I read in a West African newspaper the address of a white American Protestant Bishop, whose sphere of work lies in Africa, to his flock. This episcopalian inter- preter of the Gospel of Christian charity to the benighted African is concerned in his address with the downfall of the Portuguese Monarchy and the accession of the Republic which, he says, " opens wide every door leading to Christian work among millions of native Africans." He proceeds : " Of course Rome howls. On October 13, 1910, among weeping Jesuits, speaking of the new nation, the Pope said ' A cursed Republic ! Yes, I curse it ! ' The curse of Balaam against the people of God was turned into a blessing by Jehovah ; and so, too, will this blasphemy be turned into a blessing to the struggling people of Portugal."

Islam, on the other hand, despite its shortcomings, does not, from the Nigerian point of view, demand race suicide of the Nigerian as an accompaniment of conversion. It does not stipulate revolutionary changes in social life, impossible at the present stage of Nigerian development ; nor does it undermine family or communal authority. Between the converter and converted there is no abyss. Both are equal, not in theory, but in practice, before God. Both are African ; sons of the soil. The doctrine of the brotherhood of man is carried out in practice. Conversion does not mean for the converted a break with his interests, his family, his social life, his respect for the authority of his natural rulers. He is not left stranded, as the Christian Church, having once converted, leaves him, a pitiful, rudderless barque upon a troubled sea. He does not become, through conversion, an alien in thought, in custom, and in outlook ; a foreigner in his own land, a citizen of none. He remains African, attached to his country, looking for inspiration inwards, rather than towards an alien civilization across thousands of miles of unknown seas. No one can fail to be impressed with the carriage, the dignity of the Nigerian—indeed, of the West African—Mohammedan ; the whole bearing of the man suggests a consciousness of citizenship, a pride of race which seems to say : " We are different, thou and I, but we are *men*." The spread of Islam in Southern Nigeria which we are witnessing to-day is mainly social in its action. It brings to those with whom it comes in contact a higher status, a loftier conception of man's place in the universe around him, release from the thraldom of a thousand superstitious fears. It resembles in its progress the annual overflow of the Niger diffusing its waters over the land. The extensive ramifications of internal trade, now greatly fostered by the construction of additional roads and railways and rendered wholly safe by the *pax britannica*, leads to the multiplying of facilities for human intercourse among the various peoples of the Protectorate. The Hausa pushes ever further south his commercial operations. The Delta, and still more the Western Province, yearly attest to the widening area of his activities. Not to be outdone, his trading rival the Yoruba taps in additional numbers the markets of the north. Railway construction finds the Mohammedan labouring side by side with the pagan in the same trench. A sense of security and the increasing circulation of a portable medium of exchange in the shape of silver and nickel coinage attract to the great native markets of the Central Province, such as Onitsha, for example, the tattoed pagan Ibo and his pagan colleagues the Anams, Katundas, and Kukurukus, where they rub shoulders with the Mohammedan Hausa, Nupe, and Igarra. In and around Ibadan, Oyo, and Lagos you meet the Kano and Sokoto trader with his donkeys and pack-bullocks, and even the Tuareg with whom you parted company months before in the far north, travelling on the roads or camping for the night near some local village. The road is at once the club-house and public rendezvous for Nigerian humanity. A vast commingling, a far-reaching fusion unexampled in the history of these peoples is taking place. The expansion of an African religion which, somehow, succeeds in investing the convert with a spiritual and social standing that at once raise him among his fellows, follows as a matter of course. The Mohammedan teacher wanders over the face of the country visiting the centres of human activity, haunting the roads and market-places, unattended, carrying neither purse nor scrip, making no attempt at proselytizing beyond saying his prayers in public, not in a manner to cause obstruction, but quietly in some corner ; waiting until people come to him, literally fulfilling the command, " Take nothing for your journey, neither staves, nor scrip, neither bread, neither money, neither have two coats apiece." The Mohammedan trader or agriculturist settles in a pagan village, marries pagan women, enters the family and social circle of the community and imparts to it his faith, the women making even readier converts than the men.

This is why and this is how Islam is propagating itself and taking root in pagan Nigeria without financial outlay, without doles and collecting boxes. One of the oldest of Christian missionaries in Nigeria, a man of venerable appearance and saintly character, who for twenty-five years has laboured with hands as well as with heart and head for moral and material improvement, not of his converts only, but of their unconverted relatives, confessed to me his fear that nothing could stop Islam from absorbing in course of time the whole of West Africa. He was almost disposed reluctantly to allow that in the providence of God, Islam might prove to be intended as the half-way house through the portals of which it was necessary the West African negro should pass in order to lift him out of a sterilizing paganism and make him a fitter vessel to receive in course of time the nobler ideals of the Christian faith. Sir Harry Johnston is right, I think, when he says that "to Negro Africa," Islam has come "as a great blessing, raising up savages to a state, at any rate of semi-civilization, making them God-fearing, self-respecting, temperate, courageous, and picturesque." But Islam does more than this; it preserves racial identity. In West Africa, Christianity destroys racial identity. It should not : as taught it does.

"Picturesque," says Sir Harry Johnston, and there speaks the artist. But the word covers a profound truth. A great deal of the denationalizing or Anglicizing process which is going on and which makes bad Africans and bad Christians, is attributable to the discarding of the national dress. Why cannot the Administration and the missionary societies combine in some practical, positive form, to combat this curse of alien dress ? There is absolutely nothing to be said in its favour. The West African looks better in African dress, the robe of the Mohammedan and of many pagan Africans. It is much healthier for him. It is preservative of his racial identity ; and that is, perhaps, the most important of all pleas which can be put forward for its retention. With very slight modification—such as one sees among the native staff, and personal servants in many parts of Northern Nigeria—it can be made suitable for any form of labour, literary or otherwise. Clad in his national dress the African has a dignity which in most cases he loses almost entirely when he attires himself in a costume totally unfitted for the country, and hideous at best. Nothing to my mind is more pitiable than to visit school after school in West Africa, filled with little boys and girls and big boys and girls in an alien dress, to see the denationalizing process going on day after day and nothing whatever done to stop it. In the case of the women it is not only dignity and nationalism which are concerned, but decency as well. The national dress of the women in West Africa is classical and graceful, and although leaving more of the body exposed than is usual at home (except in the ballroom) it lacks suggestiveness. It does not accentuate the figure. It emphasizes that racial difference—not inequality, but *difference*—which it is so essential to emphasize. With the substitution of European dress, especially of the prevailing fashion, the West African woman loses much of what she need never lose, and acquires that which is of no profit to her. These things cannot be altered in a day, nor would it be possible in some cases for the present adult generation to go back to African costume. But it would in many cases, and the reform could be at once taken in hand so far as the children are concerned. Government could do much. The missionary societies could do more. The anglicised native community could do most. I believe that if some popular Government official, known and trusted, could be led to appeal, in private conference to the native staff and win them over, the movement once started would spread and have enormously beneficial results. That many members of the anglicised community would be hostile goes without saying—that is the fault of the wretched system everywhere at work. That a body of thoughtful men would not, I am satisfied by the many representations on this very subject personally made to me. I shall always recollect, in particular, the private visit paid to me in one of the great Yoruba towns by one of the leading merchants of the place. A magnificent specimen of an African, dressed in African costume and speaking our language fluently, he came with the usual touching words and gifts, and begged me very earnestly to take up the question of dress with his compatriots.

And, in conclusion, there is another and a very serious handicap upon Christianity in West Africa, in Southern Nigeria especially. Under the native social system, religion and politics—the religious organization and the political organization—go together. It is inconceivable to the native mind that they should be separate or antagonistic. Islam, again, preserves this ingrained conviction. But in West Africa the political and religious organizations of the white man are separate and distinct. The religious organization itself is split up into countless opposing sections. And in Southern Nigeria the section specially identified in the native mind with the white over-lord has for some years past played a discordant note in that white over-lord's political organization. Its representatives are almost everywhere, and upon many subjects persistently hostile critics of the Administration, begetting unrest and disloyalty to Government. The mass of native opinion concludes there is something rotten in the system presented to it, and the Islamic wave rolls on.

CHAPTER II

Is Nigeria a cotton-growing country? Is an export trade in cotton, of any large dimensions, a possibility—early or remote? I will endeavour to answer these questions to the best of my ability. I am not, however, an expert on cotton-growing, and I am in general sympathy with the work the British Cotton-growing Association is trying to carry out, although, as will be seen, I am not entirely in agreement with all its methods, either here or in Nigeria. To that extent it will be possible for any one who wants to do so to discount the views here expressed.

One of the earliest impressions one forms out there is the contrast between the presentation of the case at home and conditions on the spot. The view at home —somewhat modified by recent events—has seemed to be inspired by the idea that if the number of square miles which Nigeria covers is totted up in one column and the number of inhabitants it supposedly contains in another and these totals compared with conditions in the cotton belt of North America, then you arrive at a conclusion which enables you to speak of the " huge possibilities " of Nigeria, and even to forecast that Northern Nigeria alone " at some future date " will be able " to supply the whole of the requirements of Great Britain and to leave an equal quantity over for the other cotton-consuming countries." Four years ago a

222

prominent British statesman declared publicly that
" once the fly belt near the river was passed . . . cotton
would be grown under exactly the same conditions as
it was grown under on such a great scale in America."
He went so far as to say that the native of Northern
Nigeria was " beginning to cease to grow cotton " because
he could get British manufactured goods in lieu of his
home-grown article. Well, between these statements
and actualities there is a " huge " gulf fixed. In the
first place it can be said of Nigeria that in a part of it
only is cotton now grown, and that in a part of it only
will cotton ever be grown. To talk of Nigeria, as a
whole, being a cotton-growing country *par excellence*,
either now or potentially, is absurd. Three-fourths of
Southern Nigeria and a third, probably more, of Northern
Nigeria are quite unsuitable for cotton-growing, and this
for many reasons. To talk of Nigeria supplying the
whole requirements of Great Britain (to say nothing of
the promised surplus) is tantamount to saying that some
day " Pleasant Sunday Afternoon " excursions to the
moon will be a regular feature of the national life. Both
may become possible " at some future date," but there is
so much future about the date that such flights of rhetoric
might well be left to the compilers of gold-mining pro-
spectuses. These extravagances have not helped the
Association. The sincere and sober persons connected
with that body are merely hindered by them. As to
cotton being produced in Northern Nigeria under the
" same conditions " as in the States, and the natives of
the country " beginning to cease " to grow cotton, one
can only remark that they are too silly to deal with.

In Southern Nigeria, the deltaic region, the Eastern
Province, virtually the whole of the Central Province, and
a considerable portion of the Western Province—*i.e.*,
four-fifths of the whole Protectorate—may be ruled out
of account as a cotton field. The deltaic region will not

produce cotton. The forest belt behind it, passing (with occasional breaks) from dense to secondary growth and fading away into open country, no doubt would. But only if you cut down the forest first. To destroy the West African forest to any extent in order to grow cotton would be economic madness. Indeed, the Administration is working hard to preserve the forests from the ignorance and improvidence of primitive man, and to build up for the native communities, and in the public interest, a source of future revenue from the methodical exploitation of its inexhaustible wealth. With trifling exceptions the whole of this region is the home of the oil-palm, the most beneficent tree in the world, and such activities as the inhabitants can spare from their own requirements are given over, in the main, to the palm oil and kernel trades. It is the home of valuable cabinet woods, of vegetable oils, gums, and rubbers, and in time is likely to become a great natural nursery for the cultivation of plantation rubber and such a moisture-loving plant as the cocoa ; never, I think, of cotton.

In the Western Province large areas of forest have been destroyed ; the population is, in a certain measure, more enterprising, and a fair amount of cotton for export may reasonably be expected, especially, I venture to suggest, if certain methods now prevalent are modified. The Egba district (1869 square miles, with a population of 260,000), the capital of which is Abeokuta, a town of about 100,000 inhabitants, is the principal but not the only centre for cotton-growing in the Western Province, and here the Association has a large and well-equipped ginnery, as it has at Ibadan and Oshogbo. Out of 2,237,370 lbs. of lint cotton exported from Southern Nigeria in 1908, Abeokuta and neighbourhood was responsible for 722,893 lbs. The Egbas are good farmers and not strangers to cotton-growing for export. The industry owes its origin there to a Manchester man, Mr.

Clegg, who introduced it at the time of the American Civil War. In 1862 the export amounted to 1810 lbs., rising in 1868 to over 200,000 lbs., and continuing, I believe, at that figure or thereabouts for some years. Cotton then began to fall heavily in price, and the Egba farmer, finding no profit in growing it, turned his attention to other crops. The industry was revived on a much larger scale by the Association in 1905. The exports of cotton lint from Southern Nigeria from 1906 to 1910—*i.e.* since the Association came upon the scene—have been as follows :—

1906 ..	..	..	.. 2,695,923	1909 ..	..	..	..	.. 4,929,646
1907 ..	..	..	.. 4,089,530	1910 ..	..	..	..	.. 2,399,857
1908 ..	..	..	.. 2,237,370					

The total value of these five years' output amounts to something like £350,000. It is entirely creditable to the Association that it should have been instrumental in reviving a decayed industry in one district and creating one in others, and in five years to have fathered an export of cotton to so considerable an amount. I found the best-informed opinion in Southern Nigeria imbued with the belief that the 1911 crop will be a poor one, though better than last year's, but that the prospects for the crop of 1912 are good. The newly opened ginnery at Oshogbo is said to be doing well. The ginnery at Oyo, however, is apparently lying idle. At any rate, it had done nothing, I was there informed, ever since it was put up, some four years ago. A good deal seems to have been spent upon the experimental plantation at Ibadan, with indifferent results. It has now been taken over by the Government, whose officers, I was informed, found it in a very neglected condition.

Personally, I do not attach, in a sense unfavourable to the growth of the industry, much importance to the drop in the output. The field, it must always be remembered, is small, the entire Western Province being only

27,640 miles square, and much of it, as already stated, covered with forest. In West Africa new industries are always liable to violent fluctuations. The drop in the maize export is much more considerable than the falling off in cotton. Unfavourable seasons, too much rain or too little, late sowing, and other considerations play a determining part in these matters. Things move very slowly in West Africa as a rule. The cotton crop is not the easiest to handle. Compared with ground nuts, for instance, it entails a great deal more time and trouble. All kinds of obstacles have to be encountered and over-come which people at home have difficulty in fully appre-ciating. The experimental stage of any enterprise, especially in a place like West Africa, is bound to leave openings for error, and error in West Africa is a costly luxury. The Protectorate is under considerable obliga-tions to the Association for the good work it has done and is doing.

It seems to me that the British Cotton-growing Association may perhaps find it advisable, so far as the Western Province of Southern Nigeria is concerned, to reconsider two aspects of its policy. Fundamentally that policy is without question sound—viz. the recogni-tion that agricultural development in West Africa can only be possible on any scale worth mentioning when undertaken by the natives themselves. A policy of large plantations run under white supervision by hired native labour will not pay in West Africa, and, politically speak-ing, is virtually impossible. The Association should receive public support in resisting any pressure which might be placed upon it to alter its fundamental policy by those of its supporters who may be impatient of a comparatively slow advance—slow, *i.e.*, in comparison with the unwise optimism displayed by some of the Association's friends upon public platforms. I doubt, however, if an export trade in cotton will ever reach substantial proportions—let us say 100,000 bales per annum twenty years hence—in the Western Province unless the element of competition is introduced. Hitherto, by combining with the merchants, the Association has established a fixed buying price. In the initial stages this was a good thing. The native farmer wanted the certainty that his crop would be purchased if he were induced to grow it. Now that the industry is well on in its stride it may be seriously questioned whether the Yoruba farmer, the certainty of sale notwithstanding, will be content with the prices offered him under the monopoly agreement now obtaining. He has always the oil palm to fall back upon ; but he has, in addition, cocoa and maize. Cocoa is rapidly increasing, and the profit realized by the cultivator is a good one. The timber trade, too, is growing slowly, and the forest is always yielding fresh elements of trade. The bulk of the cotton produced in the Western Province to-day is roughly similar to " middling American," which is now quoted, I believe, at 8d. a pound, but some of the Yoruba cotton fetches up to 3d. above " middling American." It is asserted by the Association that 4 lbs. of seed cotton are required in the Western Province to produce 1 lb. of lint. The native cultivator is (now) supposed to get from the combine—*i.e.* from the Association and the merchants, as the case may be—from 1d. to 1$\frac{1}{8}d$. per lb. of seed cotton. I say " supposed," because I was informed that the actual producer had not always got the amount which he was understood to be getting. As regards Northern Nigeria, until the close of last year the native had never been paid 1d. a lb. cash, and I was given to understand that conditions had been much the same in the Southern Protectorate, except at Ilushi, where it was proved to my satisfaction that the amount of 1d. cash had actually been paid.

The Association reckons, I understand, that at this

rate every pound of lint landed in Liverpool costs the Association 6½d. I cannot check that figure. I merely quote it. But one may point out that in addition to the profit at the present price of "middling American" disclosed by this estimate, there must be a considerable profit to the Association on the seed, which, upon arrival in England, is worth, I believe, between £5 and £6 per ton. Moreover, as already stated, some of this Yoruba cotton is fetching a higher price than "middling American," and I do not think it is beyond the mark to say that, but for the fact that the Association's ginneries are not continuously employed, the Association's profits on Southern Nigerian cotton to-day would be substantial. It must be fairly obvious from what precedes that if the industry were placed upon an ordinary commercial footing like any other, with merchants competing on the spot for the raw material, the Yoruba farmer would have no difficulty in obtaining very much more than he gets at present for his crop. Cultivation, under those circumstances, would become proportionately more profitable and a greater acreage would be laid out in cotton. No doubt it would cut both ways, the native restricting his acreage when the price fell, but it may be fairly argued that no special reason now exists for treating the cotton industry on an artificial basis, that it must take its chance like any other, and like any other become subject to ordinary economic ups and downs. We cannot expect the native farmer to concentrate upon one particular crop if he can make a greater profit in cultivating another. No industry can develop healthily on artificial lines. If this suggestion were thought worthy of consideration, the Association's *rôle* could be confined to ginning, and, if asked to do so, selling on commission, or that *rôle* might be combined with buying and selling in cases where the producers preferred to deal with the Association, or found it more convenient to carry the cotton direct to the various ginneries. That, no doubt, would force the Association into competition with the merchants, and the merchants, bringing out their own gins (if it paid them to do so), might cause the Association's position to become precarious. The first alternative would, therefore, appear the most desirable, the merchants being the buyers and the Association, the ginners, and, if necessary, sellers on commission. Each force would then be operating within its natural orbit, and an unnatural alliance would cease, unnatural in the sense that one price means one market, and that one market is not an inducement to economic expansion, especially when the price of other tropical products produced by the Yoruba farmer with an open free market to deal in has been steadily rising during the last few years. The Association has always contended that its primary object is not money making, but the establishment in our oversea dependencies of an Imperial cotton industry calculated in the course of time to relieve Lancashire, in whole or in part, of her dangerous dependence on American speculators.

The other point which those responsible for the management of the Association might conceivably think over, is one that impressed me in Northern Nigeria when inspecting the beautifully kept cotton plantations in the Kano and Zaria provinces. I was later on to find that it was one upon which very strong, though not unanimous, opinions were held by persons of experience and judgment in the Southern Protectorate. A great deal of energy, and doubtless money too, is apparently expended by the Association in experimenting with and distributing seeds of non-indigenous varieties of cotton. Now, although one cannot say without careful cultivation, speaking of the north, one can at least say without perpetually improving scientific cultivation extending over a century, Nigeria is able to produce indigenous cotton, fetching to-day $1\frac{1}{4}d.$, $2d.$, and even $3d.$ per lb. above

" middling American." Does not this fact constitute the strongest of pleas for concentrating upon the improvement of the indigenous varieties instead of distributing effort by worrying about the introduction of exotics ? If these indigenous plants, without a century's scientific care, can produce cotton superior in value to " middling American," what could they not do with a tithe of the attention which has been lavished upon the industry in the States ? I know the experts will argue that the indigenous varieties make a lot more wood, and that an acre planted with American varieties will yield much more lint than an acre planted with a Nigerian variety. Not being an expert I would not venture to dispute this. All that I would make bold to query would be whether experiments tending to prove it have in Nigeria been sufficiently continuous and carried out under conditions of fairness to the indigenous cotton sufficiently conclusive to place the matter beyond the pale of discussion. Even if this were so, I am not sure that it could be taken as an irrefutable reply to the contention I have ventured to put forward. For, on the other side, must be reckoned the diseases which invariably attack all exotics, animal, vegetable, and human, introduced into the West African forest region. At every halt on my trek from Riga-Chikum to Kano, a matter of twelve days, wherever I saw cotton plantations, and often enough at points on the road, I made it my business whenever practicable to put a number of questions to the Sarikis (chiefs) and to individual farmers on the subject of cotton-growing. I always prefaced these questions with an assurance that I did not belong to the Government and that I was not a commercial man, but merely a Mallam (I believe my interpreter sometimes inserted on his own account the word " wise " before Mallam), who travelled about and wrote " books," and that my friends could therefore feel satisfied that they would not be causing me any pleasure at all by answering my questions in any particular manner—that, in short, I did not care a row of yams what their answer might be. One question I never failed to ask was whether the Government had distributed seed to that particular village or in that particular area, and if so, what result had followed the sowing of it ? Sometimes the answer was in the negative. When it was in the affirmative it was invariably the same. The Government seed had come. It had been sown. But it was " no good." Now, I disclaim all attributes of wisdom in this matter of cotton. But I beg you to believe me when I say that the Hausa farmer is no fool.*

* It is only fair to state that Mr. W. H. Himbury, of the British Cotton Growing Association, has since pointed out, in regard to the prices fetched by indigenous Southern Nigerian cotton (p. 227), that the prices here given only refer to small samples and cannot be taken as indicative of the general selling value of Southern Nigerian cotton. The official report of the Commercial Intelligence officer of Southern Nigeria, from which the figures here given are quoted, is thus somewhat misleading. But the correction does not appreciably affect my general line of suggestion. Referring to the cotton grown in the Bassa and Nassarawa provinces of Northern Nigeria, Professor Wyndham Dunstan in his recent report states that in making a comparison of the lint for the Liverpool market the standard employed is "Moderately rough Peruvian, which is a grade of higher price than Middling American."

CHAPTER III

THE COTTON INDUSTRY—*continued*

COTTON is grown extensively in parts of Northern Nigeria, not for export—outside the Hausa provinces—but for home consumption. In Kano province—28,600 square miles in extent with 2,500,000 inhabitants, more than one-fourth of the total population of the Protectorate—its cultivation is accompanied by what can, without exaggeration, be termed a national industry of weaving, manufacturing, embroidering, and dyeing the garments, both under-garments and over-garments, which the Kano people wear. But not the Kano people alone. For many centuries, for nearly 1000 years probably, the Kanawa have been famed throughout the great region comprised between the bend of the Niger and the ocean as the expert cotton manufacturers of Africa ; the most interesting region in all the Dark Continent, where divers races have ceaselessly intermingled, attracted thither by its fertile soil and abundant pastures ; Libyan and Berber, Egyptian and Semite, and the mysterious Fulani. Three-fourths of the " men of the desert," too, the fierce-eyed, black-lithamed Tuareg, descendaits of the Iberians, who roam over the vast spaces between Tripoli and the Chad, replenish their wardrobes from the Kano looms. Throughout Bornu, Wadai, and Baghirmi, in the northern German Cameroons as far east as Darfur, Kano cloths hold unquestioned sway. The Kanawa are not the only Nigerians who manufacture cotton goods ; but they are the only

WOMEN COTTON SPINNERS.

MEN WEAVING.

people among whom the industry may be truly called a national one. As carried out in Kano province this industry adds dignity, interest, and wealth to the life of the people, assists their inventive faculties, intensifies their agricultural lore, and sustains several other branches of industrial activity, binding in close alliance of material interest the agriculturist and the artisan. It gives a healthy, attractive employment to many thousand homes —employment carried on in the free air of heaven, beneath the bright sunshine of Africa. It has become a part of the national life, the pride and profit of the people. Men, women, and children participate in it, the men clearing the ground, hoeing and sowing, the women and children doing the picking, the women cleaning the lint of the seeds (on flat stones), teasing, the men weaving, tailoring, and usually, but not always, embroidering. Woven in long, narrow strips, the manufactured article is of remarkable durability and firmness of texture. The predominating dye is the blue of the indigo plant, extensively cultivated for the purpose, dyepits being common all over the province. The embroidery, both in regard to design and execution, is astonishingly handsome, and the colours harmoniously blended. A fine specimen of a finished *riga*—the outer robe covering the shoulders, with an aperture for the head and neck, and falling in folds to the knee—is a work of art of which any people in any country might be proud. It is a very heavy garment, and it is costly. But it is suitable for the cold nights and chilly mornings, and it lasts for years.

It is impossible to separate the cultivation of cotton from the agricultural pursuits of the people generally. Cotton, like cassava, onions, ochro, pepper, ground nuts, and beans, takes its place as one of the secondary crops. The people are primarily a people of agriculturists, raising vast quantities of cereals year after year for home consumption and export to other districts—guinea-corn and

millet, yams, maize, a little wheat.   In the Kano Emirate
or division—as distinct from what is known as the Kano
province—the population is exceedingly dense, and virtually the whole land is under cultivation.   I have seen
nothing more remarkable in the way of cultivation either
in France or Flanders.   And it is all done with the *galma*,
a peculiar kind of short-handled hoe, which would break
the back of an English labourer to use, but which the
Hausa will wield for hours together.   The pattern of the
galma is of great antiquity.   It came from ancient Egypt,
with the original inhabitants probably ;   the plough,
which was used in Egypt when intercourse was frequent
between the valleys of the Nile and Niger, never seems to
have penetrated so far West—a curious and unexplained
fact.

Long, deep, broad, parallel ridges cover the surface of
the land, dotted here and there with magnificent specimens
of the locust-bean tree, the shea, the tamarind, and many
other varieties, under whose shade it seems a favourite
device to grow a catch crop of pepper.   How does the soil
retain, year after year, its nutritive properties ?   That is
the secret of the Kanawa, who from generation to generation have studied it in conjunction with the elements, as the
Niger pilots have learned to read the face of the waters and
can steer a steam launch where no white man could without
running his craft upon a sandbank, especially at low water.
That they have acquired the necessary precise knowledge
as to the time to prepare the land for sowing ;   when to
sow and how to sow ;   how long to let the land lie fallow ;
what soils suit certain crops ;   what varieties of the same
crop will succeed in some localities and what varieties in
others ;   how to irrigate the land situate in the vicinity of
the waterways and planted with secondary crops in the
dry season ;   how to ensure rotation with guinea-corn,
millet, ground nuts, and beans ;   when to arrange with the
Fulani herdsmen to pasture their cattle upon the land—

so much at least the outsider interested in agricultural problems can gauge to some extent. For miles and miles around Kano city one passes through a smiling country dotted with farms, riven by fine, broad native roads lined with hedges of euphorbias and other plants.

Great care is lavished upon the cotton and cassava plantations—the two chief secondary crops. When the cotton fields are in the neighbourhood of a road, and very often when they are not, they are surrounded by tall fencing, eight to ten feet in height, usually composed of reeds and grass or guinea-corn stalks, to protect them from the depredations of cattle, sheep, and goats, all of which abound. In April and May, with the advent of the early rains, the land is cleared and hoed into furrows and ridges. Along the ridges drills are made at a distance of two and a half to three feet apart, the seed dropped in, and the ridge hoed up. In some districts, however, this custom is varied by the ridges being made after the sowing. The water lies in the hollows between the ridges, prevents the seeds from being washed away by the torrential downpour, and allows air to circulate freely, thus keeping the plants in a healthy state. A month later, when the plants have grown to a foot or more, the ground is again hoed. That is the first sowing. With variations according to localities there are successive sowings up to July and even August. The success of these late sowings depends very much upon the extent to which the land has been previously manured. Conditions are slightly different with the variety of cotton grown, but as a rule the plants are in a fit condition for picking about five months after sowing. December, January, March, and April appear to be the months when cotton is most abundant in the markets. In November and December of last year I observed that while in some of the fields the pods were bursting well and picking beginning, in others they were still in full flower ; in others, again, they had not reached the flowering stage. Speaking generally, the plantations were in excellent condition, and the absence of weeds would have done credit to an up-to-date British farmer. But the difference in vigour of plant growth was very marked—affected, doubtless, by locality and manuring or the lack of it. One of the finest plantations I saw was at Gimmi, to the north of Zaria province, and the intelligent *sariki* (chief) of that village informed me that his people not infrequently treated the plant as a perennial up to the third year, when it was plucked up. I subsequently ascertained that in the Hadeija division of the Kano province, where the soil has a good underlying moisture, the perennial treatment is carried on sometimes for no less than seven years. After the third year the annual crop decreases. When so treated the plant is invariably manured.

I found it exceedingly difficult to obtain reliable figures as to the average yield of cotton per acre in any one district, or the average acreage under cultivation ; and the Residents share the view that only continuous residence in the country by a Hausa-speaking (that is essential) European expert in constant and close touch with the farmers will permit of anything approaching exact information being acquired on the point. In the Katagum division of Kano province an acre is *said* to produce an average of 266 lbs. The average annual acreage under cotton in Katsina is *said* to be 16,000 acres. In Zaria province the soil, which is a sandy clay, the subsoil being reached at six inches, is generally rather poor, and the farmer is not so great an expert as his Kano colleague. In some places it is so poor that one hundred plants are said to be required to produce a single *riga*. In the true cotton-farming districts of the northern part of the province—such as Soba, Gimba, and Dillaya—the soil is, however, very much better, obtaining more moisture than the higher ground of Kano province and producing even finer cotton. Broadly, the problem which faces the native farmer in Zaria province is how to increase the fertility of his land. Artificial chemical manuring is out of the question ; the rains would wash it all out of the soil. Green manuring is well understood but might be improved. The introduction of one or two shallow ploughs might work wonders by showing the farmers how the subsoil could be broken up, but the experiment would have to be carefully demonstrated. The native is only affected by actual demonstration, and, so far, demonstrations inspired by Europeans designed to show the Hausa farmer how to improve his agricultural systems have done little more than provoke a smile. The white man has failed where the black man has succeeded, because the white man thought he knew local conditions and did not. A Government experimental farm was started at Maiganna rather late last year, the sowings being made in July, if I remember rightly, seventeen miles from Zaria city. This is an excellent initiative which it is to be hoped will be maintained. It is really Government work. The British Cotton-growing Association should be spared all expense of this kind. Two varieties indigenous to the southern provinces (Bassa and Ilorin) and " Nyassaland upland " were planted. I was told last November by the official in charge that the indigenous varieties were doing fairly well, but that the " Nyassaland " was suffering from red-leaf. The British Cotton-growing Association was then about to put up a large and costly ginnery at Zaria. The operation is proceeding, and a substantial quantity of cotton has already been bought. I will refer to that later on. Meantime I cannot help thinking that it might have been better to have waited a little and set up the ginnery at Kano. However, this is merely a personal opinion.

The chief varieties of indigenous cotton grown in the Kano province are three in number. The first is known under the four following names—*gundi, bagwandara,*

lutua, or *mailaushi;* the second as *chukwi* or *labai.*
These two are the best kinds, their quality being about
the same. The third is called *yerkarifi* or *yergeri.* It is
of an inferior quality with a shorter staple, usually but
not always grown where the soil is not naturally rich
enough to support the other kinds. It is the *yerkarifi*
variety, I gathered, which is more often used as a perennial.
It fetches a lower price on the local markets and takes a
month longer to mature. Cotton plants are fairly free
from insect pests, but the following are identified :
the cotton boll worm (*tsutsa*), what is described, doubt-
fully, as an ant which attacks the root (*zago*), and two
species of blight (*makau* and *madi*). The native remedy,
apart from constant hoeing, is to light a fire to windward,
upon which the dried leaves of a certain plant, and also
dried fish, are thrown. The question of indigenous
versus exotic varieties here crops up again. One hears
talk of flooding the country with exotic seed and doing
away altogether with the indigenous varieties. I refer
to Zaria, where some five hundred bags of exotic seed—
or at least non-local seed—were distributed this spring
after a palaver with the Emir and his principal headmen.
No doubt it may be all right. From the non-expert point
of view it seems dangerous. As already stated, African
insect life fastens with relentless savagery upon exotic
plant life, just as it revels in nice fresh blood out from
Europe. One season's failure with an exotic or non-
local variety, sown by instructions of the Emir's headmen
in lieu of the indigenous kind, might create a prejudice
in the native's mind that it would take years to remove.
Concentration upon improving the fertility of the soil,
and therefore the quality and quantity of the local
varieties (combined, of course, with seed selection)
would be a slower process. It is just possible that it
might be a wiser one.

The distribution of the cotton now grown in Zaria

and Kano provinces is as follows : Zaria is visited by the weavers (or their representatives) of Kano and of French territory—from the neighbourhood of Zinder principally. They buy up between them virtually the whole crop, importing live stock and manufactured goods, which they dispose of in the markets for silver coin, buying with that coin the cotton. What is not taken by the Zinder people is taken by Kano. The Kano division of the Kano province consumes all the cotton it grows. So does the Katagum division. The Katsina division exports a percentage to Kano and consumes the rest. The soil of this division compares unfavourably with that of Kano, except in the southern district, where it is even better than in Kano. In this district cotton-growing forms the principal means of livelihood of the inhabitants. The total annual output of the Kano province is estimated at about 5200 tons—3500 from the Kano division, 1000 from the Katsina division, 700 from Katagum-Hadeija. But these figures are mere estimates, and not over-reliable at that. The country is too extensive and the British occupation too recent to permit of accuracy in such matters at present. I was unable to obtain even an estimate of the Zaria output, which is, of course, very much lower—probably about one-fifth, or less than that at Kano.

As already remarked, the whole of the crop now grown is used by the local industry (except the Association's purchases this year, which I will refer to in a moment). So far this industry not only shows no signs of decreasing, but the demand, especially from the southern markets is, I was told, steadily increasing. The advent of the railway may, apart from the activities of the Association, modify the situation appreciably through the increasing influx of Manchester goods. As well-being increases—and up to a certain point it is doing and will do so as the result of our occupation—the consumption of Manchester goods will doubtless increase, but it does not altogether follow that the output of the native looms will decrease. It is curious that the Kano weavers themselves think that the railway will enlarge their market. I was informed that the natives of the south, who have been in touch with Manchester cotton goods for many years, very much prefer the Kano cloths, which although dearer, are much more durable. In the north I heard frequent complaints of the quality of the Manchester goods imported. Many of them, so I was told, were much too thin, and so heavily starched that on the first washing they became threadbare and useless. I saw nothing on sale in the markets from Manchester suited for the early and late hours of the day. Cheap prints are all very well for the hot hours of the late morning and afternoon. But the people require warmer garments than that. I used to strike camp when trekking at about 5 a.m. or 5.30 a.m., and at that time, and for a couple of hours afterwards, I was glad of two sweaters over a khaki shirt, riding. When the sun goes down it is equally chilly. The robes worn by the better-class natives are of a consistency and weight which would astonish us here.

I am persuaded that the British Cotton-growing Association is in every way worthy of support, that its ideal is a fine one and a patriotic one, and that the West African dependencies of Southern and Northern Nigeria are very much indebted to it. At the same time I should not be giving honest expression to the views I have rightly or wrongly formed if I did not enter a *caveat* against any Government action calculated to undermine or destroy the weaving industry of the Kano province. That industry may disappear as the result of natural causes. But nothing should be done by the Administration to assist its decay. Frankly, I am compelled to state that from the standpoint of the happiness and welfare of these Hausa people, our wards, the disappearance of their national industry would be deplorable. It would lower their outlook and stunt their development, and send them down in the scale of civilization. Their intelligence is of an order which would enable them under tuition to advance their methods of production beyond the hand-loom. While the duty of the Administration to lend its moral support, as it is doing, from the Governor, Sir Henry Hesketh Bell (who is most interested in this question) downwards, to any legitimate effort directed at increasing the area of cotton under cultivation, increasing the yield per acre by improving the fertility of the soil, facilitating communication and the accessibility of markets, is unquestioned, I submit that there is an equally clear call of duty on its part to encourage rather than discourage an indigenous industry of great antiquity, of wonderful promise, which is at once a source of profit to, and an elevating influence in, the life of the people of the land.

I have now endeavoured to sketch the chief factors to be considered in estimating the possibilities of a substantial export trade in raw cotton from Northern Nigeria. There remains to be examined the question of price and of competing articles of production. The British Cotton-growers' Association's *début* at Zaria has been attended with no little success. They bought this season, I believe, something like 60,000 lbs. of cotton, a considerable proportion of which, I am informed, came from the Katsina division of Kano. Whilst the Association's buyers, lent to its representative by the authorities, could not compete in price with the Kano and Zinder buyers in the big markets, they competed successfully with them in the remoter small markets of the province which buyers from the native weaving interest do not usually visit.

I hope I shall not be thought desirous of " crabbing "

the Association's efforts or minimizing what they have accomplished if I venture to point out that there would be some danger—of which the Association is doubtless aware—in drawing too definite conclusions from these first and satisfactory results. The taxes fell due in Zaria province at the time of the maturing of the crop, and the growers were anxious for cash to meet them. The Emir of Katsina is a very intelligent man and wishful of encouraging in every way he can any desires he deems the Government to entertain. His influence would be directed to giving a tangible proof of his interest and goodwill. This desire would be shared by his people, by whom he is personally respected. It would be unwise, however, to imagine that Katsina farmers will permanently be willing to send their cotton all the way to Zaria for 1*d*. per lb., when in the ordinary run of things they can get as much, if not more, than 1*d*. from the native weaving interest. If the cotton were bought on the spot the farmers might be willing to sell at 1*d*. The question of price is bound to play an important part in the interesting developments which have now begun. Taking year in year out, the local price of cotton in Zaria and Kano varies from 1¼*d*. to 2*d*. per lb. in the seed. In Zaria last November and December it varied from 1⅝*d*. to 2*d*. In Kano it kept at 2*d*. throughout November, December, and part of January, having fallen from 2¼*d*. in September. In the latter part of January it fell temporarily to 1*d*. It went up again to 2*d*. in February. The bright side consists in the possibility—the probability, perhaps— that the knowledge of a permanent and unlimited market at a fixed price, albeit a low one, in their midst will incline farmers to patronize that market (and increase their acreage), assuring them as it does of an immediate sale. Personally, I cannot but think that the Association will have to put up its price if it is to obtain substantial quantities. Competition here, as in Southern Nigeria, would undoubtedly tend to increase production, but I believe that the advent of the European merchant to Zaria and Kano is to be characterized by the same arrangement as I have already commented upon in Southern Nigeria. There is, of course, what there is not in Southern Nigeria, an element of competition in the Northern provinces—viz. the native weaving interest— and the play of these two forces, if both are allowed a fair field, will, no doubt, have a stimulating effect in itself.

Another element comes in here which is worthy of note. I refer to the price of foodstuffs. Everywhere the price of foodstuffs is growing with our occupation of the country. Round the main highways and large markets it has risen enormously in the past eighteen months. In one part of the Niger province the native farmer now reckons upon getting, I was informed, £8 to £10 per acre out of yams. Cotton at 1d. per lb. would bring him in from £3 to £4. That is rather an extreme case, I admit, nor does the whole country produce yams, and the farmers generally do not appear yet to have fully grasped the economic importance for them of the increased demand for foodstuffs. On the other hand, it is, of course, true that the sowing of cotton between the ordinary food crops is not uncommon.

I have thought it well to describe the position just as I read it, and to make certain suggestions, the outcome of personal observation and discussion on the spot. It may well be that in certain respects I have read the situation wrong and that the suggestions made are faulty. Prediction at the present time, I am convinced, must be largely made in the dark, and they are no friends of the British Cotton-growing Association who describe the outlook in Nigeria in " high falutin' " terms. It is too soon to say how matters will develop. That development will in any case be slow may be taken for granted. The

Administration is in urgent need of a properly equipped agricultural department with at the head of it the very best man that money can secure.

Reviewing the whole situation, the only definite conclusions I have been able to arrive at in my own mind are—first, that all attempts at giving an artificial basis to cotton production in the Nigerias will, in the long run, defeat its own ends; secondly, that by some means or other the price paid to the native farmer must be raised if any extension of the industry worth talking about is to be looked for. Everywhere in Northern Nigeria, whether the personal view inclines to optimism or pessimism, I found the officials without exception deeply interested in and anxious to assist in every way the effort to build up an export industry in cotton, and fully persuaded of the great importance and value of the work of the Association.

CHAPTER IV

THE LIQUOR TRAFFIC IN SOUTHERN NIGERIA

APART from religious questions there is probably no subject upon which it is more difficult to secure reasonable discussion and study than the subject of drink ; none upon which it is more easy to generalize, or which lends itself more readily to prejudice and misunderstanding of the real points at issue. That moral reformers in England and elsewhere should feel strongly about drink is natural enough. A considerable proportion of the population of this country, of France, Germany, Belgium, and other European States live wretched and unhealthy lives. They are over-worked, under-fed, herded in insanitary tenements with insufficient space, ventilation, and light, under conditions which preclude decency and breed moral and physical diseases. Their horizon is one dead, uniform, appalling greyness from birth to death. Who can feel surprise that people thus situated should seek momentary forgetfulness in drink ? The abuse of intoxicants is not, of course, confined in Europe to one particular *stratum* of society, but no one will seriously contend that the social conditions under which so considerable a proportion of the poorer classes live are not a terrible incentive to immoderate drinking. Speaking generally the drink problem in Europe is not a cause but an effect. The cause lies deep down in the failure-side of our civilization, and statesmen worthy of the name are grappling with it everywhere. Those of us who think we see beyond an effect, are striving to prevent the reproduction in tropical Africa of this failure-side of our civilization. We are striving to maintain the economic independence of the West African ; to ensure him a permanency of free access to his land ; to preserve his healthy, open-air life of agriculturist and trader, his national institutions, his racial characteristics and his freedom. We are endeavouring to show him to the people of Europe, not as they have been taught by long years of unconscious misrepresentation to regard him, but as he really is. We feel that if we can protect the West African from the profounder economic and social perils which encompass him on every side ; from the restless individualism of Europe ; from unfair economic pressure threatening his free and gradual development on his own lines ; from the disintegrating social effects of well-meaning but often wrongly informed and misdirected philanthropic effort ; from political injustice—that if we are able to accomplish this even in small measure, the question of drink, while requiring attention, becomes one of secondary importance. The West African has always been a moderate drinker. From time immemorial he has drunk fermented liquors made from various kinds of corn, and from different kinds of palm trees. It is not a teetotal race, as the North American race was. It is a strong, virile race, very prolific.

Unfortunately this question of drink has been given a place in the public mind as regards Southern Nigeria altogether disproportionate to the position it does, and should, hold. It has been erected for many sincere, good people into a sort of fetish, obscuring all the deeper issues arising from the impact upon the West African of civilization at a time when civilization has never been so feverishly active, so potent to originate vast changes in a few short years. The use of intoxicants of some kind is common to humanity all over the world. Whether it responds to a positive need of the human body or not will, no doubt, be a matter for everlasting debate. Christ Himself did not condemn the juice of the grape, since He Himself, the Sacred Writings tell us, changed water into wine at a marriage feast and consecrated its use sacramentally. Excessive indulgence in liquor, like indulgence in any other form of human appetite, is a human failing. It is not the drink which is an evil, but the abuse of it. The abuse of liquor nine times out of ten is the outcome of social discomfort and unhappiness, a way of escape, like a narcotic, from the pangs of conscience, or of misery. People at home are prone, in approaching problems connected with the coloured races, to place themselves exclusively from the subjective point of view. The inhabitant of the heat belt is given an economic and social setting similar to the European and his outlook is treated as it were on parallel lines. To that mode of reasoning, three-fourths of the evils which civilization has inflicted upon coloured races may be traced. Nothing is more curious or more saddening to observe than the unfailing success of such methods of thought translated into public action, in their effect upon home sentiment. Consumption sweeping through the ranks of a coloured people as the consequence of the educationary and religious processes of Europeanism may make a holocaust of human victims. The public remains indifferent. European marriage laws ; European ethics, or nominal ethics, in the matter of sex relationship ; the European individualistic social system grafted upon the communal life of a coloured people—these things may produce widespread human misery and immorality. The public is cold and unconcerned. European interference and innovation in social customs and usages essential to the well being, to the political and racial needs of a coloured people in one stage of development, but repugnant to European twentieth-century notions, may cause social disturbance and widespread anarchy which those who are responsible for such interference can never themselves witness, let alone suffer from. It is virtually impossible to arouse popular interest. For these and kindred disasters are very largely brought about by the uninstructed zeal of God-fearing, Christian men and women in Europe who judge other countries by their own, other peoples by their own people, other needs by their own needs, with the best of intentions and with the purest of motives ; and outside a small band of students, ethnologists and experienced officials, the public mind is scandalized and even incensed if any one ventures to doubt the excellent results necessarily flowing from disinterested action. It is disinterested : therefore it must be right. That is the popular belief and the general fallacy.

Poor Mary Kingsley, who knew her West Africa as few have ever known it and who had the true scientific mind, fought hard against this ingrained characteristic of the Anglo-Saxon temperament. But she fought in vain. Despite her charity, the geniality and the humour in which she clothed her truths, she had against her the whole weight of what is called the philanthropic school of home opinion, responsible for so much good and yet for so much unconscious harm.

" The stay at home statesman," she once said, " thinks that Africans are all awful savages or silly children—people who can only be dealt with on a reformatory, penitentiary line. This view, you know, is not mine . . . but it is the view of the statesmen and the general public and the mission public in African affairs."

And again :—

" The African you have got in your mind up here, that you are legislating for and spending millions in trying to improve, doesn't exist ; your African is a fancy African. . . . You keep your fancy African and I wish you joy of him, but I grieve more than I can say for the real African that does exist and suffers for all the mistakes you make in dealing with him through a dream thing, the fiend-child African of your imagination. Above all, I grieve for the true negro people whose home is in the West Coast . . . ."

No, you cannot excite public interest in these matters. But mention the liquor trade, describe the Nigerian as an infant in brain, incapable of self-control, down whose throat wicked merchants are forcibly pouring body and soul destroying drink which a wicked Administration taxes in order to raise revenue. Public sentiment responds with alacrity. It becomes at once a popular cry, and the most inconceivable distortions of native character and native life pass muster.

The liquor traffic is common to the whole of West Africa and requires constant and vigilant attention. For more than a century, long before the bulk of the coast line was occupied by the Powers in a political sense, spirits had been exported to West Africa from Europe together with cotton goods, woollen goods, beads, ironware, hardware, haberdashery, perfumery, salt, tobacco and a host of other articles. At first the trade was untaxed. As European political influence extended, the various Administrations found it necessary to control the traffic by placing an import duty upon spirits at the port of entry. In this policy Great Britain has always led ; the other Powers have always lagged. When interior penetration from the coast began and the scramble for Western Africa was well on its way, Great Britain's influence was responsible for the proposal that the import should be prohibited beyond a certain geographical limit interiorwards. Thus Northern Nigeria was excluded from the accessible zone of European spirit import. By general consent the trade has been looked upon as a potential danger, if unregulated, and nowhere has the determination to prevent it from becoming an active evil been so clearly recognized as in Southern Nigeria ; by successive increases of duty, and, as I shall show, by so adjusting taxation as virtually to penalize spirits of high potency in favour of spirits of weak strength. The Governor-General of French West Africa, M. Ponty, told me only last autumn at Dakar, how he desired to bring the French duties up to the British level, and what difficulties he was experiencing in doing so.

Now the existence of a permanent, outside influence, whatever its origin, directed at encouraging the Administration in this course could only be to the good. While differences of opinion must exist as to the relative importance of the matter compared with other problems of administration, I have met no one who would not regard a policy of letting in spirits free, as wrong.

There has been an immense amount of controversy over the liquor traffic in Southern Nigeria, marked in many ways by regrettable lapses and characterized by gross exaggeration. By a system of sur-taxes upon the higher forms of alcohol initiated by Sir Walter Egerton, the character of the Southern Nigerian spirit trade has been revolutionized for good in the last six years. The system inaugurated in 1905 imposed, over and above the general duty, a sur-tax of $\frac{1}{2}d.$ for every degree or part of a degree in excess of 12·4 under proof. This sur-tax was successively raised until it reached its present figure of $2\frac{1}{2}d.$, with the result that while five years ago nearly 60 per cent. of the total spirits imported varied in strength from between 45 degrees and 55 degrees *Tralles*, to-day something like 90 per cent. of the total spirits imported are just under 40 degrees *Tralles, i.e.* 28 per cent. under proof.

Not only is the general trade (*i.e.* the trade in cotton goods, hardware, etc.) increasing at a far greater ratio than the spirit trade, but the amount of alcohol imported into the Protectorate is actually decreasing, notwithstanding the enormous development of general trade and the steady opening up of the country to which the former is largely due. Here are the figures. They are official and their accuracy has been endorsed by the Secretary of State—

GALLONS OF ALCOHOL

Years		Totals		Annual average
1902–04	..	8,947,000	..	2,982,332
1905–07	..	8,746,000	..	2,915,333
1908–10	..	8,626,000	..	2,875,333

There are two methods of approaching the subject.

One consists in denouncing the traffic, regis ering a personal detestation of it, and declaring that t must cease. If that method embodies a constructive policy, well and good. If it is mere declamation, it is waste of time to discuss it. It is open to any one to *say* these things. What does a policy of prohibition involve—if it is a constructive policy? Obviously, in the first place, the substitution of the revenue derived from taxing spirits by revenue derived from another source or sources. If you are going to abolish the import of spirits by, let us sugggest, January 1, 1913, you must between now and then find three-quarters of a million sterling from somewhere else. Taxing exports will not give it you. Increasing your taxes on other imports will not give it you. You must either tax the natives directly, or you must appeal to the British taxpayer. I have no objection to a direct tax upon the natives in principle. But when the Administration has been in touch with Native Communities for half a century, and has never demanded of them any direct tribute ; when the relations of many of these Communities with the Administration are not the relations of conquered and conqueror, but those based upon Treaties of amity, commerce, and protection,—the inauguration of direct taxation is one of the most delicate and difficult policies imaginable. It must be a very gradual process, otherwise the whole energies of the Administration will be squandered in "punitive" expeditions and in the machinery for collecting an unpopular and not understood impost. I say unhesitatingly that any precipitate enforcement of direct taxation in Southern Nigeria, to come into operation at a given date, is in practical politics an utter impossibility, and this without referring to the gross injustice which would be inflicted upon the Native Communities by suddenly depriving them of a commodity which they have learned to desire and which, supplied in an easily portable form, now plays a regular part (in various ways) in their domestic economy. On the other hand, if you are going to appeal to the British taxpayer for a grant-in-aid to replace the revenue lost to the Dependency by prohibition, you *must* be in a position to *prove* to him that the trade in imported spirits is, in Southern Nigeria, a frightful evil. You cannot do this, for even the Missionaries are not agreed on the point amongst themselves. And, outside Missionary circles, opinion is, with few exceptions, in total disagreement with the allegation. Hence the demand for prohibition has no constructive side, is not practicable, and is mere declamation.

The other method of approach consists in discussing the question in the light of facts. This is the only method which can lead to constructive results, and it can be equally followed by the man who is opposed to the human race drinking alcohol on principle; by the man who believes that the spirit trade is doing great harm in Southern Nigeria; and by the man who does not believe that it is now an active evil, but fully recognizes that it is a potential one. Personally, I belong to the last category.

Now, setting aside all differences of opinion and all past controversies, what is the problem, broadly speaking? Upon the revenue standpoint, I have already touched. The ratio of taxation upon spirits in Southern Nigeria is to-day immeasurably in excess of the ratio of taxation levied upon other imports. For instance, in 1908, goods other than spirits of a value of just under £4,000,000 produced £325,470 in taxes, while spirits of a value of £332,577 produced £691,186 in taxes. Probably the taxable limit has not yet been reached. That is a matter for experts. But on that point you are confronted with the phenomenon that previous successive rises of duty have not prevented the spirit trade from expanding with the expansion of the general import trade. All that successive rises have accomplished—and this, to be sure, is a very excellent thing in itself—has been to keep the proportionate ratio which the spirit trade bears to the general trade at pretty much the same level. It should be possible, gradually, to open up new sources of revenue, and in so doing proportionately to increase the tax on spirits. But mere increases in the duty for time to time, unaccompanied by a constructive policy in other directions, only means a prolongation of the *status quo*.

Two other considerations must be taken into account. First, the international question. Secondly, the social question. As to the former, Southern Nigeria, which has been more attacked than any other West African Dependency, is, in point of fact, the most progressive in the scale and character of its duties. And Southern Nigeria is flanked by German territory on the East and French territory on the West, and the French will not come into line. Hence, if spirits imported into Southern Nigeria cost the native very much more than spirits imported into French territory, extensive smuggling must be looked for over the western border. I do not, for my part, think that this factor should prevent us from doing what we think right in our own territory. Nevertheless it cannot be summarily dismissed. The other point is, in my judgment, a much more important one. The Nigerian Pagan is a drinker of alcohol. He does not only drink "trade spirits" imported ; he drinks palm-wine, fresh and fermented, and he drinks fermented spirit from maize and other cereals. At the present moment he consumes nominally, on the basis of the 1911 census figures, a fraction of one-quarter gallon of imported alcohol per head per annum.* What he consumes per

* Annual average of *alcohol* imported in the three years, 1908-10, 2,875,333 gallons : population 7,750,000—probably under estimated. Of course this is a very crude, unscientific, and inconclusive way of dealing with the question of consumption, but there is no other that I know of. Probably, almost certainly, the actual consumption is not so great, for much of the imported spirit is stored as banked wealth, circulates, in certain parts, as a sort of barter-currency, is wasted in religious ceremonies, etc.

head per annum of his own fermented drinks no one knows. Now what will happen if the foreign supply is cut off, either by the raising of cost price to a prohibitive figure or by some other means? Will the Nigerian be content with drinking less? Will he drink more of his fermented liquor? Will he manufacture distilleries of his own? The latter suggestion is scoffed at, especially by Northern Nigerian officials who contend that even if the Southern Nigerian Pagan attempted to do so he could easily be stopped. This is an argument of men who are used to the vast open spaces of the Hausa States, and to a very efficacious system of Native rule. Conditions in Southern Nigeria are widely different. The bulk of the country is covered with forest and jungle: no inconsiderable proportion with marshy swamp. Except in certain localities, Native rule is very far below the level of capacity and authority which prevail in the North. To control and patrol Southern Nigeria in matters of this kind would be an altogether different and much more perplexing problem. Officials of experience in the South contend that if once the Southern Nigerian were taught the distilling process, it would spread rapidly, for the rough pot-still method requires little or no science, and that to deal with the practice would be a matter of immense difficulty in view of the configuration of the country. It is well known that illicit distilling has caused, and causes, much trouble in India. This danger, then, cannot be eliminated from discussion, and the product of rough distilleries erected in the bush would contain innumerable impurities which, as has now been satisfactorily proved, the imported liquor does not. I know of no evidence which would suggest that the stoppage or serious curtailment of the foreign supply of liquor would lead, as a resultant effect, to a decreased consumption of the sum-total of alcohol. The common-sense supposition is that the Southern Nigerian Pagan would consume greater quantities of his own fermented liquors. These, as already stated, are obtained from two (or three) species of palm-trees, one of them being the oil-palm of commerce, and from various kinds of cereals. There are two ways of tapping the oil-palm for wine without killing it, but these methods are not always employed by a race which has not yet developed foresight through the pressure of economic necessity, and experienced opinion, which it is impossible to set aside, contends that the stoppage or restriction of the foreign supply would lead to a great destruction of oil-palms, and to the consequent impoverishment of the people by the curtailment of their purchasing capacity represented, primarily, by the products of the palm. Here again the Northern Nigeria man is apt to declare that legislation (which, in point of fact already exists) would suffice to prevent the mischief. But, for the reason already explained, he is not, perhaps, the best judge. On the same grounds, authorities on the Southern Nigerian tribes believe that the harvests might, upon occasion, be sacrificed to the production of liquor. It is well known, of course, that in some if, indeed, not in many of the Pagan districts of Northern Nigeria (where the foreign article has never been imported) a bumper grain crop means a bumper drinking bout, lasting, at times, several weeks. An exceptionally qualified witness before the Commission of Inquiry into the liquor traffic in Southern Nigeria in 1909, Father Coquard of Abeokuta—with whom I have had the priviledge of converse—testified to his conviction that the people of the Western Province would use their maize crops to produce liquor instead of flour, and would thus bring famine upon the land, if their foreign supply of liquor were stopped. He did not stand alone in his belief, and he has twenty years' experience of that part of the country. The respective physiological effect of these fermented brews and the imported spirit is a matter of dispute among experienced medical men. People with strong opinions like Sir Harry Johnson make short work of these conflicting views, and refuse to regard any comparison as possible, but many men who have gone into the matter deeply, and who have had long experience, are emphatic as to the extremely deleterious effect of palm-toddy and *pito*. And, so far as palm-toddy is concerned, similar evidence is on record from India. Certainly my own carriers in Northern Nigeria found no difficulty on one occasion in becoming uproariously drunk upon *pito*, getting my caravan into trouble with the worthy butchers of a place called Burrum-Burrum whom they incontinently assaulted while I was camping half a mile outside the town. Socially speaking, the imported liquor is in Southern Nigeria the richer Pagan's drink. It has become in social entertainments, in festivals, and so on, the smart thing to do to offer gin to your guests. Gin takes the place of champagne with us.

These, then, are in brief the principal aspects of the liquor problem—the revenue aspect and the social aspect. There is also, it will be urged, the commercial problem. I do not attach nearly so much importance to that. There is no great vested interest to consider. The vast bulk of " trade spirits " are of continential manufacture. It is not a British industry. The British, Foreign and Native merchants who deal in spirits, as with every other class of European merchandise, are merely middle-men. So long as the spirit trade is regarded as a legitimate one, it must receive fair and equitable treatment : that is all. The opinion held by merchants as to the effect a notable restriction in the import of spirits would have upon the total bulk of their commercial turnover, differs considerably. I know of none who have any special love for the trade. I know of some who would rather welcome than otherwise a progressive decrease in the import on purely commercial grounds. There is no considerable profit on the actual purchase and sale of this branch of the trade, taken by itself, but it is an established branch of the general trade and enters into all general trade transactions.

The general line of action I would suggest for dealing with the trade in trade spirits is this—

A. Frequent analyses of the imported article. Severe punishment if bad stuff is going in.

B. Continuation of the legislation, consistently followed since 1905, of taxing, over and above the general tax, higher degrees of alcoholic strength *pro rata*. Perhaps pursuing that still further by prohibiting altogether the importation of liquor above a certain strength.

C. Keeping duties to the level of safety, raising them whenever possible, but not so highly that the dangers indicated above may become actualities, or at least until exhaustive inquiry has been held as to how far those dangers are real and can be guarded against. (See, too, in this connection, J.)

D. Not permitting the proportion which the spirit trade now bears to the general trade to increase— that means watching, and increasing the duty when possible. At every sign of the present proportion being increased, another increase of duty should be made.

E. Restricting, if possible, the present proportion, by *degrees* either by the policy of successive increases of duty ; or by an arrangement with the merchants (very difficult to bring about, owing to the advent of new firms ; but not, perhaps, impossible), whereby they would be precluded from exceeding in the spirit branch of their trade a certain fixed proportion to their general trade turn-over—the imports of each firm being calculated on a basis which would establish a decrease in the total volume of the spirit trade. This arrangement, if it were possible, would have, really, the same effect as judicious increases of duty, by making the imported article dearer.

F. The creation of a sitting committee in Lagos—sitting and permanent—the members of which would be gazetted and paid a small salary : with two branches, one in the Central and one in the Eastern Province, and (if necessary) with corresponding members in several of the more important centres—with the object of creating in each province a sort of bureau of information on the spirit trade to which every one would feel free to communicate.

G. Standing instructions to every medical officer to give attention to the subject from the physiological point of view, within his area and to furnish a half-yearly report to the Principal Medical Officer. These reports would be annotated by the P. M. O., who, reviewing the whole evidence, would give *his* report. Specific instances raised by any medical officer, might if necessary be referred to the permanent committee above mentioned.

H. A yearly report to be furnished by the Chairman of the permanent committee, and by the P. M. O. respectively, to the local Government, and published in the Official Gazette.

I. Maintenance of the prohibitory line under amalgamation ; and its deflection southwards in the Eastern Province in order to keep from the influence of the trade, the northern portions of the Eastern Province where the trade has, up to now, not, or barely, penetrated.

J. Gradual, *very gradual*, introduction of direct taxation in the Central and Eastern Provinces, working upwards from the coast line—preceded by full explanations, and the calling together of District Chiefs and Heads of Houses for purposes of *discussion*. In the Western Province, where direct taxation by the British Government would be a violation of Native law and of Treaties and Arrangements, a policy (sketched in Part II.) of re-constituting according to native law, the old Yoruba Kingdom, and reviving through the Alafin, the tribute which in native law is due to him, and eventually controlling the expenditure of the proceeds through the Alafin and the heads of the various Yoruba States. These respective proceedings being taken with the object of *gradually* making us independent, or virtually independent, of taxation on spirits as a source of revenue.

That is, broadly, the constructive policy I venture to recommend. It might have to be modified here and there. But in its main lines I believe it to be sound.

I must, in conclusion, register my belief, based upon a mass of published evidence—which can be found in the Report and minutes of evidence of the Commission of Inquiry (C.D. 4906 and C.D. 4907) ; much private evidence extending over a number of years ; upon limited but unfettered personal observation, and upon personal conversation with many officials, doctors, railway engineers, educated natives, and resident missionaries, etc. —that the Nigerian Pagans of North and South are, as a race, moderate drinkers, keen traders, able agriculturists, hard workers, well endowed with the gripping senses, of fine physique, virile, fine specimens of humanity. I do not believe that drink, whether imported or local, has undermined them in any way. Sentimentally I dislike the liquor trade and wish it did not exist, because if it has not yet done harm, it has, at least, done no good. But as it does exist, I urge that it shall be treated as a problem of actuality from a statesmanlike point of view, and that no unreasonable and unnecessary crusade against it shall be permitted to inflict injustice and harshness upon the Native Communities. If it is ethically a sin that Europe should originally have introduced distilled liquor into West Africa generally, the West African must not be made to pay for it, that is all—now that the imported spirit has taken root as a factor in general trade and social life. The West African has paid heavily enough as it is for European sins. Further I confess to a very great logical difficulty in understanding the justice of preventing the Pagan native from drinking a gin free from impurities of manufacture and from the higher alcohols, and allowing both the European and the Europeanized native to drink champagne, whisky, brandy, and liqueurs.

As an antidote to any dangers of over-indulgence in drink among the mass of the people which may exist, the spread of the Mohammedan religion is automatically the most effective, from the purely social standpoint ; and this, not because of any special virtue attaching to Islam in itself, but because Islam in West Africa has become an African religion which does not denationalize, and does not produce the social unhappiness which denationalization brings in its train, and because it teaches abstinence from alcoholic liquors.*

* It may, perhaps, be well to emphasize, in view of the printed statements describing the writer as the "champion of the liquor traffic" and so forth, which are so freely made in certain quarters, that the above remarks are concerned solely with the liquor traffic *in Southern Nigeria*—not in West Africa as a whole. They deal with specific facts affecting a specific area of West Africa and with specific circumstances surrounding those facts which have formed the subject of public controversy.

INDEX

INDEX

INDEX

INDEX